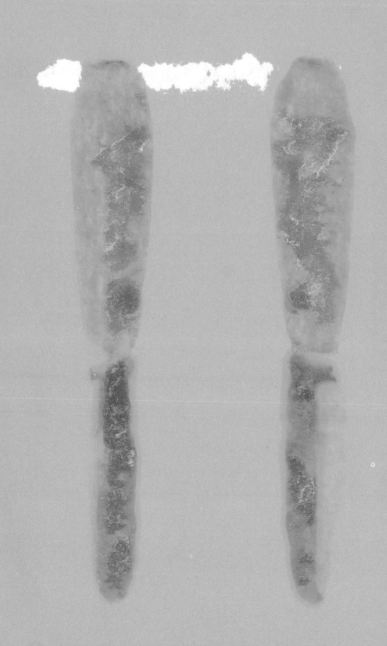

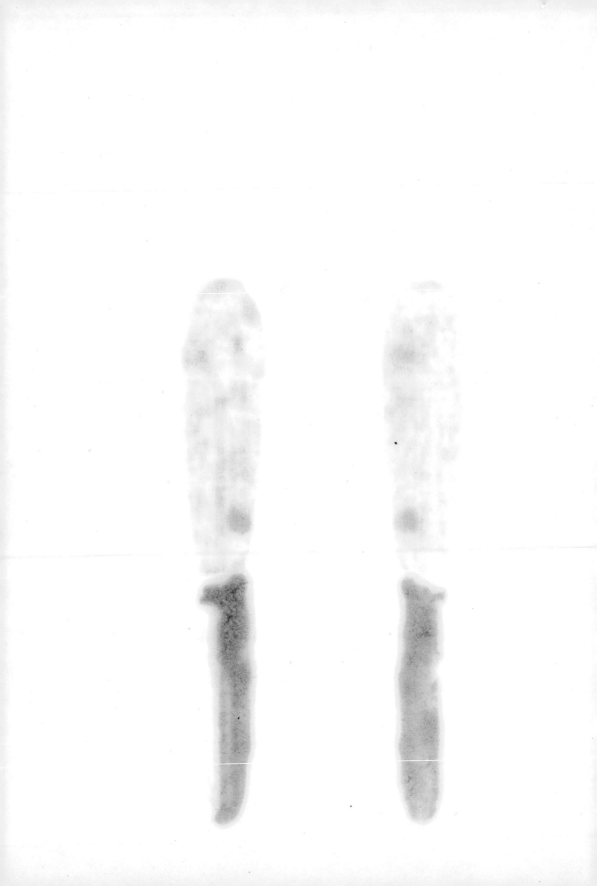

MAMMALS
OF THE OCEANS

MAMMALS OF THE OCEANS

Richard Mark Martin

G. P. Putnam's Sons
New York

The close knit family
relationship among most
seals is particularly strong
between mother and child.

First published in the United States of America in 1977
by G. P. Putnam's Sons, 200 Madison Avenue, New York, NY10016

Designed and produced by London Editions Limited,
30 Uxbridge Road, London W12 8ND

Library of Congress Catalog Card Number: 76-56957
SBN: 399-11953-1

Printed and bound in Yugoslavia

Contents

Dedication

For Mij – In memory of walks and whales, seas and surf

Preface

This book is not intended as a scientific treatise. I have not dwelt on obscure physiological details that would only be appreciated by advanced students of zoology or anatomy. I was not interested in writing a textbook, but a book which might in some small way enhance the stature of the magnificent and much abused mammals that live in the sea.

I have had to consult many sources for reference, qualification and enlightenment. I have had to be constantly on my guard against the misinterpretations of others and the not inconsiderable number of false assumptions which are passed down from one book to another like intellectual heirlooms. I hope I have eradicated all such faults from this edition but await resignedly to be thwarted; it is astonishing how much present day scientific 'fact' is rooted in ancient legend.

In the course of my researches I have received much indirect help from the many authors who have already published works on these animals; I am indebted to them and to the various other people who have given freely of their time and knowledge. In particular, I want to acknowledge the kind assistance I received from Dr Wolfgang Gewalt, Director of the splendid Duisburg Zoological Gardens in Germany, where I observed exemplary conditions for captive dolphins and two wonderful specimens of Beluga.

My friends helped in more personal ways and gave me much encouragement without which I should not have been able to complete my task. My thanks to Gordon Fielden for his unceasing enthusiasm and good humour through many upsets and frustrations, to Robin Wright for his kindness, and to Mij, to whom the whole thing is dedicated, for her long-sufferance.

The Friends of the Earth is one of the most aware and most valuable of organizations, and they deserve the fullest support of everyone interested in seeing the complex beauty of our planet preserved – it has an incalculable amount of ruthless enemies. FOE, personified by Angela King, has kindly provided me with much valuable information on subjects connected with commercial whaling, against which it crusades continually and energetically. Some of the recent legislative successes which help to protect the whales are due principally to the efforts of FOE. There are branches in Amsterdam, Anchorage, Frankfurt, Honolulu, London, Paris, Rome, Seattle, Stockholm, Washington and Zurich.

Lastly, may I express my gratitude to those gentle giants who dwell beneath the sea for giving me so much pleasure, and who, by their sunny natures, provide an illustration of patience and tolerance that all humanity would do well to imitate. It should not really be too difficult – when we have suffered as a race what the whale has suffered, then we might have cause to grumble.

Introduction

Mammals which live in the sea are very different from the rather more typical forms of land-based mammals, which most of us tend initially to visualize. Asked without notice to name a mammal, we should in all probability plump for a dog or some other familiar animal equally well-endowed with hair.

Indeed it was not so long ago that the scientific definition of a mammal suggested that hair was a necessary qualification. Nowadays mammals are broadly defined as warm-blooded animals which rear their young on milk secreted from special organs on the mother's body, known as mammary glands. It is still true, however, that all animals that have a covering of hair are mammals; but the reverse proposition, that all mammals are hairy, is not true.

There are a few wildly different forms of naked or near naked mammals. We ourselves qualify, as Desmond Morris has so astutely pointed out, and so does a strange African rodent called the Naked Mole Rat; and so, to all intents and purposes, do the elephant, rhinoceros, hippopotamus etc. We, however, wear clothes; Naked Mole Rats live beneath the hot Somali desert, and the others also come from the warmer regions of the globe.

Even so, the hairless land mammals are very much in the minority, and that may well be why such a familiar creature as the dolphin is seldom recognized as being a mammal – that, and the fact that it lives in water.

It has been one of the more enlightening aspects of my work to study the effect these animals have on the ordinary paying members of the public at various oceanariums I have been to. The number of children whose knowledgeable fathers have told them 'Of course, they're fish,' must be quite sizeable. How many, I wonder, go through life under this impression, handing out similar pearls of wisdom to anyone unguarded enough to seek their advice?

It is in the whale order, Cetacea, which with its ninety-two species is the largest group of marine mammals, that we find the widest ranging and most perfectly adapted group of mammals to have cast off their outer fur. Some members are absolutely naked while the remainder retain only the vestigial and apparently forgotten bristle here and there, usually near or on the head. The second largest order, Pinnipedia, the seals, sealions and walruses, comprises thirty-two species and is nearly as widely distributed as the whales. Many of these, however, possess very dense, short coats. The sirenians, Sirenia, are by far the smallest complete order of marine mammals, totalling only four species, and they are almost as hairless as the whales. There are other mammals, such as the Sea Otter and the Polar Bear, which live in or are dependent on the sea, and for convenience I have grouped these 'aberrant' species together.

The pinnipeds, though wholly dependent on the sea as a source of food and for all but the most restricted locomotion, spend much of the year in the littoral zone of the coastline, especially the eared seals or otariids, of which the sealion is a familiar example. They are, strangely enough, in general far less aquatic than the two species of marine otters – which are nevertheless usually omitted from works on ocean life. On the other hand, those mysterious, lazy and gentle vegetarians of the tropical shallows, the sirenians, are almost as perfectly adapted to an aquatic existence as any of the whales.

It may not be generally known that all marine mammals were derived originally from ordinary terrestrial quadrupeds. Without this basic knowledge our efforts to familiarize ourselves with these animals come up against certain difficulties.

A casual observer of nature might, without giving the matter much thought, find the idea of air-breathing mammals living in the sea mildly interesting. A specialist in a different branch of natural history might take a greater but still not very great interest in the subject. Even to a large proportion of amateur and professional mammalogists it is a subject often bypassed in favour of the more accessible and accommodating land species.

Understandable as this is, it has led to one or two unfortunate results. One in particular, and it was not until beginning to work on this book that I became so acutely aware of it, is the lamentable lack of literature available on the subject of marine mammals; the amount written on all the cetaceans hardly compares, for instance, to that written solely about the mole.

The reasons for this are obvious enough. To study effectively oceanic creatures in the wild, especially when they are as large, rapid and far-ranging as seals and whales, you have to be either extraordinarily lucky or extraordinarily wealthy or one of the privileged few who actually work below water – and not many of those are interested specifically in mammals. Hence, most of our knowledge comes from either captive or dead specimens; and this is seldom the most profitable way of acquiring information on such matters as social orders, habits and functions, hunting techniques, distribution, natural mortality, migration and a hundred other problems.

This, however, was just one of the reasons which first prompted my deep attachment to all mammals which live in the sea – this mystery and remoteness. And yet it was in the zoo, marineland and dolphinarium, where those precious qualities are notably absent, that I have best been able to get thoroughly acquainted with some of these animals. I have worked or studied in various institutions of this sort and have visited many more; in Germany and Holland I have encountered the exemplary captive conditions for marine mammals equalled only by the Americans.

I offer the above not as an apology but as an explanation. Many of my observations in captivity have had to be sensibly pruned or embroidered before they could be submitted as part of a practical hypothesis for an animal in the wild. I hope with this book not to stagger science but to promote interest. If some influential body had had the courage to recognize sooner the very real plight of just one example, the Blue Whale, that largest of all animals would not now be on the very verge of extinction.

It is solely due to public demand that we now have our league table of vertebrate legal protection, which begins at the top with birds, and works down to the hapless snake at the foot. People do not like seal pup slaughtering; but it is only occasionally brought to their attention and so is quickly forgotten. But, as the saying goes, 'worse things happen at sea'. Because the victim is not a cuddly baby, and because the deed is practically never witnessed by the television camera, the booming business of whaling goes on almost unabated.

I have no wish, as some naturalists evidently have, to go along for the ride on a whaling expedition. I know well enough I should be physically sick. Perhaps the only circumstance justifying my presence would be an opportunity to record the gruesome spectacle on film, and I can imagine all too vividly from the reports of the number of whales caught and processed in 'successful' expeditions just how gory a business it must be.

My encounters with sea-going mammals happen, I am glad to say, under happier circumstances. That they are normally unexpected says much for the excitement of the moment and the unpredictability of these animals. I can safely say that some of the most triumphant and satisfying moments of my life have been spent in the company of wild whales and seals.

One meeting I had some years ago with a Common Seal was particularly exciting – not because it was an exceptionally breathtaking occasion but more because of the sheer charm, warmth, and benevolence that animal in those surroundings seemed to reflect. It was late September, and I was camping near the shores of a tidal loch in western Scotland. It had been a very hot day and I was busily employed in a private battle with a dense swarm of large mosquitoes, which seemed to prefer my particular blood-group to anyone else's, when I heard some curious gurglings, splashings and humanlike groans emanating from the calm water. I had heard some voices coming from around a headland earlier and supposed that what I now heard was a sub-aqua club indulging in their hobby. Grateful for a chance of losing the mosquitoes, I wandered down to the beach. It was a few minutes before I saw anything, and when I did I thought I had been correct in my supposition, for a dark, glistening back, like a diver encased in a wetsuit, appeared momentarily out of the water. I stood idly watching for a few moments, and then to my complete stupefaction was suddenly confronted by a neatly domed head and magnificent white moustache at a mere six yards range; a large pair of melting eyes gazed at me somewhat sadly for what seemed an age. Eventually,

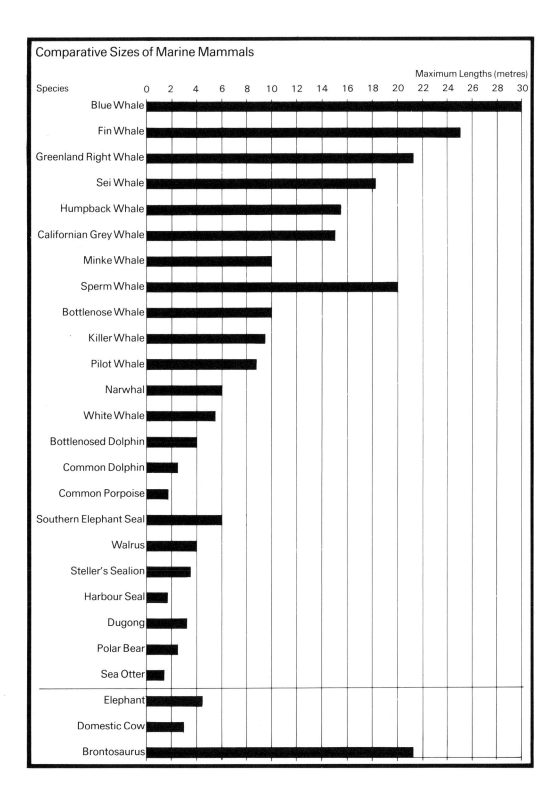

Comparative Sizes of Marine Mammals

Maximum Lengths (metres)

Species: Blue Whale, Fin Whale, Greenland Right Whale, Sei Whale, Humpback Whale, Californian Grey Whale, Minke Whale, Sperm Whale, Bottlenose Whale, Killer Whale, Pilot Whale, Narwhal, White Whale, Bottlenosed Dolphin, Common Dolphin, Common Porpoise, Southern Elephant Seal, Walrus, Steller's Sealion, Harbour Seal, Dugong, Polar Bear, Sea Otter, Elephant, Domestic Cow, Brontosaurus getting tired of my lack of activity, the seal carried on playing and wallowing in the water, snorting happily to himself, quite unconcerned by my rude staring. He remained until dusk, and I have been eternally grateful to him ever since, for I feel it was that meeting which finally cemented my deep love for these mystical and misunderstood clowns of the oceans.

Introduction to the Habitat

1

The Oceans

Sand-strewn caverns, cool and deep,
Where the winds are all asleep;
Where the spent lights quiver and gleam;
Where the salt weed sways in the stream.

from 'The Forsaken Merman' by Matthew Arnold

When we assert that the world is becoming too small for us or that there is nowhere left to explore, what we are trying to say is that we consider there to be insufficient *land* for all our multifarious activities. That may be, but let us remember that over seventy per cent of the world's surface – nearly 140 million square miles – is covered by salt water. Even this figure becomes insignificant when we compare it with the world beneath the surface.

Unlike the land masses, all seas are interconnecting, although to living organisms a combination of factors such as temperature, depth and salinity interact to create very real obstacles to free movement. Apart from such physiological considerations, the actual topography of the oceans is diverse, magnificent and menacing.

The mean depth of the sea is over 12,000ft (compared to an average land height of only 2250ft) and in the deepest parts – the trenches – the depths range from 23,000ft to over 33,000ft, the recorded maximum being 37,782ft in the Mindanao Trench. (Mt Everest in comparison is 29,028ft high.)

To understand the world of the marine mammal best one has first of all to know something of its environment. On a superficial and geological level it can be divided into three main regions: the continental shelf (including the littoral zone), the continental slope, and the ocean floor. Such impassive labels, though, do little to evoke the drama of the submarine world, and it might be as well to examine these regions with a little more interest.

The continental shelf is the immediate submarine continuation of dry land; it is generally of gradual elevation, moulded by erosion, and covered with a deep deposit of river sediments. A multitude of animals and plants prosper in these sunlit waters (the euphotic zone). Most of the following invertebrates are found on the continental shelf or in surface waters: sponges (*c.* 5000 spp.); hydroids, jellyfish, sea anemones and corals (nearly 10,000 spp.); lampshells (*c.* 260 spp.); molluscs (*c.* 45,000 spp.); bristleworms (over 4000 spp.); sea spiders (*c.* 500 spp.); arthropods (*c.* 8500 marine spp.); and echinoderms (*c.* 5400 spp.). Besides the invertebrates, there are well over 11,000 species of marine fish, plus various turtles, sea-snakes and birds. And there are the mammals that are the subject of this book.

As far as botanical life is concerned, the plant or *phyto*plankton has been aptly described as the pasture of the sea. It consists of microscopic, free-floating plants such as diatoms and flagellates, and this mass of plant life (nourished by photosynthesis through the action of the sun on chlorophyll) is the foundation of all oceanic life and perhaps of terrestrial life as well. It is here that the food chain begins. Phytoplankton and the animal plankton (*zoo*plankton) which grazes upon it are collectively known simply as plankton, and as such form the basic food, either directly or indirectly, of all marine life. It is indeed so nourishing and inexhaustible that it alone sustains the Blue Whale (*q.v.*) – the largest animal ever known to have lived. This huge whale and the other mysticete whales feed directly upon the plankton, as do such large fish as the Whale Shark (up to 60ft long) and the Basking Shark (30ft). The food preferences of most other marine animals is more conventional, and the larger invertebrates and shoaling fish constitute the central rungs of the ladder.

Naturally the continental shelving varies considerably in width and depth but on average it is seventy-eight miles wide and terminates at a depth of 430ft from where the rapidly descending and darkening continental slope (the bathyal zone) plunges down towards the abyssal ocean floor (the abyssal pelagic zone). Going down the continental slope the pressure increases rapidly, the aspect becomes starker and plant life vanishes altogether. At a depth of 3000ft no atmospheric light can penetrate, and a world of pitch darkness takes over. The familiar fish are replaced by scavengers and strange predators which hunt one another. Geographically, the slopes are quite staggering – they are great escarpments, the grandest on all earth. On an average, these continental boundaries plunge down to a depth of some 12,000ft but in certain areas (e.g. off the Philippine and Marianas Islands) they plummet straight down to a depth of over 30,000ft. It is not only their height and steepness that make the continental slopes so remarkable; they also possess canyons, valleys and so on such as we associate with terrestrial landscapes.

At the foot of these escarpments, the descent begins to level out along the continental rise, and the vast abyssal plains, or ocean floor, begins; towards the centre are the mid-oceanic ridges (submarine mountain ranges). Even at these depths, where the pressure is as much as three tons to the square inch, sufficient oxygen is brought

down from the surface by oceanic circulation to sustain life. Conditions are permanently near freezing, but animals can survive and indeed thrive. They do not of course have to tolerate the enormous pressure; the pressure inside the animals is the same as that without; as the different types do not ordinarily need to stray beyond comparatively restricted limits, they have no need to adjust to varying pressures. Factors such as this limit both vertical and horizontal free movement; a deep sea animal confronted by an oceanic ridge can neither go round it nor over it.

Male Weddell Seal at its breathing hole in the Antarctic ice. Seals keep such holes open through regular use, though this may prove a source of danger since man and, in the Arctic, Polar Bears use them as ambush points. However, they are safe from Killer Whales, which do not venture under solid ice.

A thick layer of sediment, in places over two miles deep, covers the ocean floor; it has been built up over hundreds of millions of years by what Rachel Carson, in her magnificent book *The Sea Around Us* (1951), described as 'the long snowfall'. The tiny particles endlessly drifting and floating down include all manner of substances from volcanic dust to the siliceous remains of minute organisms, from fragments of shells and skeletons to grains of sand and terrestrial silt. As the sediment imperceptibly built up and the ocean floor sagged beneath its weight, page after page of history was laid down. These pages can now be turned and read with the aid of core samples, and they make fascinating reading. The long snowfall continues today, and must do so until the end of the world.

Oceanography is perhaps the most rapidly expanding of all sciences. The blind rush for oil has added further impetus to its already con-

Harp Seals hauled out on a jigsaw of ice floes off the Labrador coast. Such 'terrain provides the seals with considerable protection from attacks both from below and above and gives them adequate escape routes.

siderable momentum. Besides oil and fish, the sea offers many other valuables, perhaps not willingly nor openly, but they are there all the same. Not the least of these is the plankton, the very food and life of all oceans. No-one knows just what effect the drastic over-fishing of the great whales has had on the balance of nature in the sea or on the plankton itself. This subject is discussed further in Chapter 5.

It is tempting to assume that the scarcity of great whales has had a beneficial effect on the plankton. However, I view with horror the proposals put forward by the Russians for the harvesting of Krill. Krill (*Euphausia superba*) is a shrimp-like crustacean about $\frac{3}{4}$in. long; it occurs in vast swarms and is the principal animal component of the plankton in Antarctic waters; it feeds on single-celled diatoms and other microplants which abound in the polar seas. Krill has long been regarded with hungry eyes by the world's nutritionists; it has been described as the 'richest source of marine protein in the world' (and the word 'marine' could easily be omitted).

Any proposal to harvest this most important of all ecological cornerstones by sterile machines must be contested at all levels. Without doubt the great whales provide not only the safest (in ecological terms) but also the most economical means of harvesting plankton – if harvest it we must – but first of all they have to be allowed to rebuild their numbers. Whales return to their environment, through their corpses and their excreta, such essential biochemicals as natural

organic matter for bacteria to attack, natural oxidation, organic nitrogen and ammonium ions etc. A factory ship can only steal from nature; the sea can become 'bankrupt', like a store which is preyed upon without restriction by shoplifters. If Krill is exploited indiscriminately the consequences would be dire not only for the whales but for all marine life, and possibly for ourselves as well.

During springtime and the consequent lengthening of the day, the phytoplankton multiplies dramatically and can noticeably colour the sea red or brown. This phenomenon occurs especially in enclosed seas such as the Red Sea (which thus acquired its name). The open oceans, on the other hand, are subject to the worldwide movements of pelagic currents which dissipate and scatter the free-floating diatoms; the flagellates and most zooplankton are only capable of limited vertical self-propulsion, to save them from sinking below their food supply, and are borne along by the currents without resistance. Many species of plankton migrate vertically to the surface at night, and sink down in the daytime, some of them to a depth of 1500ft.

This then, very briefly, is the mysterious, gloomy and somewhat frightening world the whales, seals and sirenians returned to, and the story of their success is told in the following pages.

The voracious Killer Whale pursues its prey in the Ross Sea off the Barne Glacier. Judging by the comparative violence of the shock waves, the Killer Whale would seem to be closing in.

17

2 The History of Sea-going Mammals

Evolution

And the rainbow lives in the curve of the sand;
Hither, come hither and see;
And the rainbow hangs on the poising wave,
And sweet is the colour of cove and cave,
And sweet shall your welcome be:
O hither, come hither, and be our lords.

from 'The Sea Fairies' by Alfred Tennyson

There are three main orders of marine mammals – Cetacea (whales), Pinnipedia (seals) and Sirenia (sirenians). Apparently their ancestors all returned to the sea independently of each other, and in different ages and parts of the globe. Moreover, and most important, they are all derived from different stock.

The ancestral order of *all* living mammals (apart from Monotremata which are thought to have evolved separately from the primitive Docodonta) is Pantotheria. In the Jurassic period (about 150 million years ago), when the mammalian break-away from pure reptilian stock first began, there were five orders of primitive mammals. Three were evolutionary 'dead ends', but the other two, Pantotheria and Docodonta, began to evolve and explore all the possibilities of their newly-acquired advantages: warm-bloodedness, speed and agility, complex brains, better heat retention, live young (retained within the womb and born in an advanced stage), prolonged maternal care and, above all, intelligence.

Even so, this was still the age of the great dinosaurs, and their sheer size dominated the primitive mammals for about eighty million years. The mammals were forced to use all their resourcefulness to avoid and hide from the great reptiles. In retrospect, this cannot have done the mammalian tree much harm. It must certainly have stood them in good stead, and when the mysterious reptilian decline started, they were the obvious successors. So, about seventy million years ago, before the beginning of the Tertiary period, the mammalian world erupted. Pantotheria divided: the marsupials went one way

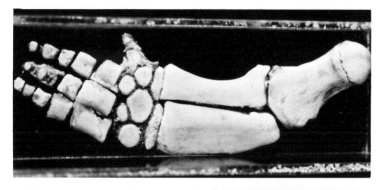

top This skeleton of a Common Porpoise's flipper shows well how the typically mammalian forelimb has become evolutionarily adapted. The proportions of the 'hand' have become relatively lengthened and those of the forearm correspondingly shortened.

below Top view of the head of a Beluga or White Whale. The solitary blowhole performs the function of the nostrils, and it has migrated to the top of the head to facilitate breathing.

independently while the insectivores branched and blossomed, and evolved into the versatile placental mammals we know today. The insectivore mainstream sent out conquering tributaries wherever there was a vacant ecological niche, and there were many.

One such niche was the sea. When the competition grew a little too vigorous on *terra firma*, or the earth became for some reason unsuitable, and the living gleaned from fresh water proved none too fattening, the sea must have appeared an ideal, an irresistible alternative. The adaptive and versatile young mammals could neither ignore the challenge of the sea nor its rewards.

Obviously much of what follows is conjectural; it is almost impossible to be positive about events so long ago that took millions of years to come about and about which there is little geological evidence. However, certain things are quite well authenticated. It is almost certain that the whales were the first to invade the sea, about sixty-five million years ago, followed by the sirenians, some five million years later, and most recently the seals, in the Eocene epoch, about fifty million years ago. It is immediately apparent that the order of evolution corresponds accurately with the respective degrees of specialization. In other words, the whales have now overcome all obstacles and are as much at home in the sea as any animal; the sirenians, while being totally aquatic, are confined to estuaries and the coastal shallows of the tropics, while the seals are still dependent on dry land for certain essential functions but at the same time are extremely successful marine animals. At this stage we need not be concerned with the other marine forms of different land-based orders (see Chapter 9).

As I have said, the three totally committed orders adopted the sea independently. Once in the sea they could well have found themselves in competition and radiated adaptively towards different goals to reduce the competitive element.

The cetaceans almost certainly had a common ancestor with the Archaecoceti or zeuglodonts – primitive and extinct forms of marine mammals. Zeuglodonts were similar in many ways to whales but less specialized. While it is probably true that they had a common ancestor, it is impossible for whales to have derived from any known form of zeuglodont. A. Brazier Howell in his book *Aquatic Mammals* (1930) believes that the two diverged at tangents from the same stock – the route taken by the zeuglodonts proving itself eventually to be the less successful. Exactly the same kind of periotic bones found in whales have also been found in the skulls of zeuglodonts, and in no other mammal, living or extinct.

The ancestral stock of the cetaceans *and* zeuglodonts is highly problematical. Some workers believe it to be bear-like, others horse-like (or more descriptively, perhaps, tapir-like – and tapirs are of course today very aquatic). I myself prefer not to speculate. It is fairly certain that the stock of today's whales was a small animal, but whether it took to the sea directly or by way of fresh water is another debatable point. I personally think that the invasion of the sea was a gradual one, via swamps, freshwater estuaries, etc. All reasonable indications point to this more cautious procession; moreover, I believe the cetaceans separated into the toothed and baleen whales also at this stage of their development, the baleen whales being attracted by the massive quantities of plankton which they found virtually untapped in the cold polar seas. The fish which till then had had the plankton to themselves now faced not only the competition of the primitive great whales but also the menace of the emerging toothed whales. While the whales' ancestors tackled the plankton, the dolphins' concentrated on the vast schools of shoaling fish, which were almost as abundant as the plankton. It was presumably at a later date that the Sperm Whale and the other squid-feeders discovered the rich source of food lurking in the bathyal zone, developed their impressive diving powers, and so avoided any competition with their odontocete relations.

While the whales were conquering the oceans, the sirenians were beginning to emerge in the estuaries of tropical rivers. With no carnivorous inclinations, they were content to idle away their days browsing on the aquatic vegetation which proliferated in these estuaries and along the littoral zone of the coast. The absence of any

The eared seals, unlike the true seals, are still able to use their hindlimbs to speed up their movement over land. Though retaining firm links with land, seals now regard the sea as their true environment. Here a herd of Californian Sealions races to reach water in a moment of panic.

serious predators gave them an easy-going nature. It is only now, through man, that they are suffering for this 'oversight'.

If all we know of cetacean ancestry is that it was carnivorous, we are able to be a little more positive about that of the sirenians. They have certainly descended from plant-eating ungulates, and their present day affinities, together with studies of fossils found in the African region, indicate very strongly that their actual forefathers were the early proboscideans (ancestors of today's elephants). All four sirenian species are now seriously threatened with extinction.

The sirenians, it may be assumed, progressed peacefully towards a completely aquatic existence.

Until quite recently the seals were thought of as nothing other than specialized members of the order Carnivora. This theory has now been outmoded, and they are quite rightly allotted their own order (Pinnipedia). It is, though, fairly obvious that their origins lie with the carnivores, from whom they probably diverged about fifty million years ago, but conclusive evidence dates no farther back than about half that time – to the beginning of the Miocene epoch.

The seals, while comparatively young as an order, are in some ways the most successful of all the marine mammals, if only through the advantages they have retained by keeping some contact with dry land. Of course this can also be to their disadvantage, and it seems that the seals are progressing, as did the whales, towards total marine commitment. Perhaps once the call of the sea has been answered and the journey begun, it is found to be down a one-way street with no waiting.

Seals possess the alert, combative fierceness of true carnivores. Dolphins, too, are carnivorous, yet one cannot fail to observe their sweeter natures and general friendliness. I have never known a dolphin attack anything other than food, yet I know to my cost that a seal, like any wild cat or dog, will unthinkingly snap at anything within reach. Their limits of tolerance and irritation are not very high.

Status
& Distribution

3

Oh then a longing like despair
Is to their farthest caverns sent;
For surely once, they feel, we were
Parts of a single continent.
Now round us spreads the watery plain –
Oh might our marges meet again!

from 'To Marguerite' by Matthew Arnold

The most important factors governing the distribution of any animal are the availability and abundance of food and the suitability of the climate and terrain. Status is determined by the success of the species and by the size and nature of the particular ecological niche which it occupies. To borrow an example from another branch of the animal kingdom, the Lesser Flamingo (*Phoeniconaias minor*) lives where there are sufficient quantities of microscopic animal life to sustain it. That happens to be in certain inland alkaline lakes of Central Africa; the Lesser Flamingo is therefore restricted to these areas. It is gregarious because so much of its preferred food is crammed within such a relatively confined area, and also to ensure safety from predation. Animals which have to roam far in order to glean a living cannot afford to share their slender pickings, and so adopt solitary or family life-styles. This is, of necessity, an over-simplification; each species is a law unto itself, but each even so will follow certain rigid guidelines and only stray from them in order to cut a corner or to explore a 'byway'.

Man has thrown the entire subject of animal status into confusion; in theatrical terms, he is now the self-appointed leading actor-cum-director (and thinks he is also the producer). He continually upstages, fires and recasts the other players to such an extent that many do not know where they are or what role they should be performing. The deletion of just one part can throw the remainder into total disarray; they may, if allowed, expand to accommodate it, but they are just as likely to miss their cue and lose their way in the ensuing turmoil.

Until man arrived and trespassed on the oceans, the whales and other marine animals had worked out their individual roles very exactly, and the whole play ran like clockwork with every intention and prospect of a long and successful run; but as any actor knows a new director can cause havoc.

All oceanic life stems from the plankton which, as already described, multiplies in the polar and sub-temperate waters of the world. Whether the whales feed on it directly or on the planktonic fish, it follows that their main areas of congregation will be in the higher latitudes. Most seals are fish-eaters (and the Crabeater Seal feeds directly on krill) and therefore a similar distribution also suits them.

The warmer and tropical pelagic areas are obviously not devoid of fish or small invertebrates but the huge schools of shoaling fish are not present in such numbers and large gatherings of carnivorous mammals are also proportionately fewer. The dolphins found in the tropics usually occur in widely-scattered small schools and are great travellers.

Their wonderful powers of heat-retention have ensured that the circumpolar whales and seals seldom, if ever, need to leave the cold waters which to us seem inhospitable. The Polar Bear (*q.v.*) was similarly attracted to the Arctic, and developed its own ways of keeping warm and surviving the bleak conditions. The universal prey-species are those found in the deeper zones of the sea, where the temperature and conditions are more constant and not subject to the vagaries of climate or the violent extremes of seasons. The discovery of cuttlefish, enormous squids and other cephalopods many fathoms beneath the surface motivated the Sperm Whale in particular and opened up for it an almost boundless world. Nowadays the Sperm Whale is one of the widest ranging and most successful of all marine mammals. The Weddell Seal (*q.v.*) could conceivably have enjoyed a similar cosmopolitan distribution had it not been tied for reasons of reproduction (and seclusion) to the Antarctic ice-fields, where it is one of the commonest species.

The herbivorous sirenians are restricted to their tropical and sub-tropical coasts by their food supply and for reasons of safety. They hardly have the equipment to survive for long should they stray beyond their rather narrow boundaries. The sirenians are a classic example of animals forgotten by progressive nature and living in an ecological backwater. They have probably never been very numerous in spite of a compact and ideal habitat.

Conversely an animal like the Rough-toothed Dolphin occurs world-wide; but its wide distribution does not necessarily signify a dense population. The Crabeater Seal, in contrast, is confined to the Antarctic coasts, yet is the most numerous of all seals and possibly of all marine mammals. Ironically, the very expansiveness of the great whales' range is now a factor inhibiting their recovery. Should many schools be depleted, as often happens, the individuals lucky enough to escape will not necessarily be compatible. And the chances of two

compatible individuals meeting up at the right place and time in an area like the North Atlantic is going to be fairly remote. (Bear in mind also that, the Minke Whale apart, all great whales are further handicapped by breeding only every second year.) To help offset this communication problem, which could be serious even with numbers at full strength, certain safeguards exist. The uncanny range of sounds or calls these leviathans are able to produce is something still not fully understood. We can appreciate the sounds on an aesthetic level and have made some scientific inroads, but there is undoubtedly much to learn. It has often been asserted (not unreasonably) that some of a whale's calls, those lower in pitch, are so far-carrying through an aqueous medium that they may be picked up by another whale hundreds of miles away. This extraordinary vocal (and auditory) ability coupled with set migration routes and destination areas helps to compensate somewhat for the vastness of the range.

Evidently some mechanism to prevent the animals from becoming lost on their journeys has been developed; but how whales navigate is a mystery far from solved. Perhaps when we know more about the migration of birds, and of such mysteries as the emigration of the juvenile cuckoo, we shall be better equipped to tackle the problem of the whale. Do they similarly use the stars and the moon, or some other method unknown to us, like the flow of currents which we know follow set courses? Perhaps a mixture of factors such as salinity, temperature, taste and organisms or matter borne along by the currents interact to guide a school of whales along its path. Certain

There is little that this Weddell Seal can do. Its floe has become separated from any safe means of retreat across the ice, and with the two attacking Killer Whales it would have no chance in the water.

25

species we know follow coastal routes, and this is of course the safest and surest form of sea-navigation. Sadly, though, this habit has also speeded the decline of some species: humans were quick to notice and anticipate this supply of food and provisions which so conveniently transported itself right into their laps every year.

The four members of the *Platanistidae* (river dolphins) together with the Amazonian White and Irrawaddy Dolphins have either become adapted to an estuarine and freshwater environment or simply remained behind when their more adventurous congeners probed the sea so many millions of years ago. Studies of comparative anatomy favour the latter hypothesis (see Chapter 6). However, rivers or, more accurately, estuaries in both the Old and New Worlds support the river dolphins (three species in South America and three in Eastern Asia). One is forced then to ask the obvious question: is it feasible that the toothed whales had more than one ancestor, and that these took to the water at more or less the same times on opposite sides of the world? It seems highly unlikely; in which case some dolphins must have crossed the Pacific at an early stage in their development and taken up residence in estuaries similar to those they had left on the other side (not necessarily in a single lifetime). The Amazonian White and Irrawaddy Dolphins presumably have moved back to freshwater, since they are members of confirmed marine families.

The distribution of whales is impossible to set down accurately; the problems are similar to those encountered in describing the exact ranges of birds, but birds are considerably easier to observe. The majority of birds are closely tied to land, and their ranges can be recorded in terms of the countries, districts etc. with which all are familiar. Oceans are uninhabited by humans and appear to our eyes featureless, lacking specific, named regions. At best we can say that such and such a species inhabits, for example, the western part of the Atlantic; we do not know precisely when or how far it moves away, nor any of the other details generally associated with an animal's range, status and distribution. Seals, while on dry land, present no problems, but once they take to the sea an equivalent situation is created. The best way of familiarizing oneself with the overall distribution of most species is, I think, to approach it as it were from the opposite direction. There follows here a series of tables designed to show the species which can reasonably be expected to appear in the waters of the main zoogeographical regions. It does not pretend to be exhaustive, nor could it be with our present lack of knowledge, but it should help at least to narrow down the specimens sighted from ships or found stranded on beaches. It also helps to indicate the dispersal of families. It will perhaps be necessary to refer at the same time to the systematic list of all species at the end of the book.

Holarctic Region

Ziphiidae	Beaked Whales (some)
Physeteridae	Sperm Whales
Monodontidae	White Whales and Narwhals (exclusively)
Stenidae	(only *Steno* Rough-toothed Dolphin)
Delphinidae	Typical Dolphins (only a few, some others marginally)
Phocaenidae	Porpoises (few)
Mysticeti	Baleen Whales (all except three)
Thalarctos	Polar Bear (exclusively)
Enhydra	Sea Otter (exclusively)
Otariidae	(only *Callorhinus* Northern Fur Seal and *Zalophus* Californian Sealion)
Odobenidae	Walruses (exclusively)
Phocinae	Northern Seals (exclusively)
Monachinae	Monk Seals (some)
Cystophorinae	Proboscis Seals (some)
Trichechus manatus	N. American Manatee

Neotropical Region

Inia	Geoffroy's Dolphin
Stenodelphis	La Plata Dolphin
Ziphiidae	Beaked Whales (some)
Physeteridae	Sperm Whales
Stenidae	(*Steno* Rough-toothed Dolphin and *Sotalia* spp. Amazonian and Guyana White Dolphins)
Delphinidae	Typical Dolphins (many, especially *Cephalorhynchus* spp.)
Phocaenidae	Porpoises (some)
Balaenopteridae	Baleen Whales (some)
Balaenidae	(only *Eubalaena australis* Southern Right Whale and *Caperea* Pygmy Right Whale)
Otariidae	Eared Seals (principally *Otaria* and *Arctocephalus australis*)
Lobodontinae	Southern Seals (some)
Monachinae	Monk Seals (some)
Trichechidae	Manatees (except *senegalensis*)

Ethiopian Region

Ziphiidae	Beaked Whales (some)
Physeteridae	Sperm Whales
Stenidae	Dolphins (some)
Delphinidae	Typical Dolphins (many)
Phocaenidae	Porpoises (some)
Balaenopteridae	Baleen Whales
Balaenidae	(as *Neotropical Region*)
Otariidae	Eared Seals (principally *Arctocephalus pusillus*)
Dugong dugon	Dugong
Trichechus senegalensis	West African Manatee

Oriental Region

Platanista	Gangetic Dolphin
Lipotes	Chinese River Dolphin
Ziphiidae	Beaked Whales (some)
Physeteridae	Sperm Whale
Stenidae	Dolphins (most)
Delphinidae	Typical Dolphins (many)
Phocaenidae	(only *Neomeris* Finless Black Porpoise)
Balaenopteridae	Baleen Whales
Balaenidae	(as *Neotropical Region*)
Dugong dugon	Dugong

Australasian Region

Ziphiidae	Beaked Whales (many)
Physeteridae	Sperm Whale
Stenidae	Dolphins (some, especially *Sousa lentiginosa*)
Delphinidae	Typical Dolphins (many)
Phocaenidae	Porpoises (occasionally *Phocaena vomerina* and *Neomeris*)
Balaenopteridae	Baleen Whales (most)
Balaenidae	(as *Neotropical Region*)
Otariidae	Eared Seals (some)
Lobodontinae	Southern Seals
Dugong dugon	Dugong

I have not yet specifically mentioned the numerous species whose survival is endangered – partly because, being a subject of such importance, it calls for special treatment. Chapter 13 deals in part with the rarities; additional references are made throughout the book and especially, where appropriate, in the *Species Biographies* at the ends of Chapters 6, 7 and 8.

Design

4

*Diviner than the dolphin is nothing
yet created; . . . by the devising of
Dionysos they exchanged the land for
the sea and put on the form of fishes.*

from 'Halieutica' by Oppian (fl. 3rd cent. AD)

Some of the drastic modifications needed to transform an earth-bound quadruped into something resembling a fish can be readily appreciated. Yet the transformation was apparently managed with consummate ease. Time of course was on its side; if a species battled for existence, it did so over millions of years and not, as it does today, over a handful. And if a species died out, as many did, it was the result, one might say, of a democratic decision: an event, given the fair test of time, inevitable and essential to the plan of nature. Unsuccessful species had to be sacrificed to benefit the majority. Nowadays extinction has been debased; it is no longer a purely natural process.

The first thing a prototypal marine mammal had to ensure was that, once in the water, it would not drown. Most mammals are innately able to swim, if not always very proficiently, and any animal intent on an aquatic existence would soon develop its swimming ability. Gradually the tail, if it possessed one of substance, would gain ascendancy over the more powerful *hind* feet, owing to the unavoidable swaying of the hindquarters while swimming in a dog-like fashion.

In all adult cetaceans and sirenians the hindlimbs have now totally vanished. A vestigial femur is present but that is all that remains of the pelvic girdle. This small bone is not attached to the backbone but is lost within a mass of muscle.

In the whales, the horizontal propulsive movement of the emerging tail flukes evidently veered to a vertical one; or, more likely, the ancestor was of an active disposition and early began swimming with an action akin to that of a human's butterfly stroke – similar in fact to the method employed by river otters. Whatever the origin, the whales' present means of locomotion immediately sets them apart from fish.

The seals, instead of growing a pair of tail flukes like the whales, modified their hindlimbs into fin-like appendages which are sculled laterally. (I am mainly concerned in this chapter with cetaceans and sirenians, essentially the *marine* mammals, but the Pinnipedia are sometimes used for comparison. They are covered in their own right in Chapter 7.)

Apart from perfecting the 'propeller', the early marine mammal had to streamline its body by reducing, moulding or removing all prominences such as the scrotum, external pinnae and the forelimbs – which were given the role of stabilizing organs and accordingly became flipper-like, the humerus, radius and ulna being shortened and the five digits united within a common sac.

While the hindlimbs atrophied and forelimbs were converted into rigid paddles, the trunk was refined into a torpedo or teardrop-like shape. The neck is now so shortened as to be to all intents and purposes non-existent, and the head appears as a direct continuation of the body. The anterior section, fashioned by the play of water, has achieved various shapes which are a compromise between the necessary remodelling and the essential and individual cephalic functioning. Toothed whales need only the typically strong jaws of carnivorous animals, and the foremost part of the head (the snout) was fashioned with few restrictions by the all-important search for the speed and litheness essential in the pursuit of fast-moving fish. The skulls of odontocetes are strange in that they are slightly asymmetrical; the left and right-hand sides are of unequal proportions.

Baleen whales were destined to be large through many factors: the nutritive value and relative inactivity of their superabundant food, and the sudden freedom they found from the stresses and strains of gravity. In fact, there appear to be no restrictive influences at all on their enormous size; and who is to say that they may not grow larger still, if allowed to survive?

There is no such thing as a specific streamlined shape; the term simply implies the attainment of easy motion (not *necessarily* speed) with the least expenditure of effort. A racing car is streamlined, but so is an express train; their difference in shape is decreed by the dissimilar jobs for which they are designed. Similarly, a snake is more superbly streamlined than a cheetah, yet the cheetah is considerably faster – it is a mammal built for speed and has a phenomenal energy output; a snake does not require speed but does need to move easily through dense vegetation. Streamlining of the baleen whales may not have given them the sinuosity of the dolphin but it moulded the animal well enough to enable it to cleave the water as quickly as necessary, which in the case of the finbacked whales is very swiftly indeed. They cruise at about 12mph and can achieve speeds of 30mph over short distances, which is generally too fast even for modern whaling boats.

In the shaping of the mysticete head, account had to be taken of

The tracks left by the awkward progression of a Grey Seal across sand. The fore-flippers provide balance and traction, but the hind ones drag along uselessly

the immense quantity of baleen forming in the mouth, and this resulted, I think, in a remarkable compromise, which can be appreciated from studying a whale's profile – perhaps not immediately appreciated, as we have first to remove the familiar picture from our minds and substitute a vision of a mammal.

A dorsal fin, it would seem, is useful without being critical. The more nimble odontocetes have developed them, but not all the mysticetes or the sirenians; and the pinnipeds presumably are not sufficiently specialized. As we have seen, streamlining in terrestrial species takes many forms and is subject to many opposing stimuli; underwater these stimuli are clearly fewer, since a similar basic shape was arrived at quite independently by such heterogeneous animals as the extinct *Ichthyosaurus* (Reptilia), the dolphin (Mammalia) and certain sharks (Chondrichthyes). We can assume then that the present form of the dolphin is as near perfect as possible.

An aquatic body form should ideally be rather cigar-shaped, with both ends tapering. Some of the cetaceans, such as the Sperm Whale with its astonishing mass of rostral tissue, indicate that the stimulus for a blunt face can be more powerful than that for a tapered one. This stimulus, which must be extremely strong to invalidate the call for streamlining, can still not be satisfactorily explained. One theory suggests that the function of the accentuated forehead of most odontocetes, or 'melon' as it is known in the whaling business, is that of a shock-absorber, protecting the delicate frontal area of the brain-case from the pressure experienced as it moves swiftly through water, and that in the case of the Sperm Whale it may now be an instance of an exaggerated evolutionary trend, perhaps like the tusk of the Narwhal (*q.v.*).

However, an animal would hardly develop such an unwieldy protuberance unless it fulfilled some vital need. Many people now believe it to be a device for directing and focusing into a narrow beam the various sonar sounds which are made in the glottis. Others believe that it serves some physiological function, possibly connected with the migration of the nostrils to the top of the head and the ability to dive deeply. This is discussed in more detail below, as is a third theory, that it gives buoyancy to the disproportionately large head.

The situation of the blowhole(s) is one of the most interesting and definitive of the many external transformations undergone by the whales. Internally the transformation is not quite as amazing as it might seem; it has been brought about basically by the remodelling and lengthening of the premaxilla, forming a beak, and the sympathetic shortening of the nasal bone or muzzle, with the resulting upward shift of the nostrils, which in the toothed whales have merged into a single orifice sometimes situated to the left of centre.

An animal intent on moving rapidly through water will not want to reduce speed and raise its head above the surface every time it needs to breathe. Such a handicap would be intolerable on migration and when chasing fish or fleeing from enemies. As it is, all cetaceans are able to roll out of the water to breathe without slackening pace; the exhalations and inhalations are extremely rapid and explosive. The Sirenia and Pinnipedia are in the process of similarly realigning their nasal orifices.

It might be assumed that, through the attentions of parasites and sessile growth, constant immersion in water would render any fur literally unbearable; in which case it would be eliminated early in the animal's aquatic development. Certain qualifications are necessary, however, because the Sea Otter (*q.v.*) in particular is almost as exclusively aquatic as the whales. (Seals haul out regularly and are then able to dry out and groom their pelts.) Presumably the cetacean ancestor had a coarse pelage which the early whales would not have been able to keep clean; nor would it have served them well as an insulator or as an aid to smooth movement through water. The Sea Otter has a remarkably fine and velvety fur, as have the fur seals, which also spend prolonged periods in the sea.

Instead of the dense and luxurious underpelt of the fur seals, the whales developed a thick layer of blubber (see Chapter 6) which can serve them in times of food shortage. Blubber must however have other functions. If it were solely for insulation and food storage, the sirenians would not be so amply endowed. They live in a warm climate (and incidentally have very little tolerance of low temperatures) and being herbivorous can seldom need to be short of food. It is unconvincing to state that the blubber in some way assists buoyancy, since it could be argued that the ability to dive deeply and easily is of prime importance to most whales and, for that matter, to the Walrus. Perhaps there is a physiological explanation, as there may be too for the 'melon' and the fat organs which members of the Odontoceti are prone to develop.

The ability to make prolonged and sometimes deep dives was obviously of paramount importance if whales were to make a success of an aquatic existence. Fundamentally their skill lies in being able to hold their breath long enough to allow themselves time to achieve the object of the dive, which is nearly always the acquisition of food. Their inherent strength and streamlining helps to take care of the rest. Diving proficiently, however, raises not only problems of duration but also of depth. Whales (and some seals) have to be capable of surviving often quite rapid and severe changes of pressure with no ill effects; furthermore they have to be able to ascend quickly, and this raises the question of decompression or caisson sickness which quite needlessly baffled many people for a long time.

Human divers rising too rapidly from a depth of about 200ft are liable to suffer from the painful and sometimes fatal disorder known as the 'bends'. The reason, as most people know, is the absorption of nitrogen in the lungs by the blood under pressure; when the pressure is suddenly reduced (i.e. while surfacing) the dissolved nitrogen explodes from solution causing bubbles to form in the blood, as when the cap is taken off a bottle of soda water. If these bubbles appear in the fatty tissues covering the nerve fibres, as they are very likely to, paralysis can result, and if they are carried to the heart, forming an air lock, then the diver dies. Whales of course need to surface rapidly but for them the problem of caisson sickness does not arise. Whereas a human diver has a continual supply of oxygen and therefore nitrogen pumped into him for the duration of his dive, a whale has only the amount with which it originally sounded, and so has only very little to cope with. Even so, any nitrogen which *is* present is thought to be absorbed by an oily foam secreted by special glands in the breathing passages.

The spouts or blows of whales arise, partly anyway, from circumstances brought about by the above. In medieval times whales were thought to spout water, and pictures showed them doing this. More recently the spout was believed, and still is in some quarters, to be solely caused by the condensation of the warm breath when exhaled. While this will certainly contribute to the spout in a cold atmosphere, it does not explain its appearance in warm and tropical areas. A more advanced idea is that the oily foam mentioned above mixes with the breath (and a certain amount of water which must inevitably get into the orifices) on each explosive exhalation and appears as a fine, misty vapour, varying in height, shape and angle, if not from species to species, certainly from family to family.

We must now consider the outstanding ability of whales to descend to great depths. Seals cannot as a rule stay submerged as long nor dive as deeply as the whales, though considering their more recent specialization they do exceedingly well. Sirenians, and also the river dolphins, have no need to make long and deep dives, and have not developed this technique very far.

The mechanics of the vascular system and how it can prolong a dive are discussed on later pages. There is no basic difference between the equipment of a seal and that of a whale. But however well designed the apparatus is for conserving and rationing oxygen, it does not explain the staggering depths achieved by some species. The Sperm Whale, largest of the odontocetes, is known to be capable of reaching the abyssal ocean floor. A skeleton was hauled up, entangled in a submarine cable, off the Colombian coast in 1932 from a depth of 3700ft. It had presumably been searching for squids when its lower jaw got caught in the cable, which then became wrapped round one flipper, the body and the tail; one can imagine the terrible struggle that must have ensued. At such a depth, the pressure (weight of water) would be savage – about 123 atmospheres (1800lbs per square inch). A human diver, even one equipped with breathing apparatus, has difficulty in descending below 150ft. And for every 30ft down, the pressure increases by about one atmosphere (over 14.7lbs per square inch).

The main danger to a whale in a pressure of a hundred atmospheres is that water will be forced down the air passages into the lungs. To combat such an eventuality certain safeguards have been evolved. Any mammal that spends much time in water soon develops the power to close its nostrils at will, and before long (in evolutionary terms) it is the closed position which is maintained involuntarily and not the other way around. I have observed seals and whales closely and am in no doubt that the closed position is the relaxed one. Apart from the strong external nares closing the blowhole, there is also a system of valves formed by air sacs round the nasal passages which help to seal off the lungs.

It might be thought that whales would be in danger of choking when swallowing under water. Although man can swallow underwater, choking can occur if he is not careful. (Terrestrial mammals have to be able to eat and breathe simultaneously.) But a whale runs no such risk; the epiglottis at the base of the tongue is extended, fitting perfectly into the nasal passage or larynx and effectively sealing it off. This safety mechanism must be especially important when feeding at great depths under enormous pressure.

The Sperm Whale's huge barrel-shaped head, housing the spermaceti organ, 'junk' and an enormous quantity of fine oil has been the cause of much speculation in the past, and it still defies a neat explanation. The 'junk' (so christened by whalers) is a mass of fibrous tissues lying between the spermaceti organ and the jaw. Some of the more plausible reasons for the existence of the spermaceti case have already been mentioned, but two merit more attention, and it is possible that both have played some part in shaping it.

The nasal passages of the Sperm Whale have separated, possibly through the crowding of the spermaceti; the left is the shorter (although still a few yards long) and probably the chief conductor of air during breathing. The right nasal passage, which meanders somewhat before joining the blowhole by means of a very small aperture, is particularly interesting: its posterior section is enlarged to extraordinary proportions and can be dilated with air. It is thought possible that some physiological function is served during a deep dive by air being forced into this passage from the lungs (which are relatively small compared to a man's). Accumulated carbon dioxide, which triggers the breathing reflex, has to be stored by a whale or seal when it is diving deeply. (It is not lack of oxygen which panics a drowning man into gulping down water but the action of carbon dioxide on the 'respiration centre' of the brain.) Spermaceti oil has a good carbon dioxide absorption potential, and it is possible that under pressure some carbon dioxide diffuses from the blood into the oil where it is stored safely until flushed out as the whale pants on surfacing, when the process would be reversed. There must surely be some connection between the Sperm Whale's abnormally large spermaceti case and its ability to dive deeper and for longer than any other marine mammal.

A more recent theory comes from the National Institute of Oceanography. It suggests that the spermaceti case acts as a kind of buoyancy tank. The density of water is such that the deeper a whale descends the more buoyant it becomes and the more energy it has to expend. As the whale travels downwards and meets increasingly colder water, the spermaceti is thought to contract and solidify (as it does on exposure to air), thus becoming denser and helping to offset the increased buoyancy experienced by the animal. Conversely, when the whale wishes to ascend, blood may be pumped through the capillaries, warming up and mollifying the spermaceti, which will then bring the whale to the surface, since it has become lighter than the water.

The sheer size of the spermaceti case and head of the Sperm Whale should be stressed: in a large male, the length of the head is two-fifths of the total, so the cephalic equipment must be at least one third of the animal's body length, say nearly 20ft long. The amount of oil contained in the spermaceti organ and junk can be as much as twenty-seven barrels, although fifteen is more usual. Sickly specimens have been caught which are devoid of any spermaceti oil whatsoever, but that is extremely unusual.

Senses

Just as a terrestrial animal needs to know the whereabouts of itself, its food, its companions and its enemies, so too does an animal living beneath the sea. In the case of a mammal, whose senses have been designed for an atmospheric condition, certain modifications are essential if they are to provide as good a service under water.

Sight becomes less important, since visibility, even in the upper reaches, is severely restricted. No matter how clear the water, an object further than about 50ft away is invisible. At 30ft down only one tenth of the atmospheric light remains, and the deeper one goes the darker it becomes until soon enough all light is extinguished. Even so a whale, seal or fish can see more efficiently underwater than can a human; the actual eye has been modified – most importantly the lens has become almost spherical, thereby achieving greater focusing power. Because the refractive indices of water and corneal tissue are the same, the light is not bent as it passes between them as it is in the air. But for humans under water the eyesight no longer operates so effectively. Because there is no corneal refraction the image is focused *behind* the retina, causing longsightedness and consequential blurring. (The use of a mask counteracts this.)

In order to protect the cetacean eye from pressure during deep dives, the sclerotic membrane is thick and tough, and a protective oily substance is secreted from the corners of the eye, saving it from

wear and friction.

The position of the eye in relation to the head also varies from family to family. All great and pilot whales have orbits set more or less at right angles to the body axis; they are therefore only able to see to either side and have a blind spot on the front and rear which used to be exploited by whalers. Most odontocetes however possess acute stereoscopic vision similar to that of the pinnipeds (*q.v.*), and their eyes are easily recognizable as those of mammals, since they do not have the glassy quality of fishes. We may conclude, then, that despite the difficulties encountered in their habitat, most whales and seals make the fullest possible use of their optical equipment. It is still clearly not enough, though, to compensate for the poor visibility.

An exceptionally keen sense of hearing atones for any lack of vision, and this is aided by the excellence of water as a conductor of sound. (Sound travels four times faster through water than through air, and

A whaler flenses round the top jaw of an upturned Humpback Whale. The 'curtain' of baleen growing from the top jaw, the throat furrows (a distinctive feature of finback whales), and the skin protuberances, each with two tactile bristles growing from it, are clearly visible in the photograph.

with much less absorption, which means it travels further.) A human diver's acoustic sense is completely upset in such an unnatural medium, and it becomes impossible to pinpoint the source of any particular sound. A whale's ear however is extensively refined, albeit along the usual mammalian principle of outer, middle and inner ear and transmitting the sounds to the fluid of the inner ear, from where, by way of the cochlea, they are relayed to the brain. A whale hears similarly but the construction of the ear differs substantially.

To begin with, there is no external pinna; all that is visible of the ear is a tiny aperture leading into a tapering meatus, extraordinarily narrow for such an enormous animal. (Howell was only able to fit a *matchstick* into that of a 75ft finbacked whale.) The meatus closes in the centre, and is continued for a short distance by a succession of tissues before it widens again to make room for the laminated ear plug. This ear plug serves to block the meatus when the whale dives. Immediately behind the earplug there is an elongated tube which is part of the complex eardrum and is called the 'glove finger' because of its shape.

The sound waves or vibrations travel down the meatus and are conveyed to the inner ear through the tissues and ear plug, both of which are better conductors of sound than the surrounding blubber. A whale has certain advantages over us in locating the source of a sound. The reason why we cannot hear accurately under water is basically that the sounds reach our sense cells in a random fashion and by all manner of routes through the skull. The head no longer serves as a barrier to the sound waves and this results in them reaching both ears simultaneously. The ear of a whale, though, incorporates a number of devices (such as rigid bones, oily foam, air sacs and non-conductive tissues) which isolate the ear from the skull, cutting out all sound save that which travels down the meatus.

Most people know by now that dolphins emit a more or less continuous series of high-frequency clicks as a means of locating and identifying various objects. The frequency is in fact so high (up to 100 kilocycles) that man, who only hears up to about 20 kilocycles, cannot pick them up at all. Indeed, dolphins, which can detect sounds of up to 153 kilocycles, are second only to bats (up to 175 kilocycles) in sound sensitivity. Sperm Whales also use echolocation to catch their prey of squid. It is difficult to see how else they could manage at the depths they frequent. I see no reason why the baleen whales should not also employ some form of sonar. They certainly have sufficiently sophisticated equipment. Other aspects of cetacean communication are discussed in Chapter 12.

Senses of taste and smell are predictably of less importance to animals living in water and swallowing their food whole. But that of touch is probably highly developed. Apart from the obvious pleasure experienced and shown by dolphins when patted and stroked, many cetaceans also possess either stiff and sensitive hairs or hair follicles

on the snout and lips, which are richly supplied with nerves and are very likely sensitive to water turbulence and pressure when diving. By such means a whale could learn much, from its speed of movement to the turbulence created by underwater rocks which it might otherwise blunder into. In another way, the tactile sense could serve the whale as a failsafe device should its sonar fail; but more probably the two are used in combination. Much of our knowledge about whales, especially the larger ones, is inevitably deduced from corpses, never the best way of studying a living animal. Very few cetaceans have been studied in captivity. Apart from the small dolphins (most of which are not studied, only exploited), serious work has been done on such species as the Beluga and even young Californian Grey Whales, but these are the exceptions. It is difficult to see how the great finbacks and right whales are ever going to be properly understood.

The specialized dental formation of the upper jaw of a Crabeater Seal enables it to sieve krill, on which it depends, through its fine teeth. Other seals have to be able to chase, catch and grasp slippery fish, and in consequence their teeth are more robust.

5 The Role of Mammals in the Sea

Big floes have little floes all around about 'em,
And all the yellow diatoms couldn't do without 'em,
Forty million shrimplets feed upon the latter,
And they make the penguins and the seals and whales much fatter.

Griffith Taylor

Strange as it may seem to those who still consider their place to be on dry land, mammals do perform important services to the marine environment. Unfortunately the subject of ecology, even this single aspect of it, is so vast and complex that I can do no more here than whet the reader's appetite.

Mammals introduced a new and unique element into the marine world when they invaded it over fifty million years ago. Being warm-blooded, they had a great advantage over the fish and invertebrates, and were from the earliest days destined to be the largest and most successful creatures in the sea. True, fish are by far the most numerous of the vertebrates, and in many ways they assume the same role as terrestrial rodents. But little can compare with the variety of the mammals: the intelligence of the dolphins, the power of the great whales, the mildness of the sirenians, and the vitality of the pinnipeds. The same qualities that promoted the land-tied mammals to the top division of organic life were bound to do the same for those in the sea, provided they were able to cope with the natural conditions they were to encounter. This they were well able to do. It says a lot for the power of evolution that a type of animal moulded exclusively for a life on dry land could not only relinquish it and elect to live in the sea but could also triumph over it so emphatically.

A few basic statistics will put the marine biosphere into perspective. We have already learnt of its size; let us now consider its occupants. It is surprising that only one-fifth of all animal species live in the sea, which means that four-fifths live on and off the much smaller land mass. Of greater significance, out of approximately seventy-five classes of animals, all but four have representatives in the sea (about thirty-five are exclusively marine). Therefore while we immediately notice that the sea has a great diversity of animal life, it provides accommodation only for relatively few species. The reason for the occurrence of so many *classes* in the sea is that they originated there –

only the most adaptable and resourceful animals were able to leave it. Why, though, are there so few *species*? I have been at pains earlier to point out that the sea cannot be regarded as a gigantic bowl of water in which all the occupants may roam about at will – there are some redoubtable obstacles to free movement; but having said this, it is still true that there are not nearly so many as on land, nor is the sea subject to such geographic and climatic extremes. The result of so many barriers on dry land is isolation, and the effect of thousands of topographical variations is specialization. Only the most adaptable animals are able to survive the rigours of terrestrial evolution, and these have constantly to keep pace with their changing world. The stresses and competition of land life demand a higher psychological order and conformability than those of marine life, which is relatively immutable.

Thus tropical waters, where the competitive element is greatest, encourage diversity, while the colder waters and deeper zones are conducive to large populations of comparatively few, sometimes very ancient, species. The competition is much reduced and, from an ecological viewpoint, the environment is less harsh. So for marine mammals the road was wide and straight (at least until man appeared at the far end like a lunatic policeman).

During their formative years in the sea, the mammals can have had few, if any, enemies, a fact which must have greatly enhanced their prospects. A sophisticated large predator would surely have made short work of the novice re-entrants. It has taken one of their own kind, the Killer Whale, to realize their potential as a food source. Small wonder that it is a remarkably successful species with such an un-limited and untapped food supply to contemplate. Only the Great White Shark approaches it in voracity, and these two animals, with the possible addition in Antarctica of the Leopard Seal, have an almost free rein. It is, though, only the Killer Whale who preys directly on the great whales in addition to which, of course, it also consumes many fish, seals, dolphins etc.

Just what effect man has had on nature in general we shall probably never know. What he has done to the sea defies speculation. He is steadily contaminating it with chemicals and effluent (and yet he is still quite happy to catch and eat its fruits), killing off its inhabitants, and now violating its floor in his greed and panic to secure its oil and minerals. We are in the paradoxical but not unusual situation of scientific research following what it ought to be leading.

The great multiformity of mammals in the sea – cetaceans in par-ticular – is worthy of note. The three main orders (leaving aside for the moment the interlopers, discussed in Chapter 9) contain just about everything, from the Killer Whale, most terrifying of all oceanic creatures, to the peaceful and vegetarian sea-cows; from the gigantic plankton-filtering baleen whales to the intelligent and comical fish-catching dolphins; from the highly organized societies of sealions to

above A male Elephant Seal, apparently asleep, flicks sand over its body, presumably an instinctive action to help cool its skin, which can overheat when out of water.

opposite A seal, even an otariid like this Californian Sealion, can look out of place on dry land. Once swimming, however, it is transformed into an agile, swift and beautifully streamlined sea animal, which has the appearance of literally flying through the water.

the lone wanderings of the fearsome Leopard Seal.

All these animals do the greatest service to their environment. The fertility of the sea is maintained only through the biochemical cycles (the carbon, phosphorus and nitrogen cycles), and the nutritive content in the waste products of so many large mammals would hardly be forthcoming from any other source. The ecology of the oceans must by now be so geared to the needs and by-products of mammals that their disappearance would do immeasurable harm. Most seals are in no great danger at the present time, and the biological value of the sirenians, living as they do in an ecological backwater, cannot be very great; it is the large whales that pose the most disturbing questions.

The order contains the largest animals ever known to have lived, and they were once (last night in evolutionary terms) uniquely abundant and far-flung. Now, with so many reduced to remnant populations – pockets here and there overlooked by man – their worth must be greatly diminished.

Let us take for an example the colossal Blue Whale. As the *Red Data Book* says, 'a hundred years ago they could be encountered in all the seven seas'; their effect alone on the biosphere would have been considerable. If one Blue Whale consumes four tons of Krill daily, how much would the world population have got through, and what happens to the Krill now that the Blue and other baleen whales have been virtually eliminated? (See Chapter 10.)

There is a certain amount of admittedly fairly circumstantial evidence suggesting that the waters of the Arctic and Antarctic are proliferating with small fish which, if true, may not in itself be too harmful, provided that the milieu does not, as it were, burn itself out. The question is, is enough organic matter being put back into the sea to ensure the continued multiplication of the all-important phytoplankton? We may know one day. The advent of factory ships processing plankton into cakes of protein bodes worse, in my opinion, for the balance of marine life than all the hunting of whales, seals and fish put together.

Krill in the southern oceans is composed almost exclusively of one species, *Euphausia*, whereas in the north a mollusc called *Clione* or the Sea-butterfly is the principal food of many baleen whales, especially of the Greenland Right Whale. The food chain of the large whales could hardly be shorter: phytoplankton—zooplankton (Krill)—baleen whales (although they do also consume other foods, see Chapters 6 and 10). Toothed whales form the summit of a longer chain: phytoplankton—zooplankton—fish—squid—Sperm Whale is a simplified example.

Killer Whales almost certainly play the oceanic role of the wolf in weeding out sickly whales and seals. So closely related are the populations that their numbers have declined, especially in the north, with the demise of the great whales' stocks.

6 Dolphins & Whales

The Cetacea

Where the sea-beasts, rang'd all round,
Feed in the ooze of their pasture ground;
Where the sea-snakes coil and twine,
Dry their mail and bask in the brine;
Where the great whales come sailing by,
Sail and sail, with unshut eye.

from 'The Forsaken Merman' by Matthew Arnold

Can there be anyone who is not inspired and astonished by the incredible world of the whale? Animals as amazing as these demand a special treatment and I cannot but help give them it. Facts and figures alone, awesome as they are, would only be half the story. For above all, even more important than the quick brain of the dolphin and the phenomenal size of the great whales, is their character; and animal character is not an easy thing to define.

Although there are a great many species of whales – nearly a hundred – many are unstudied. We know of the Blue Whale through its sheer size, the right whales through commercial hunting, the Killer Whale through its rapacity and ferociousness, the Bottlenosed Dolphin through its circus antics, and the porpoise through its relationship with boats, but of the remainder we have only vague and scattered accounts, much of them hearsay and legend.

There cannot be another group of animals – certainly not one so widespread and comprising such strikingly large members – that is so difficult to observe. Very many people live their whole lives without ever seeing a whale in the wild. The nearest most will ever come to knowing these animals is while watching performing dolphins.

Whales are of course the most totally committed of all marine mammals, never willingly leaving the sea. Their history and evolution has been discussed elsewhere. The most important thing to remember is that the whale was once a land mammal. During a laborious and hazardous Tertiary Period its ancestors discarded many of the refinements they had acquired during their initial retreat from the sea. It almost seems as if on leaving the sea they decided that a terrestrial existence didn't suit them, and so returned to it. The process would have taken something in the order of fifty million years. Such a span of time is really beyond our imagination. After all, eighty years is a life-time, 1000 years an age, and 5000 years takes us back to pre-history! Yet 5000 years is insignificant in terms of a million, and the matter of a moment in terms of fifty million.

In order to return to the sea, whales had to overcome some severe obstacles. The fundamentals of life had to be approached from an entirely opposite direction, yet whales still remain as much mammals as we are. Pioneer whales needed to live in the sea without drowning; to discard the legs they had been at such pains to acquire; to stream-line their bodies and modify their skeletons; to develop feeding techniques and alternative diets; to grow tails resembling those of fish; to keep warm (as coarse fur is useless for this purpose in water); to condition their brains on long dives to suffering surfeits of carbon dioxide with no ill effects, while at the same time allowing sufficient oxygen to reach the essential organs; and to bring forth their off-spring, suckle and nurse them over long periods, and rear them to independence. Somehow, they managed to conquer all these obstacles and many smaller ones.

The massive size of the whalebone species (*Mysticeti*) came about in an almost incidental way, and had little bearing on their evolution. Feeding, as they do, on the relatively inactive plankton – which calls for no speed, agility or ferocity to gather – and being permanently suspended in an atmospheric medium – which demands no strength of leg or wing – there is theoretically no restriction to their size. Indeed, with their style of life and their consequent peaceful nature, if it were not for the forbidding bulk of the great whales they would be prime targets for all oceanic predators. As it is, the great whales are the strongest, gentlest and least offensive of all large animals.

The suborder of toothed whales (*Odontoceti*) contains eighty species, greatly outnumbering the mysticetes, of which there are only twelve. Its distribution is worldwide and includes several species of dolphins which inhabit freshwater rivers and estuaries. The large majority of odontocetes are generally known as dolphins and por-poises. Exceptions include the Sperm Whale, which is by far the largest of all toothed whales, attaining a length of 60ft and as such is the only leviathan or great whale in this suborder; also the White Whale or Beluga, the Narwhal and the Killer Whale or Grampus.

Most species possess more than 200 teeth (including one with the mammalian record of 260), which are very similar in appearance and cannot be divided into incisors, canines and molars like those of other mammals. However, a few species have only very few teeth – in some cases a single pair. Although the teeth, which are conical, are usually extremely simple in design and structure, those of some members of the *Phocaenidae* (porpoises) have chisel-shaped crowns and certain ziphioid (beaked) whales have teeth which are curiously flattened and twisted. The Narwhal is well-known for its extraordinary spiral unicorn-like tusk (actually the upper left canine) which in males can protrude for more than $7\frac{1}{2}$ft ahead of the animal; very rarely females display a smaller version of this peculiarity.

Most odontocetes feed on such animals as fish and squids, and most have friendly and confiding natures. The Killer Whale here is the exception – as it is in many contexts – though I have seen some extraordinarily tame and friendly grampuses, and know a girl who regularly swam with one. This particular whale seemed to prefer his swimming companions unclad! I do not think this animal would have taken readily to strange humans entering his territory, and possibly the absence of a swimming costume ensured that the girl always appeared the same and was as such easily identifiable.

Toothed whales have a single blowhole or nasal opening on top of the head, while the whalebone species have retained a double one. The migration of the nostrils to well back on top of the head (except in the sperm whales) demonstrates very adequately the sort of adaptation whales had to make in order to adopt the sea as a permanent home. One has to imagine and speculate on how they managed to achieve it. Fossil evidence is not very helpful; it shows us only primitive forms of whales, though true whales nevertheless. The current and most acceptable theory supposes that at a very early stage in mammalian evolution a type of cloven-hoofed animal took to living in fresh water, whence it gradually and imperceptibly invaded the sea. There is not to my knowledge any definite proof that the odontocetes and mysticetes have a common ancestor, but we must assume it for the time being.

R. Kellogg (1928) asserts, very reasonably, that the terrestrial ancestors of the whales must be sought amongst Cretaceous remains. It seems pointless to argue whether or not the biserial whales separated before or after they entered the water. There are many conflicting beliefs on this point; and the fact that remains of the *Odontoceti* have been located in the Upper Eocene whilst the earliest signs of mysticete activity have been found no farther back than in the more recent Oligocene is no real indication of the latter's more recent development. It is possible that their divergence occurred in the transition from a freshwater existence to a marine one; that is to say that the early mysticetes may have delayed for longer in the rivers, retaining dependence on dry land, while the odontocetes ventured into the sea.

However, the toothed whales, whatever the reason, pursued a carnivorous course and in so doing determined their smaller, more nimble size and their relatively larger brains. Although the larger toothed whales such as the Sperm Whale, pilot whales and bottlenose whales are strictly in the same suborder, we can recognize here a further 'unofficial' distinction. These medium-sized whales feed mainly on squids and cuttlefish, and therefore have to be able to dive to very great depths; the Sperm Whale can descend to over 3000ft. Their size seems proportionately greater than that of their fish-eating cousins and proportionately less than that of the planktonic or 'browsing' great whales. The size of the brain varies similarly. The Sperm Whale's brain is no more than four times greater than that of a dolphin, while its body is about nine times larger.

Typical of the odontocetes is the large dolphin family (*Delphinidae*) of thirty species, which is only one of the six groups in the dolphin superfamily (*Delphinoidea*), which contains fifty-seven species altogether. Surprisingly, perhaps the Killer Whale and pilot whales are also large dolphins, and are included in the *Orcinae* – a cosmopolitan subfamily of eight species. The average dolphin is about $7\frac{1}{2}$ft long and is a swift, intelligent hunter of fish. Dolphins can be distinguished from the smaller porpoises by the shape of the head; the dolphin's head is lengthened by a narrow 'beak', while the porpoise's face is blunter. Dolphins also possess a dorsal fin which sweeps backwards to a sharpish point, while that of the porpoise is more squat and triangular and is set farther back on the body.

Dolphins are gregarious and highly vocal creatures, communicating and co-operating by a wide variety of sounds. This aspect of their lives is discussed in detail in Chapter 12. They show great social responsibility and family unity. Dolphins tend to favour the warmer and tropical waters of the world, only a few species venturing into the temperate and polar regions.

Down the years there has been much poetical and factual material set down concerning dolphins, or more precisely concerning two species – the Common Dolphin and the Bottlenosed Dolphin. Many people are unaware that there are a great many more species than these two, and it must be admitted that very little is known about most other species of dolphins – which vary substantially in habits and appearance. I will try adequately to cover the above two species in the *Species Biographies* later in this chapter, and many of the more general aspects of the cetacean biology have already been dealt with elsewhere. Here I am more concerned to tackle some of the lesser known species, which certainly should not be ignored.

Systematically the river dolphins are rather difficult to define, but they are of tremendous interest as they help to show the direction along which the highly sophisticated marine dolphins must have travelled. They are in a sense living fossils in much the same way as the Coelacanth. There are four species from South America and South-East Asia; a further species, the Irrawaddy Dolphin, from the *Orcinae* subfamily, also habitually frequents rivers in Asia. They are of average length and coloration, and are almost certainly primitive forms. This becomes apparent from even a superficial glance and without going into more detailed anatomical discourses, interesting as they are.

Externally, the river dolphins differ from their maritime cousins in the following ways: the head is more 'lumpish' and has not withdrawn into the trunk as in the remainder of the Cetacea (in fact the cervical vertebrae are longer and atypically unfused) – the streamlining appears still to be in process; also the dorsal fin has scarcely begun to emerge, and the tail flukes would hardly befit an oceanic existence. But the most curious difference, and the one that most readily sets these animals apart, is the formation of the mouth, which is very reminiscent of a crocodile's. It is a long, pointed 'beak' with the teeth very prominent. The eyes have more or less atrophied, certainly in two of the species – the Chinese River Dolphin and the Gangetic Dolphin. The latter is said to be virtually blind and to find its food by probing about in the mud on the river bottom. This species and the Geoffroy's Dolphin from the Amazon and its tributaries also retain a pectoral limb in which the individual digits are still clearly defined. Neither the Geoffroy's Dolphin nor the La Plata Dolphin have lost all traces of their former fur, and they still retain a few vestigial hairs round the mouth.

Another anomaly of the river dolphins is their apparent inability to remain submerged for more than about one minute. Certain internal features also illustrate the differences between these and the marine dolphins. One that I find particularly significant is that only the *Platanistidae* among the toothed whales have a caecum (a blind gut leading from the alimentary canal – very important in the digestive processes of *herbivorous* animals).

The ziphioid or beaked whales form a cosmopolitan group of larger toothed whales, some of which are extremely rare. The two species of bottlenose whales – one from each hemisphere – attain a length of over 30ft and are distinctive in appearance as well as in size, although it is difficult to see how they acquired their English name; in profile, the forehead rises almost vertically from the mouth. They live in small schools of up to ten individuals and display a highly developed sense of loyalty, much to the satisfaction of whalers who hunt the northern species, and who, on wounding one, can more or less bank on securing the entire school. Bottlenose whales descend to great depths – at least up to 2600ft – in search of their prey, which consists mainly of squids and cuttlefish; they can stay submerged for up to two hours on shallow dives but only for about fifteen minutes on deep ones. A pair of rounded teeth shows on the tips of the lower jaw in elderly males.

Ziphioid whales as a family only *appear* to be deficient in teeth; the fact is that the teeth are mostly non-functional, especially in the upper jaw, and are often (notably in the female) hidden in the gums. Characteristic of these animals is the very pointed beak which in some species (the Sowerby's and Gray's) is extraordinarily exaggerated. Other external features include two throat furrows which converge anteriorly, a dorsal fin which is situated behind centre, and a body which is often scarred.

The Cuvier's Beaked Whale – another large species, 18–30ft – occurs throughout the pelagic regions of the world with the exception of the polar waters. Stranded specimens have been found on many European coasts, especially in the Mediterranean. It travels in large compact schools of up to forty individuals, which surface for periods of ten minutes before sounding again for upwards of half an hour; it also undertakes long migrations. An even larger species is the rare Baird's Beaked Whale from the North Pacific, which can attain a length of 40ft.

As the great whales become rarer, the medium-sized species, such as the beaked whales, are certain to be hunted with increasing determination.

It is generally accepted today that the differences between the river dolphins and the beaked whales (and of course the sperm whales, White Whale and Narwhal) on the one hand and the *Delphinoidea* superfamily on the other are sufficient for their separation. This being so, we now come to the main dolphin families – the *Stenidae*, *Delphinidae* (including the *Cephalorhynchinae*, *Orcinae* and *Lissodelphinae* subfamilies) and *Phocaenidae*. These are all exclusively sea-going mammals (with the exception of the Amazonian White and Irrawaddy Dolphins [*q.v.* above]) of which the Common and Bottlenosed Dolphins, Killer Whale, Pilot Whale and Porpoise are the best known (*see Species Biographies*).

This still leaves a large proportion of little-known animals. Amongst them, the solitary Rough-toothed Dolphin is the only world-wide representative of the *Stenidae*. It is average in length and appearance, except for a few spots of contrasting shades on the darker upperparts and whitish underside. There are 20–27 teeth in each ramus of the jaw. It is not a common species despite its wide range and is little studied.

The main dolphin subfamily (*Delphininae*) includes the following lesser-known species. The Euphrosyne Dolphin of the Atlantic and North Pacific is similar to the Common Dolphin in appearance but has a heavier beak and distinctive black streaks along the pied flanks. The Bridled Dolphin of the Atlantic and Indian Oceans has a profile similar to that of the foregoing species and possesses more spots than the Rough-toothed Dolphin; it is a fast swimmer and is often seen in small schools playing in the bow waves of ships. The White-sided Dolphin of the North Atlantic is well-named and occurs as far north as the Arctic Circle; it usually lives in large schools of up to 1000 individuals. The White-beaked Dolphin also comes from the North Atlantic and European waters and lives in even larger schools – up to 1500 individuals. It is found in cold waters also but tends to be more southern than the previous species, which it resembles quite closely apart from its curious white 'snout'.

The wide-ranging Risso's Dolphin, deserves somewhat more attention, thanks mainly to just one individual. For nearly a quarter

A pair of Common Dolphins in Cook Strait leaping in perfect formation from the mirror-like sea.

of a century from 1888, in and around the Cook Strait in New Zealand, a Risso's Dolphin (christened *Pelorus Jack*) commanded much international attention by his antics and friendliness towards humans (despite once being fired at by a rifle). He would rub up against their boats, and postpone fishing as soon as he heard one approach. In 1904 he was even responsible for an Order in Council which prohibited the taking of any of his species. No other individual animal has ever to my knowledge been protected by such legislation. The Risso's Dolphin as a species differs from the other typical dolphins in that it lacks the characteristic beak and therefore has the blunter appearance of a pilot whale. Apart from that, it is also slightly larger and can reach a length of 13ft. Although they usually live in smallish schools, gatherings of 100 have been seen.

One of the most interesting groups of dolphins is the *Orcinae*. Although small in number, comprising only eight species, it contains such fascinating animals as the Killer Whale, False Killer and Pygmy Killer; the Irrawaddy Dolphin, and the four species of pilot whales. Some of these are looked at in more detail in the *Species Biographies* at the end of this chapter. The False Killer is the same shape as its better-known namesake but considerably smaller. It also lacks the conspicuous white markings which immediately set the Killer Whale apart. The False Killer is similarly worldwide in distribution, but it sometimes congregates in enormous schools of several thousand individuals; strandings often involve more than one specimen at a time.

The *Phocaenidae* is a family of seven species of porpoises (a term, incidentally, often applied in America to any species of dolphin) which inhabit most pelagic regions of the globe. Apart from the 'Common' Porpoise, which is found in most northern waters, it is a principally southern family. Porpoises usually live in small schools and prefer coastal waters to deep oceans. They seldom exceed 6½ft in length, and if a small whale is seen offshore or sporting around a pleasure boat, it will almost invariably be a porpoise. Porpoises occasionally venture up rivers and estuaries and have even been found living in inland lakes.

The *Mysticeti* suborder of great whales provides an example of over-specialization; but, although their size has rendered them ideal targets for human predators, it has not yet had any detrimental affect on what might be termed their natural hopes of survival. If the great whales do become extinct it will be due not to any ecological factors, but to man's commercial greed. It is possible though that their extinction will have dire consequences on the oceanic biochemical cycles. One cannot emphasize too strongly that their severely reduced numbers are not the result of any ambiguity or 'miscalculation' in nature's great plan; there can be no parallel with the demise of the dinosaurs.

In studying these giants one must guard against being overwhelmed by their size, which can overshadow all manner of interesting and important features, many of which have already been discussed in Chapter 4. It might be helpful here briefly to recapitulate some of the basic aspects of their design.

The streamlining, so important to an aquatic animal, makes the best of their undeniable size, and some grotesque looking mammals have resulted. In actual fact, streamlining entailed the drastic modification of the pectoral limbs; the complete degeneration and disappearance of hind limbs, external pinnae and fur; the emergence of horizontal, flattened tail flukes and, in some species, of a dorsal fin. The head, as a unit, had to undergo the greatest secondary adaptation: the front and back portions of the skull became greatly shortened and telescoped, while the central section grew out of all proportion. The necks of all cetaceans are also shortened. In some species the cervical vertebrae are even fused. Baleen whales do not require mobile necks, but the smaller fish-catching odontocetes are capable of a certain amount of independent head movement. The eyes are relatively small, deepset and situated at the corner of the mouth. A thick layer of blubber (up to 20in.) has replaced the fur for purposes of insulation and also serves as a reserve food supply. Because blubber can be readily fashioned it greatly expedited the streamlining process.

The teeth of the mysticetes never break through the gums, and in their place there are triangular horny plates of baleen which hang down from either side of the palate and serve to trap the Krill, of which they consume vast amounts daily.

Neither speed nor maneuvrability is of great importance to these whales but their strength, which is a by-product of their size, is phenomenal. It is perhaps just as well, from a sea-going human's viewpoint, that they are also extremely gentle; they certainly seem to be aware of their own immense power. The sort of barbarous cruelty and wholesale slaughter they suffer would not be tolerated against any land-living animal, but because it goes on out of sight of the world on the high seas few even know about it.

There are three families of mysticetes. The Californian Grey Whale is the sole member of the *Eschrichtidae*; there are six species of finbacked whales in the *Balaenopteridae*, including the rorquals, Blue and Humpback Whales; and finally there are the five right whales (*Balaenidae*). Most of these merit individual attention, for their rarity if for no other reason. The right whales, however, are amazingly little known; it seems that the only things considered of interest were the best method of killing them, and their distribution.

The right whales were so called simply because they were the right whales to hunt; apart from their huge yield of baleen, they also had the useful attributes of swimming slowly and of floating when dead. They are unmistakable animals. The massive head (one third of the total body length) is characterized by the arched upper jaw from which the baleen is suspended.

The Bowhead or Greenland Right Whale (see *Species Biography*) is the best known, and even after lengthy protection is still in danger of extinction. The closely-related Black or North Atlantic Right Whale, the North Pacific Right Whale and the Southern Right Whale are also discussed in detail, collectively. The extremely rare Pygmy Right Whale is only known from a few strandings on the shores of southern seas; as great whales go, it is rather small, only growing to about one third of the size of other right whales (i.e. some 20ft). Alone among right whales it possesses a dorsal fin.

The only great whales which typically display sebaceous dorsal fins are the appropriately named finbacked whales. Each of these, with the exception of the Bryde's Whale from the South African seas (only identified as a separate species in 1913), is allotted an individual biography, but there are certain facts common to all. Members of this family are often known collectively as rorquals – a name derived from the Norwegian rørhval, which means pipe-whale and refers to the characteristic longitudinal furrows or pleats which run from under the lower lip along the chest and into the belly. The mouth aperture is not arched as in the right whales, but more or less straight, and the baleen plates are correspondingly shorter. The pectoral fins are more pointed and rorquals are altogether sleeker in appearance than the right whales.

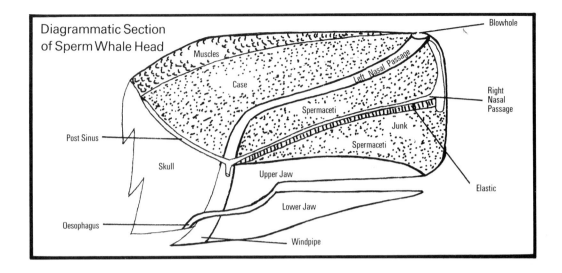

Diagrammatic Section of Sperm Whale Head

Sperm Whale or Cachalot (*Physeter catodon*)

Distribution: Worldwide, but prefers the warmer areas. Probably crosses the equator in order to get the benefit of the summer in each hemisphere. Tends to congregate where food is plentiful, i.e. where warm and cool currents meet.

Status: Decreasing in numbers owing to commercial whaling but still quite plentiful. Estimates of populations vary greatly but most hunting takes place in the North Pacific; in this area the number of males has reputedly fallen from 167,000 to 69,000, and that of females from 124,000 to 100,000. Global estimates are as high as half a million individuals.

Description: Largest of the toothed whales. Bulls 40–65ft (mostly 50–60ft); cows 29–37ft. Bulls maximum weight 50t; cows 13t. The circumference of a bull's body is 29–37ft and the tail is about 16ft wide.

The colossal barrel-shaped head gives this whale a bizarre appearance. The narrow lower jaw, which contains some fifty large teeth, is greatly overshot by the upper, which shows no teeth; the effect of this is superficially shark-like. The single blowhole is situated to the left and front of the head.

Coloration varies considerably but is mostly bluish-grey above and paler below. No dorsal fin; instead there is a series of tubercles towards the rear, of which the most forward (the 'hump') is the largest.

Habits: Can dive to 3000ft and stay below for seventy-five minutes or more. On surfacing the hump emerges first, and the whale's spout is directed about 45° forward. After a deep dive remains at or near the surface for at least fifteen minutes, in which time it will breathe more than fifty times and may make between thirty and fifty shallow dives.

A slow swimmer, but manages a maximum 15–20mph when pursued; usually it proceeds at a leisurely 3–5mph. Lives in mixed schools of about 15–20 individuals (rarely up to 200); sometimes young bulls will gather together, but a solitary Sperm Whale is almost invariably an old bull.

The species has occasionally been seen to leap clear out of the water, presumably for fun. Before diving deeply the tail comes high above the water, and it is this ominous sign which has been called 'the hand of God' by open-boat whalers who fear this moment more than any other.

Females do not wander as far afield as the males and tend not to venture beyond the 40° latitudes; animals found in colder waters are usually males. Migrations do occur, and whalers have witnessed schools of Sperm Whales travelling in a 'fast' and determined manner, and have been unable to catch them.

Food: Mostly deep sea squid (e.g. *Architeuthis*) and cuttlefish (see Chapter 11). The whales living in the Far East seem to subsist mainly on cuttlefish; as many as 20,000 of their indigestible chitinous jaws have been found in a single stomach, and out of a total of over 1500 stomachs examined over 80 per cent contained nothing other than the remains of cuttlefish.

Reproduction: Polygamous. Mating takes place in warm seas when harems are formed. Gestation is 10–12 months. Cows seek out an area of clean deep water in the lee of an island to give birth. There appears to be no special season for any of the reproductive acts.

At birth a Sperm Whale measures nearly 13ft. It is suckled for about a year. Males mature when approximately 30ft in length, and females at about 25ft. Longevity is not known, but there is a 32-year-old specimen on record.

Special features: The Sperm Whale (famed from the stories of Moby Dick and Jonah) is unfortunately too bountiful for its own good. Though it lacks the baleen which was the downfall of the other great whales, it possesses such treasures as an immense quantity of blubber and nearly one ton of spermaceti – a fine colourless oil found amongst the mass of tissues within the head, which solidifies to a white wax on exposure to air and is used in many industrial processes.

Another product is ambergris (used as a fixative in the perfume business); this is a clay-like substance occasionally found inside the gut of these whales. Sometimes ambergris, which soon loses its offensive odour when removed from the whale, is found washed up on beaches after having been voided naturally by the whales. It is extremely valuable. A lump weighing 400lbs found on a beach in St Helena fetched £20,000; some Norwegians found a piece weighing

330lbs inside a Sperm Whale and earned themselves £27,000. There is some disagreement over the origins of ambergris. Many believe it to be the equivalent of a pearl in an oyster, a secretion manufactured by the whale to prevent the irritation brought about by the sharp beaks of squid and cuttlefish, which are frequently found embedded within it. There is, however, no certainty about its exact purpose and origins.

The sheer bulk of the Sperm Whale, the largest of the toothed whales, can be well appreciated from these two stranded specimens. Sperm Whales have no dorsal fin but a series of humps down the last third of the back. The powerful tail flukes drive the whales down to enormous depths in search of squid.

Pygmy Sperm Whale (*Kogia breviceps*)

Distribution: Worldwide but prefers tropical waters. Stranded specimens have been found once on the Dutch and twice on the French coast.

Status: Considered rare.

Description: $7\frac{1}{2}$–13ft. Very much smaller than the Sperm Whale. Possesses a dorsal fin. Head is similarly barrel-shaped but comparatively small and does not extend so far forward. Coloration similar. The lower jaw has 20–30 sharply pointed backward-curving teeth.

Habits: Little studied. It is thought to be slow and unsociable.

Food: Presumably mainly cephalopods and possibly fish, on the evidence of the teeth – which also rarely appear on the upper jaw.

Reproduction: Unknown.

Special features: Believed to wander widely. It is considered by some authorities to be an impoverished or freakish form of the Sperm Whale. Apparently not hunted owing to small size and insufficient numbers.

White Whale or Beluga (*Delphinapterus leucas*)

Distribution: Arctic and northern coastal waters; it seems to prefer areas in the vicinity of river mouths. Migrates south in the winter. Most southerly sighting is off French coast. Favoured areas are off the North American, Canadian and Alaskan coasts. It will occasionally venture long distances up rivers.

Status: Relatively common.

Description: 12–18ft. The only completely white whale. It has no conspicuous dorsal fin and has a very short and blunt snout with down-curved mouth. Each jaw usually possesses 18 teeth. Single blowhole. Completely hairless at all stages of development. This species is unusual amongst the Cetacea in having a true and distinct neck in which the cervical vertebrae are free and not fused. The fore-limbs are noticeably broadened.

Habits: Dives deeply, and lives in small schools of up to thirty individuals which are often part of a much larger herd (perhaps up to 1000 individuals, certainly as many as 800). Schools comprising only bulls have been recorded, as have schools of cows and calves.

I have a reliable account of one Beluga remaining submerged for seventy minutes; its normal pattern, however, was to submerge for only 2–3 minutes after which it emerged three or four times for air. This particular animal was found far up the Rhine in the spring of 1966, and was observed exhaustively. It had a definite day/night rhythm, sleeping from dusk at 2100–2200 hours until around 0800 hours the following morning. It preferred to rest in shallow water near the shore. After about a month it found its way back to sea, and was seen swimming strongly, though it was considerably thinner. It was reported to be 'apparently unbothered' by the quite severe pollution of the river.

Food: Crustaceans, squid, cuttlefish and fish. One specimen in Duisburg Zoo, Germany, consumes 15–25lbs of mackerel daily, and to date has lived happily for over four years.

The Beluga is preyed upon by the Killer Whale; the Polar Bear and large sharks must also take a certain number.

Reproduction: Little is known about its reproductive cycle, except that at birth the calves are dark grey, later changing through a spotted appearance to yellowish-white.

Special features: The White Whale has many points of interest. Its unusual body colour could possibly have come about for reasons of camouflage in its Arctic environment. The conformation of its neck has already been mentioned.

This species is often alleged to have a very vocal nature, and has

even been dubbed the 'sea-canary'; other accounts speak of strange, cattle-like cries. I have consulted Dr Wolfgang Gewalt about this (he has studied this species in Duisburg Zoo almost daily for many years, and has also lived among them off the Alaskan coast), and he informs me that he has never heard it. 'I cannot understand', he says, 'how the old mariners could have named them sea-canaries, because they are evidently not very enthused to singing. Occasionally he grounds or whistles a little, but not as often, for example, as the Bottlenosed Dolphin.'

The Narwhal is closely related to the White Whale. Its size can be gauged by the two men inspecting a stranded specimen. The function of the single tusk is not understood. As the skull shows, it is an elongation of the left upper canine tooth which spirals forward in an anticlockwise direction.

Narwhal (*Monodon monoceros*)

Distribution: Arctic and northern coastal waters; prefers ice-bound areas. Occasional strandings as far south as England and Holland.

Status: Relatively common.

Description: 13–20ft. Apart from the extraordinary tusk of the male, the Narwhal closely resembles the Beluga, and is only a little darker on the back; it also has many dark spots, mainly on the upperparts. Males are paler than females. Both sexes are hairless. The female, like the male, has two teeth in the upper jaw, but these seldom break through the gums. The male's tusk is discussed below; other teeth are vestigial.

Habits: The Narwhal is generally agreed to be a lively, fast and alert animal, living sometimes in enormous herds numbering thousands, but more often in smallish schools. They are reported to dive to

1300ft and to stay below for at least thirty minutes, but frequent, shallower dives are more common. On surfacing and spouting a shrill whistle is often heard, even from far off. Cows call to their calves with deep moaning sounds.

Food: Mainly cephalopods and molluscs.

Reproduction: Little known. Calves are a uniform bluish-grey at birth.

Special features: In the fetal state there are a pair of small, non-projecting upper canines; usually in the male the right one develops no further (and neither does in the female). The left one however grows forward through the upper lip and extends, on the same plane as the body, for as much as 7ft in an anti-clockwise spiral.

Various explanations have been advanced for this strange feature. Some suggest it is used as an ice-breaker when the Narwhal finds itself under ice; some that it is used to impale prey; and others that it serves to rake up food from the sea-bed. If any of these were true, why should the female lack such a useful implement? (Narwhals often travel in sexually segregated schools.)

A more reasonable theory is that the tusks are used by the males in courtship and fighting. There may be some truth in this, for they seldom remain undamaged, and the tip of a tusk has been found in the body of another Narwhal. I think it unlikely, though, that these animals charge one another, as it has been suggested, like ancient knights on horseback.

Perhaps the tusk will be found to be a useless overspecialization, perhaps even a hindrance, threatening the very survival of the species. Presumably it first grew in response to some stimulus and to fulfil some such need as is suggested above; but tusks, antlers and similar appendages sometimes acquire 'evolutionary velocity' and develop beyond the point of real usefulness. Such growths are thought to have caused the extinction of some ancient species, including various elephants, the Sabre-toothed Tiger and the Irish Elk. The exceptional growth is possibly stimulated by the male sex hormone; or the sexual disparity could be induced by an inhibitional factor in the female.

As in the Beluga, the Narwhal's cervical vertebrae are unfused, although externally the neck is not so obvious.

Common Dolphin (*Delphinus delphis*) (*see also following species*)

Distribution: Worldwide but prefers warmer regions of the Pacific, Atlantic and Indian Oceans and the Mediterranean and Black Seas. Avoids the polar regions.

Status: Common.

Description: 6–8ft. The Common Dolphin is variable in colour but usually has a very dark brown back and white underparts with yellowish-grey wavy streaks along the flanks. A graceful animal with a very narrow beak. A distinct dorsal fin is set about midway along the back. This species can be distinguished from the somewhat similar Bottlenosed Dolphin (*q.v.*) by its slender shape. Each ramus of the jaw usually contains between 40 and 50 sharp, conical and backward-curving teeth.

Habits: Gregarious – associating in large and small schools. A fast and agile swimmer (possibly capable of at least 30mph); often seen sporting round ships, playing and riding on the bow waves, and leaping clear out of the water.

Although able to dive to quite substantial depths, it is usually content to make only relatively shallow dives. It does, however, inhabit deeper pelagic waters than the coastal-loving Bottlenosed Dolphin. Like other small dolphins it cannot make prolonged dives and generally surfaces every few minutes, breathing rapidly and highly efficiently. Dolphins surface in a rolling manner, coming obliquely out of the water and re-entering in the same wheel-like motion. Common Dolphins are extremely frisky creatures, and are frequently seen gambolling with floating objects and such animals as turtles in the sea. They will even play with a fish in much the same way as a cat plays with a mouse.

Dolphins have been said to make regular migrations but all evidence points to their remaining faithful to a home territory.

Food: Mainly small surface-living fish such as pilchards, but will also consume many other small animals, mainly crustaceans, molluscs and cuttlefish. The Danish biologist Eschricht has recorded that he found the ear stones of 7596 recently consumed fish in one stomach.

Reproduction: The reproductive life of dolphins is especially well studied, thanks largely to the magnificent American marine aquariums – in particular the Marineland in Miami, Florida – which have provided the facilities for almost armchair scientific observation. Detailed information on this or any aspect of dolphins is best obtained from one of the many excellent books which concentrate solely on these animals. I have only space here to record the salient facts and figures.

Dolphins often pair up for the courting season, but whether or not they establish permanent pair bonds in the wild is obviously difficult to establish. Copulation is a wonderfully refined and sensitive affair with what seems like real love transmitted between the two participating individuals.

Gestation takes about a year. A pregnant dolphin will often keep a little distance between itself and the remainder of the school as the moment of birth draws near; it will sometimes choose a companion female, who performs the functions of a midwife, and who remains in close attendance.

At birth a dolphin is astonishingly well developed, as of course it needs to be to survive and take its place immediately in the ever-moving school. Nevertheless, drowning must be a real danger to any newly-born whale, and in order to overcome this inherent danger three main precautions are taken. First, births take place in the upper layers of the water; secondly the actual parturition is unusual in that the baby dolphin emerges tail-first (the risks involved in a normal head-first delivery are obvious, given that a dolphin birth regularly takes over half an hour and sometimes as long as two hours. There is one recorded head-first birth. The calf did not die, almost certainly because it only took a few minutes to fall free. I do not think this freakish birth negates the above argument.) And, finally, as soon as the calf is free of its mother, she whips round, breaking the umbilical cord, and is on hand to help her baby to the surface for its all-important first breath. Quite often the baby, by feverishly thrashing its tail, makes its own way up, taking only a few seconds. The attendant females then help to protect the new addition from sharks and the males (who can be a nuisance). The appointed companion enjoys a place of special privilege over the other females.

The newly-born dolphin is a full third of its mother's length and a perfect replica in almost every respect. It weighs a little over 24lbs and has a rather large head which shows a few hairs. The teeth are not cut for a few weeks but within twenty-four hours the baby has found its mother's teats (situated on the belly) and has had its first feed of milk squirted into its mouth by muscular contraction.

The mother and her companion show exceptional dedication and tenderness during the initial three months of the rearing process, guarding the baby constantly and never letting it stray more than about 10ft away. Normally the young dolphin takes up a position besides the mother's dorsal fin and, for some reason, shuts its outside eye as if not to be frightened by anything it might see! The companion sometimes takes up an equivalent position on the other side of the baby so that it is protected on both sides.

Lactation lasts approximately eighteen months, although by the age of six months a dolphin can probably ingest a certain amount of solid food. Dolphins are believed to live for more than thirty years.

Special features: Just because the Common and Bottlenosed Dolphins predominate in stories and reports of these animals, it is not fair to assume that they are necessarily the most interesting – they are simply by far the best known. No doubt all dolphins, if we knew about them, would be equally absorbing. It is more than likely, indeed, that a great deal of what is true about the Common and Bottlenosed varieties is true also about most other species.

People who are only superficially acquainted with dolphins (through dolphinaria, etc.) may well believe that the most interesting thing about them is their attitude towards human beings, and this is certainly a fascinating subject, and one I have endeavoured to cover adequately in Chapters 11 and 12. Among the more interesting of dolphins' biological features is their remarkable sense of social responsibility, already referred to in the section on reproduction.

An individual's involvement in its community extends from caring for newly-born calves and injured comrades to the problems of the aged and infirm. Healthy animals have often been seen to nurse elderly ones who find it difficult to keep up with the school, and will even nudge sick specimens to the surface and support them there so that they may breathe, just indeed as they do babies. There have been many instances of mothers in particular supporting dead or stillborn babies at the surface for long periods, and also some remarkable accounts of injured or distressed dolphins being the subjects of intense concern to their healthier companions, who assist them in all manner of ways.

There are even reports of drowning humans having been pushed ashore and supported by dolphins, and many sailors, down the ages, have firmly believed that dolphins will drive away sharks from a man in difficulty in the sea. I do not doubt that dolphins have helped humans, but whether the assistance has been intentional or incidental is quite another matter.

Common Dolphins 'porpoising' in the Sea of Cortez, Mexico. It is debatable whether this familiar gambolling is simple *joie de vivre* or whether it has some special physiological function.

61

Bottlenosed Dolphin (*Tursiops truncatus*) (*see also preceding species*)

Distribution: Worldwide but prefers warmer waters; fairly abundant along the western shores of the Atlantic Ocean.

Status: Perhaps not quite so plentiful as the Common Dolphin.

Description: 9–13ft. Longer and plumper than the Common Dolphin (*q.v.*). Upperparts purplish-black fading gradually to white below. The eye is set in the dark part of the face, and the mouth has an upward, grinning curve to it. Each ramus of the jaw has 20–26 teeth, similar to those of the Common Dolphin.

Habits: Similar in many ways to the Common Dolphin but perhaps not quite as playful in the wild. Not seen around ships so often. Prefers coastal waters to the oceanic wildernesses.

Food: As for the Common Dolphin. The most serious enemies of dolphins are sharks; presumably Killer Whales will also take what they are able to catch.

Reproduction: See Common Dolphin. Twins are occasionally produced and dolphin hunters claim to have found twin fetuses in pregnant cows.

Special features: (see also Common Dolphin). The dolphin is a highly vocal creature and much work has already been done on all aspects of its vocabulary (see Chapter 12). Dolphins do indeed 'speak' to each other; and it has been shown that they are capable of uttering and receiving all manner of instructions and communications. It has not actually been established yet that they are able to hold conversations, but even this would hardly be a surprise. It must be remembered that while we live in what seems to us to be a pre-eminently visual world (although it is our ears that usually first alert us to either danger or occurrences – simply because they are *constantly* monitoring a 360° field of vision – our eyesight is generally used in a confirmatory role), a dolphin exists in an essentially aural one. That is not to say that sight is of no importance to a marine mammal, just that hearing is very much more important. After all, theirs is a world of murky half-shadows and, except in the uppermost zones, one of perpetual twilight and severely limited visibility.

The commonest dolphin sound is a whistling one, used continually as a contact-call and also, in varying intensities, for displaying emotions such as fear, excitement and anticipation. Other calls frequently heard are various rasping and whining sounds and a loud jaw-clapping, used by both sexes for purposes of threat and intimidation.

Dolphins, in common with a few other animals such as bats, also make use of a form of echo-location or sonar. The mechanics of this phenomenon hardly need explanation here; most people must be

aware of the rudimentary principles of Asdic and radar. In animal terms, it is simply the act of emitting a range of sounds from ultrasonic to slightly lower-pitched clicks (up to 400 per second) and of picking up and translating the echoes as they rebound off anything within range. In this way dolphins in dark water are able to 'see' what is around them just as efficiently as we can on a sunny day.

As Anthony Alpers mentions in his book *Dolphins* (1960), this need not astonish us. We ourselves are equipped with the ability to 'sense' a wall or a lamp-post in the dark. This may sound ludicrous but I have experimented upon myself rather crudely and it is certainly true. Dolphins and bats have developed the hazy impression we experience to a fine art, and to a very great extent rely solely upon it. It is an amazing revelation to witness a blindfolded dolphin locating various tiny objects, avoiding fine wires and nets, and even catching fast-moving fish. The ability is presumably learnt subconsciously when young.

It can no longer be denied that the dolphin is intelligent, perhaps remarkably intelligent, although scientific research has only begun to touch on the matter of their brain-power. But we do know that the brain of a Bottlenosed Dolphin has almost the same capacity as that of a human; moreover, for every twelve inches of a dolphin's body length it has seven ounces of brain (a human has only about one and a half ounces more). In actual size, a dolphin's brain is about half as large again as a man's, although it must be borne in mind that a dolphin is a substantially larger animal (an average specimen weighing some 400lbs). Even more significant, though, is the fact that the cerebral hemispheres are also proportionately large – the cerebrum, as it is often called, is the paired enlargement of the fore-brain. It is the part which, in mammals, covers most of the middle and hind-brain, and the outer layer or cortex is responsible for intelligence and the co-ordination of functions and activities.

This Bottlenosed Dolphin at the Marineland, Florida, shows the superb design of aquatic mammals. The streamlining shown by the musculature, tail flukes, breast flukes, 'beak' and dorsal fin is very evident.

Killer Whale or Grampus (*Orcinus orca*)

Distribution: Worldwide but prefers the Arctic and Antarctic, also the temperate regions of the Northern Hemisphere.

Status. Not rare, but declining in some areas.

Description: Males 20–30ft; females only a little shorter (until recently it was believed that females never exceeded a length of 15ft). Unmistakable large pied whale with huge pectoral fins (up to one sixth of the body length) and extremely high and pointed, vertical dorsal fin, sometimes approaching $6\frac{1}{2}$ft high in an old male. Blunt head with striking white patch above and behind either eye. General coloration pattern is black above and white below, clearly demarcated. The white extends into the black in the shape of an oval just behind the dorsal fin.

There are usually twelve strong teeth (oval in section) in each ramus of the jaw. The exposed part of the tooth is over 2in. long and interlocks with the opposite set.

Habits: The Killer Whale is well known for its rapacity and fearlessness. It is an extremely fast predator, hunting in moderate-sized, well organized schools which show an abundance of cunning, strength and ferocity, exceeding even those of the Great White Shark. It is superbly streamlined and believed to be the fastest swimmer in the sea, although it is hard to believe that it is faster than the dolphin in full flight. Aquatic maximum speeds are almost impossible to even estimate accurately. Killers, though, often swim very slowly, taking a fresh breath every few seconds, at which time the high dorsal fin is clearly visible above the surface.

Food: Surprisingly, predominantly fish and squid. However, the Killer Whale is the greatest carnivore in the sea and will attack and eat almost anything. Other mammals are evidently preferred by some specimens; an individual caught in the Bering Sea was found to have the remains of thirty-two adult seals in its stomach, and another, thirteen porpoises and fourteen seals. That such prey is sometimes swallowed whole is confirmed by the finding of a complete 10ft dolphin in one stomach.

Even the great whales are not safe. Schools of Killers will select one (sometimes a calf) and pursue it relentlessly, hanging on to its tail flukes and fins, and darting at the corner of its mouth; the tongue is the prize Killers go for first, and as a great whale's tongue can weigh over two tons, it is hardly a morsel even for these hungry beasts. Killer Whales will also attack great whale carcasses being towed

top The White Whale (or Beluga) is aptly named, though the young have a mottled skin and are hard to tell from the young of the closely related Narwhal. Note the rounded breastflukes.

below The Bottlenosed Dolphin forms a close attachment to its young. For the first three months after birth, the mother will seldom allow the baby to stray more than about 100 feet from her.

opposite top A school of Spotted Dolphins. Mammals of the Atlantic, they belong to the genus *Stenella* which comprises the smallest of the dolphins.

opposite below A rare shot of a Commerson's Dolphin — one of a distinctively pied group, sometimes called 'skunk dolphins'. They are found in the colder waters of the Southern Hemisphere and feed on crabs and cuttlefish.

above Fully committed marine mammals, these Pacific Bottlenosed Dolphins demonstrate how superficially close they have externally become to fish.

left Pilot Whales (or Blackfish) are possibly the most intelligent of all dolphins, their mental capacity exceeding even that of the much studied Bottlenosed Dolphin. They sometimes congregate in huge schools, but sadly this makes them also easy to slaughter in huge numbers.

top Californian Grey Whale. Once thought extinct, their numbers are now estimated at about 10,000.

top right Krill, a type of shrimp measuring about 6cm (2½in.), abounds in Antarctic waters, sometimes colouring the sea red. Enormous quantities of this and other tiny creatures are needed to sustain the gigantic baleen whales.

right A dramatic and somewhat menacing shot of the infamous Killer Whale which, if not quite the monster that we like to imagine, is still a formidable and rapacious predator of the high seas.

bottom At a whaling station in South Georgia the flensing begins. Land stations such as this, at Grytviken, now only play a minor role in commercial whaling. Man can now chase, kill and process entire herds of whales on factory ships far out at sea.

behind factory ships.

Reproduction: Little studied. Gestation is probably about one year, and a newly-born calf measures a little over 6ft.

Special features: The only whale that regularly catches and kills other warm-blooded prey. In spite of its undeniable ferocity in the wild, it becomes extraordinarily peaceful towards human beings in captivity, and will even share a pool with dolphins – a natural prey. Killer Whales are little hunted commercially.

Pilot Whale or Blackfish (*Globicephala melaena*)

Distribution: Cold and temperate regions of the Pacific and Atlantic Oceans, especially Arctic and European waters. Some evidence suggests that it prefers coastal areas.

Status: Not rare.

Description: 14–28ft. One of the very few all black whales, the only coloration being an occasional grey stripe on the under belly. The most characteristic distinguishing mark is the markedly protuberant and domed forehead (see below). The pectoral fins are long and narrow and there is a large dorsal fin.

Habits: Essentially a gregarious species – often living in vast schools numbering thousands, usually under the leadership of a single old and very large male, which is followed blindly by all those in its school.

Navigates by echo-location but is sometimes confused by gradually shelving coasts and is consequently stranded in large numbers.

Its spout on surfacing is accompanied by a barking sound.

Food: The design of its head, or more specifically the rostral frontal bulge overhanging the mouth, suggests a diet of bottom-living inactive prey. However, it has been shown to live mainly on squids and other cephalopods.

Reproduction: Little known, presumably similar to that of other dolphins.

Special features: The Pilot Whale has been hunted for centuries, notably in the Faeroes. This is a cruel and bloody ritual, and entails the driving of an entire school into an estuary, cutting off its retreat, and barbarically slaughtering as many individuals as possible.

Greenhorn great whalers used occasionally to 'practise' on Pilot Whales, and the important booty from these animals was the large amount (as much as five gallons per animal) of fat to be found in the adipose tissues in the forehead. This was rendered to a fine oil and used as a lubricant for delicate machinery such as watches; it was

Two Indian Pilot Whales (or Short-finned Blackfish) photographed in the western Indian Ocean. This species is also quite widespread in the Atlantic.

thirty times more valuable than ordinary blubber oil, and is still today one of the most refined of all oils and used in precision instruments. The biological function of the adipose cushion of whales is still not understood, and this question together with that of the Sperm Whale's spermaceti organ is discussed in Chapter 4.

This species lacks the bi-colouring found in most other whales, which are darker above and lighter below for reasons of camouflage. The Blackfish is largely a nocturnal feeder and so has little need for such camouflage.

Porpoise (*Phocaena phocaena*)

Distribution: Coastal waters of the Northern Hemisphere.

Status: Common.

Description: 4–5½ft. One of the smallest of all whales; weighs only about 110lbs. Lacks the sleekness of the *Delphininae*, and has a blunt head with no distinct beak. The black upperparts merge into white below. The dorsal fin is squat and set towards the rear of the body. Each ramus of the jaw has between twenty-two and twenty-eight chisel-crowned teeth partly hidden in the gums.

Habits: Porpoises usually travel in small schools (rarely up to 100 individuals), occasionally even in pairs, and seldom stray far from the coast. They are regularly in attendance near ships, and enjoy sporting and cutting across the bows, much to the delight of passengers. On other occasions they will keep pace with ships from a distance, and one can see them travelling in that beautifully fluid and easy rolling motion as they cartwheel out of the sea to breathe ('porpoising'). When fishing they submerge for up to five minutes and then surface a few times to breathe before resuming.

Porpoises occasionally venture up rivers and even reach inland lakes.

Food: Mainly fish such as herring, cod and salmon, but will also take crustaceans and squids.

Reproduction: The single young, which at birth measures about 30in., is produced around June. It grows very quickly, like most marine mammals; the mother's milk contains between 40 and 50 per cent fat.

Special features: The flesh of the Porpoise was once considered a delicacy, especially in medieval Britain, and the oil was also valuable. Nowadays it is scarcely hunted at all, although I expect a few still succumb to 'sportsmen' with rifles. It is the whale most frequently stranded on European coasts.

Californian Grey Whale (*Eschrichtius glaucus*)

Distribution: Migrates from the Arctic to the Californian coast to breed.

Status: Once thought to be extinct but has been rediscovered and is

The moment of birth of a Bottlenosed Dolphin at the Marineland, Florida. The mother rolls on her side and the baby is born *tail* first. It is then quickly taken to the surface to prevent drowning. An 'auntie' or 'midwife' dolphin is often in attendance.

now strictly protected. It survives in greatly reduced but increasing numbers (*c.* 10,000). In 1851 an American naturalist, Charles Scammon, estimated that 1000 Grey Whales passed down the Californian coast every day on migration; twenty years later the number was down to about forty and early this century the species was believed to be extinct. This area was its last stronghold and from an estimated population of 30,000 in 1853, the species was virtually wiped out.

Description: 40–50ft. It is not one of the largest of the mysticetes, but it is the most primitive and therefore has the longest neck. Like the right whales, it has no dorsal fin but a series of low bumps on the back near the tail. It has a smallish head and two or three shallow grooves on the throat. The baleen is short and thick, with coarsely frayed inner edges.

Habits: Makes regular migrations as described above. Its habit of venturing within sight of land to breed almost caused its extinction. Now it helps to save it, for the migrating Grey Whales have become a great tourist attraction.

In the days of intensive whaling, the Grey Whale changed its habits and avoided the coastal areas. At the same time they earned themselves the name 'devil-fish' among whalers and a reputation for fierceness and aggression – attacking boats with little provocation. The Grey Whale was reputed to be stronger than the right whales, and faster than the Sperm, and one harpooned would charge frantically about, capsizing boats and drowning men. They could hardly be blamed. Besides human predators Grey Whales also suffered much harassment and depredation from Killer Whales.

Food: Bottom-living planktonic animals such as amphipods. Used to be known as the 'mussel-digger' because its snout was often covered in mud. It apparently feeds by sifting mud through its coarse and widely-spaced baleen fringes.

Reproduction: The mother/calf bond is very strong in whales, and much of the viciousness this species is accused of arises from this bond. Whalers would harpoon a calf and tow it towards the shore, knowing very well that the agitated mother would follow, when she could be killed in shoal water.

Thankfully, this is a murky page of history that has now been closed. Nowadays the Grey Whale is protected, and the Mexican Government has turned Scammon's Lagoon, Baja California, into a Nature Reserve, banning all vessels in the calving season.

Special features: The Californian Grey Whale used to have a considerably wider range, and was once hunted in the North Atlantic, where it is now extinct. A skeleton has been found in the Zuider Zee, and the species still occurred along the eastern coasts of America in

The head of this Californian Grey Whale appears to be infested with barnacles. The large slow-moving whales are sometimes plagued in this way. Not only do the barnacles spoil the whales' streamlining, they also appear to irritate them, and whales have been known to seek brackish water in an attempt to discourage and remove the marine barnacles.

the eighteenth century.

If stranded, most large whales are crushed or suffocated by their own weight, but Grey Whales reputedly wait quietly for the tide to come in and refloat them. It is at this time, when stranded whales and dolphins might be thought to be safe, that they are very liable to drown. There is insufficient water for them to swim, and consequently they are unable to raise their blowholes from the water.

Lesser Rorqual or Minke Whale
(*Balaenoptera acutorostrata*)

Distribution: Worldwide, but prefers the coastal regions of the Arctic and Antarctic, also temperate waters to a lesser degree. Minke Whales are confirmed wanderers, and sightings have occurred in the Mediterranean, Black, Adriatic and Baltic Seas. Found farther south than other finbacks, and rarely seen in the tropics.

Status: Coming increasingly under pressure from commercial Whalers. It seems to have a gloomy future.

Description: 25–33ft. Males average 27ft; females 29ft. The smallest of the finback whales. Gracefully streamlined with a small head which appears triangular when viewed from above. Pronounced dorsal fin, and fairly large pointed pectoral fins, which on specimens living in the Northern Hemisphere have a white band round them. From fifty to seventy longitudinal furrows on the white underside of the throat and breast. The short baleen plates are especially dense and finely frayed. The mouth aperture is almost straight.

Habits: The Minke Whale seems to prefer coastal waters. It is a fast swimmer, often plays around ships and is attracted to them. With whaling in its present state, this is a tragic habit: many of the ships they try to befriend will doubtless greet them with an explosive harpoon.

Usually solitary or in small schools, which may in turn form part of a larger group of perhaps 20–50 individuals. The higher the latitude, the greater the abundance of food, and therefore the larger the school. Migrates regularly, at which point the sexes tend to segregate.

The spout is indistinct but the actual exhalation can be heard from far off. The whale makes a series of shallow dives before sounding deeply for up to five minutes. The tail does not clear the water in the act of diving.

Food: Krill, especially the younger stages of *Euphausia superba*. If unable to find sufficient shrimp, it will also consume copepods and small fish (anchovies, etc.).

Reproduction: Migrates to warmer waters to breed. Very high pregnancy rate – nearly 90 per cent, and most females give birth annually when mature. Set against this is possibly the shortest life span of all Balaenopterids – less than fifty years. Sexual maturity is attained at seven to eight years, physical maturity at about twenty years. (Age of whales can be determined by counting the number of laminations in the waxy earplug.)

Special features: Owing to their smaller size, Minke Whales were for a long time virtually ignored by the big whalers. Now, due to the over-exploitation of the larger species, the Minke Whale is coming increasingly into the firing line. An annual quota is fixed by the International Whaling Commission but this is virtually meaningless since the two largest whaling nations (Japan and the USSR) refuse to abide by it.

The Minke Whale has also been hunted on a smaller scale for many years in such places as Newfoundland and Norway. Large numbers are harpooned in Newfoundland each year, and also off the Norwegian coast while passing by on migration to the Barents Sea; unfortunately it is the cows and young who suffer most as they are the first to arrive and swim closer to shore.

Sei Whale (*Balaenoptera borealis*)

Distribution: Similar to Minke Whale but keeps to deeper and more temperate waters. Since disappearance in Antarctica of the great whales, it has begun travelling south to feed on the unusually abundant Krill.

Status: Approximately 100,000. About half their original population. Between 1963 and 1967 their population was reduced by about one third.

Description: 40–50ft. Similar to but longer and more slender than

Minke Whale. Other differences: smaller pectoral fins, less white on the underside and an irregular demarcation between that and the dark upperparts, and throat furrows not extending so far back. The dorsal fin is clearly visible when the whale surfaces.

Habits: Gregarious and a fast swimmer (maximum of at least 35mph). The spout rises to about 10ft; after a few breaths, the whale sounds for up to ten minutes.

Food: Similar to Minke Whale, but more fish and cephalopods. Known in Japan as the 'sardine-whale'.

Reproduction: Migrates to warmer waters to breed, during which time it lives mostly on its accumulated blubber, as do most migrating great whales. Births occur every second year, as with all other mysticetes except the smaller Minke.

Special features: The Sei Whale has suffered more than any other species as a result of the over-exploitation of the Blue and Fin Whales, and since 1965 has been greatly overfished and is declining alarmingly.

Common Rorqual or Fin Whale
(*Balaenoptera physalus*)

Distribution: Worldwide, prefers temperate and cold seas up to the pack-ice. Wanderers are seen in tropical waters and quite frequently in the Mediterranean Sea.

Status: Reduced to less than a quarter of its estimated original population; some 80,000–90,000 probably exist today. Economically of great importance but is being caught in decreasing numbers since the stocks began to diminish rapidly in the 1960s.

Description: 60–80ft. The second largest cetacean; compared to the larger Blue Whale it is more slender, has a slightly larger dorsal fin and a white belly. Differs from all whales in being asymmetrically coloured: upperparts grey, underparts white but the lower jaw has a grey left-side (the right-side is white). Inside the mouth and on the tongue, the right-side is pigmented but not the left. Otherwise similar to other rorquals.

Habits: Gregarious but can be found singly. Alternates one long and deep dive with a few shallow ones. It can stay submerged for half an hour but 10–15 minutes is more usual. On surfacing, its spout reaches a height of 20ft (appearing as an inverted cone); it breathes rapidly several times and rests for a couple of minutes after a prolonged dive. On sounding, the dorsal fin shows but not the tail, and a patch of turbulence appears on the surface caused by the tremendous upward thrust of the tail flukes.

This photograph shows very clearly the nostrils of a finback whale in the Sea of Cortez wide open to inhale before sounding. It is at these moments, when the whale is compelled to come up for air, that most harpooning takes place.

When undisturbed, the Fin Whale swims at a steady 10–15mph but can attain 20mph if pressed.

Food: Mainly Krill but if necessary will also consume shoaling small fish; to catch these it sometimes turns its head on one side. About 3t consumed per day.

Reproduction: After a gestation period of eleven months the calf is born and measures about 13ft. It is suckled for about seven months. Although a single calf is the rule, more have been produced, including, at least once, sextuplets. Otherwise much the same as other rorquals.

Special features: The Fin Whale, second largest animal ever known to have lived, felt the full brunt of the whaling industry. After the decline of the Blue Whale its numbers were dramatically reduced, many thousands being killed every year.

An observer describes part of a Fin Whale hunt: 'The whale is rolling and driving forward by strong thrusts of its tail flukes. A shot is fired. . . . The whale is hit and the water foams wildly. The ship slows down and we see the harpoon in the neck of the whale.

'The pain forces the animal to swim ahead. . . . The water is now red with blood. There is a second shot and the whale is hit by a grenade which explodes inside it. This is the cruellest moment in the most cruel form of hunting ever devised by man. The whale is now dead and turns over on its back.' Insult is then added to injury. 'Now an iron tube is forced into the whale's abdominal cavity, and the pump drives compressed air . . . into the body of the whale inflating it like a tyre.' That is whale-hunting at its best – usually it takes half an hour or more for the whale to die.

Blue Whale (*Balaenoptera musculus*)

Distribution: Worldwide but prefers cold and temperate waters. The vast majority live in the Antarctic Ocean with only a small number in the Northern Hemisphere.

Status: The most seriously endangered of all whales, it may be already beyond recovery. There is an optimum stock level for a species like this below which the reproductive rate is so inhibited (in such a vast range) that the stock cannot maintain itself. A few hundred years ago there was a population of well over 200,000 and they were found in all the seas of the world, but now fewer than 9000 exist.

Description: The largest animal ever known to have lived. Maximum recorded length over 108ft – a female killed off the coast of Scotland in 1926; average length about 100ft. Weight about 150t and girth nearly 46ft. The whole body is bluish-grey with pale mottling, although sometimes the underparts are coloured yellow by a growth of diatoms. 80–100 furrows on the throat; over 700 plates of black baleen. The dorsal fin is small and set far back; the tail flukes are about 21ft wide.

Habits: Shy, lives in groups of only two or three. Undertakes long migrations to and from the sub-tropics where it spends the winter. It usually swims at 6–12mph but can attain well over 20mph if chased.

Dives deeply for up to twenty minutes, after which it makes a series of shallower dives of about fifteen seconds. Its spout is similar to the Fin Whale's but rather higher and is visible for up to five seconds. On sounding, the tail only breaks surface at the commencement of a deep dive.

Food: An estimated 4t of Krill, mostly *Euphausia superba*, every day. Most whales migrate to the Antarctic waters every spring to reap the abundance of this food. Occasionally will consume other items such as small fish.

Reproduction: Migration north from the Antarctic feeding grounds begins in late summer. The calves, born every second year after a gestation period of one year, measure about 23ft and weigh in the region of $2\frac{1}{2}$t. The single calf is suckled for six months and consumes on average half a ton of very rich milk (35 per cent fat) every day. It grows rapidly and puts on about 220lbs daily. At one year old the calf will measure about 50ft, and is fully grown in another year. Males are mature when they reach a length of 75ft; females at 80ft.

Special features: Should the extinction of this phenomenal animal ever come about, as well it might, it will be the worst tragedy of all in the history of man's exploitation of nature. In 1930 some 29,000 were killed, and in the sixty years that have passed since Antarctic whaling began about 350,000 Blue Whales have been slaughtered.

Some authorities consider the occasional small mature Blue Whales

caught in the Antarctic to be a distinct subspecies (*B. m. brevicauda*); others assert that they are a convenient excuse to bypass the complete protection the Blue Whale now enjoys.

Humpback Whale (*Megaptera novaeangliae*)

Distribution: Worldwide. Undertakes definite migrations along fixed routes to and from its breeding and feeding grounds (see below).

Status: Seriously endangered but now protected. Numbers have dropped from an estimated 111,000 to little over 5000.

Description: 36–53ft. Different in appearance from all other whales; rather plumper. Black upperparts and very pale below with black markings. Extremely long pectoral fins (one third of total body length) with scalloped anterior margins. There are numerous tubercles and protuberances on these fins and the head. The dorsal fin is not very pronounced and from it to the tail stretch a series of low humps. 14–30 deep throat furrows. Over 600 plates of dark grey baleen.

Habits: Lives in small, slow-moving schools. Often leaps from the water in a playful manner but will also at times rest motionless. Dives deeply for up to thirty minutes, followed by the usual series of shorter, shallow dives. The spout is explosive but does not reach as great a height and disperses more quickly than the Blue Whale's.

There are possibly eleven separate populations – four of them in the Northern and seven in the Southern hemisphere. Each one travels from the polar feeding grounds along set routes to breed in the coastal waters of tropical lands. Much affection is evinced during mating.

Food: As for other finbacked whales.

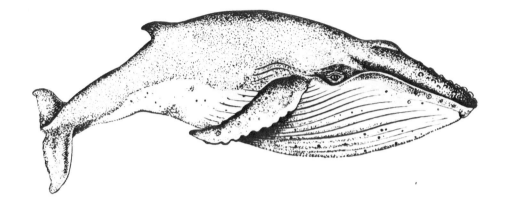

Reproduction: Gestation is the normal twelve months. At birth the calf measures about 15ft. It is suckled for five and a half months. Maturity is attained in 15–17 months. This species, especially when young, is probably preyed on to quite a large extent by Killer Whales.

Special features: The Humpback Whale is an extremely vocal species and indulges in 'songs' – that is to say, complete sequences of different notes that are repeated almost exactly. Some songs last only a few minutes (the known shortest takes six minutes) while others exceed thirty minutes. Each individual would appear to have its own song, and they are 'recycled' almost without break, the gap between finish and start being no longer than that between two notes. It is a magical and eerie sound to listen to, and in my opinion one of the most beautiful in the world, perhaps second only to the baying of wolves.

The Humpback Whale and its incredible songs have been made famous by the American Dr Roger Payne. Despite its great size (up to 30 tons) it is one of the most agile of the great whales, often somersaulting in the sea and at times completely leaving the water.

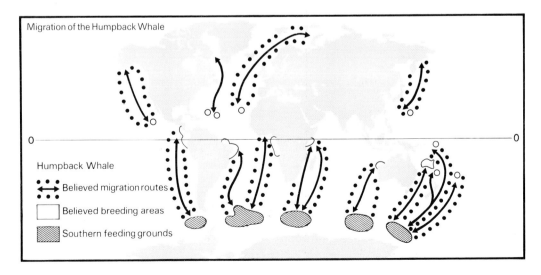

Migration of the Humpback Whale

Humpback Whale

Believed migration routes

Believed breeding areas

Southern feeding grounds

In common with all great whales, the Humpback has been hunted almost to extinction with only a few thousand surviving. Its habit of migrating along coastal routes contributed to its own downfall. Since it began to be protected midway through this century, some populations at least seem to be holding their own.

Greenland Right Whale or Bowhead
(*Balaena mysticetus*)

Distribution: Arctic waters near to drifting pack-ice. Most northerly of all the mysticetes.

Status: Extremely rare.

Description: 50–70ft exceptionally up to 80ft. The enormous head, with arched upper jaw, makes up one third of the total length. No throat furrows or dorsal fin. Pectoral fins very broad. Coloration black apart from a grey area near the tail and a white chin. About 700 black baleen plates are suspended from the upper jaw, each one over $10\frac{1}{2}$ft long (compared to only 20in. in the average finbacked whale).

Habits: Nowadays usually lives alone or in pairs but is sometimes found in schools of up to fifty individuals. In the olden days of whaling it was reported to be gregarious. The females and young usually live apart from the males. Can dive very deeply – 5000ft has been suggested, although 3500ft is more likely – and stay below for 30–60 minutes. On surfacing it will relax and perhaps make some shallow dives lasting 5–10 minutes. Its spout is double in formation and usually directed forwards (occasionally backwards). On sounding its tail appears above the surface at the last moment.

Food: As for other mysticete whales.

Reproduction: This species is unique amongst the *Balaenidae* in that it does not move to warmer waters to breed. It has become so well adapted to its environment that it has overcome one of the last problems facing the planktonic great whales – that of compromising between the Krill-rich polar feeding grounds and the warmer but less nourishing waters the young need in early life. (Unfortunately for them, this evolutionary advance also made them ideal targets for the whalers, who were not forced to chase them about all over the oceans.)

A newly born Greenland Right Whale has a considerably thicker layer of blubber than that found in the young of finbacked whales; in fact it is half as thick as that of the adults. This species is believed to mate in late summer; the young (two have been seen with one female) is born after a gestation period of $9\frac{1}{2}$ months.

Special features: The Greenland Right Whale, apart from having a tremendous amount of fine baleen and high quality oil, was relatively easy to capture; neither was it as dangerous to hunt as the Sperm Whale. Its persecution in the Arctic was a natural development after the overfishing of the North Atlantic Right Whale and its consequent rarity. A small vessel could cover its expenses for the whole season from the proceeds of a single Bowhead.

Some authorities believe this species to be almost extinct; at best there can be only a few thousand, mostly in the North Pacific. It has been fully protected (except locally by Eskimoes) since 1935.

North Atlantic, Black or Biscayan Right Whale
(*Eubalaena glacialis*)
Pacific Right Whale (*E. sieboldi*)
Southern Right Whale (*E. australis*)

Distribution: North Atlantic, North Pacific and the Southern Hemisphere respectively.

Status: All severely depleted and endangered, but hopefully beginning to recover since protection in 1935.

Description: *c.* 65ft. Generally blackish and similar to the previous species. *E. glacialis* is shorter by a few metres and has on the snout a peculiar patch of horny, roughened skin (the 'bonnet'). In the crevices of this skin lives an amphipod crustacean, the Whale Louse, often found in great numbers. Apart from these lice, which incidentally also occur on the Bowhead, animals such as sea-anemones and other crustaceans adopt these whales as hosts (see Chapter 10).

Habits: Similar to Bowhead but a little quicker through the water. Unlike the Bowhead, these species do migrate to warmer waters to breed, often along coastal routes, which of course made them vulner-

A Southern Right Whale erupts from the sea, displaying its paddle-shaped breast fluke. They are called Right Whales because they were the right whales to hunt. The Southern species is native to the southern Indian and Atlantic Oceans, and was once numerous off South Georgia.

able to the attentions of whalers.

Food: As for other mysticetes.

Reproduction: Similar to the Bowhead, except that they migrate to warmer waters in the winter to breed. Cows give birth every second year.

Sealions
Walruses
& Seals

7

The Pinnipedia

The song of pleasant stations
Beside the salt lagoons,
The song of blowing squadrons
That shuffled down the dunes,
The song of midnight dances
That churned the sea to flame –
The beaches of Lukannon –
Before the Sealers came.

from 'Lukannon' by Rudyard Kipling

All seals, whether they are true or earless seals (*Phocidae*), eared seals (*Otariidae*) or of the two races of walrus (*Odobenidae*), closely resemble one another in their physiological characteristics, which have been discussed in detail in Chapter 4.

They can be distinguished from other marine mammals by obvious physical features such as, in most species, a dense fur coat and, in all species, their retention of four limbs which, though greatly modified, still indicate in positive terms their terrestrial ancestry (see Chapter 2).

Seals, while less specialized for an oceanic existence than whales, are nevertheless superbly adapted for their own particular environment. They are very much creatures of coastal waters and the littoral zone, and unlike the other main groups of marine mammals still need to come ashore to mate, give birth, moult or simply to rest. This reliance on dry land or floating pack-ice ties them for substantial periods of the year to the coastline, and although one occasionally encounters seals far out to sea – up to thirty miles – there seems little to lure them there except possibly during long migrations or for hunting in times when food is scarce.

Phocid seals are almost certainly of older stock than the otariids and, to a lesser degree, walruses, which are often considered to be transitional between the two. This is inevitably a matter of conjecture; the scarcity of fossil evidence is both frustrating and possibly misleading. However, it can safely be assumed that the Pinnipedia emerged early in the Eocene era – approximately fifty million years ago. There is considerable controversy over their true antecedents.

Phocid seals are not so well equipped for terrestrial locomotion as the other two families, which suggests either that they are phylogenetically older and so more fully adapted to an aquatic existence, or that they have evolved from a different species. Is it because they are awkward and clumsy out of water that they spend less time on land or *vice versa* ?

Seals of one sort or another are by far the most familiar of the marine mammals to most people – in most parts of the world. They are found almost throughout the world and may be encountered in coastal regions in almost any latitude, but this is by no means a random distribution. The phocid seals, by virtue of their vastly superior capacity for retaining heat, are found predominantly in the cold waters of the Arctic and Antarctic or in regions influenced by cold currents. They are rather scarce in tropical and subtropical waters (the three species of rare monk seals being exceptions), and it has been suggested that tropical waters present actual physical barriers to them. Personally I feel this rather overstates the case; it is quite possible that planktonic abundance in polar waters, and the consequent proliferation of fish and crustaceans, makes their dispersal unnecessary. They must also have crossed the equator at some stage in their evolution, perhaps quite recently.

It is difficult to know whether the conditions shaped the animal, the animal shaped itself to suit the conditions or whether there was a combination of both. We can fairly safely assume that phocid seals gradually invaded the more lucrative colder waters as their resistance to it increased. Presumably, then, their prehistoric forebears first took to the sea in a temperate region.

The eared seals are not so problematical. They have, it would seem, always lived in the warmer areas of the world. They differ in important ways from the true seals, and can conveniently be subdivided into a further two groups: the fur seals and the sealions. Their mode of swimming, and therefore the extent to which their limbs have become adapted for this purpose, is very distinctive. This subject has been dealt with in greater detail in Chapter 4, but it may be as well to recapitulate the major points which are specific to the pinnipeds.

Among the several methods and combinations of methods used by vertebrates for swimming, by far the most effective is provided by sculling movements of the caudal regions, such as are employed by the majority of fish. The reasons are simple enough: there is no wasted movement; each action is to some degree propulsive, and recovery strokes which not only waste energy but also have a braking effect are entirely avoided. Animals such as fish, salamanders, crocodiles and cetaceans have all developed this form of propulsion, which is known as 'body fusiform'. In its most advanced form it makes no use what-

Kerguelen Fur Seals *(Arctocephalus tropicalis gazella)* in South Georgia. Like all species of the genus *Arctocephalus* they are mammals of the southern oceans. The effects of their movements over the tussock grass can be clearly seen in in this photograph.

Mother Weddell Seal and pup
at ice hole.

top right Common or
Harbour Seal mother with
pup pick-a-backing'.

centre right Crabeater Seals
on an ice flow in the
South Seas.

bottom right The Weddell
Seal is a fearless, nomadic
inhabitant of Antarctic
waters, diving to great depths
in its search for fish.

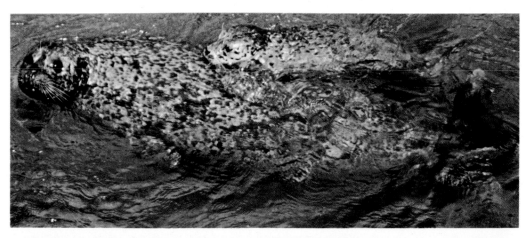

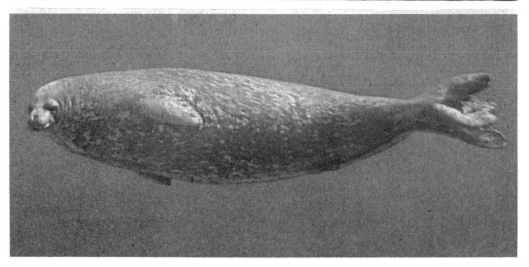

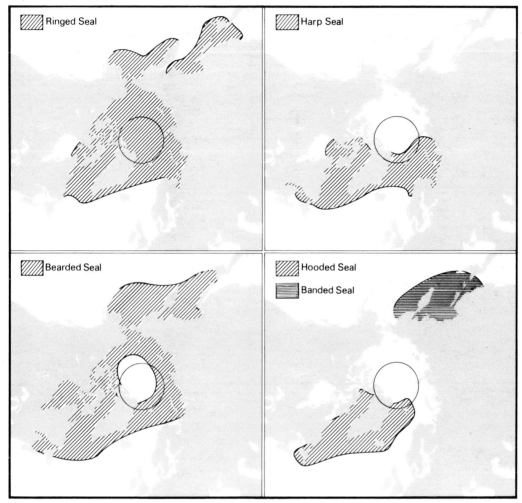

soever of pectoral appendages – the 'tail' becomes all important.

Among seals, we find some absorbing variations on body fusiform. When any animal enters the water and swims with a paddle-action such as that of a dog, it inadvertently wiggles its hind-quarters and tail (if it has one) to and fro. If the tail is substantial it will gradually gain ascendancy through evolution and take over the swimming impulsion from the feet – which were anyway hardly adequate. This is precisely what must have happened with whales, which have now lost all trace of their hind limbs.

The pinnipeds – literally 'fin-footed' – have not achieved this peak of aquatic perfection; instead their hind limbs have become modified into tail-like appendages which, in the case of phocid seals, constantly point backwards. The bulk of the flipper is now retained inside the body wall, but the manus is still five-fingered. Phocid seals in particu-

These Galapagos Sealions, hauled out on the lava of Fernandina under the shade of mangroves, are a race of the Californian Sealion. They seem happy to live at peace with an iguana and several red rock crabs.

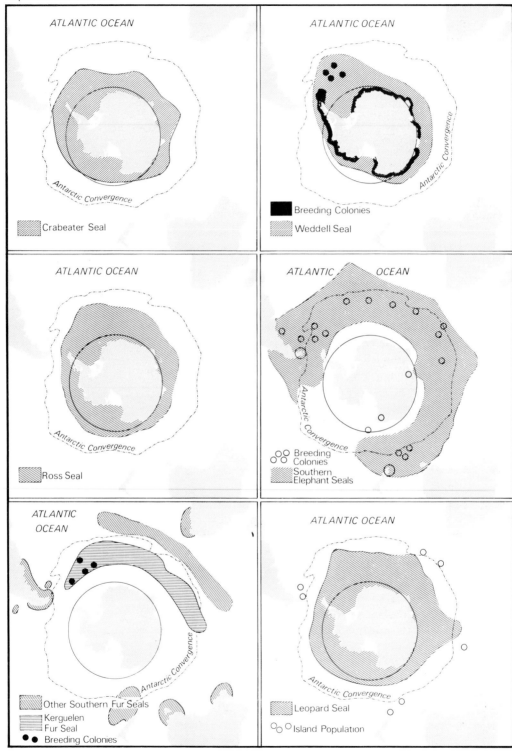

lar are little hindered by this arrangement, which presumably (because of an insufficient tail) was a chance occurrence in the formative stages of the animals' adaptation to an oceanic life. Indeed, their mode of swimming, with the soles of their hind feet pressed together, looks remarkably similar to that of a large fish. All evidence suggests that it is just as effective.

The eared seals and walrus, whose hind limbs have not become quite so specialized and who can on dry land rotate them forward to a plantigrade position, seem to have gained the best of both worlds. While the phocid seals propel themselves exclusively by means of their pseudo-tails, the fur seals and sealions have achieved comparable performance through their fore limbs; hence their more muscular and bulky forequarters. The hind limbs of these animals are used during swimming mostly for steering and equilibrium.

Although scientifically this method should be less successful, the *Otariidae* may in practice be as fast as the true seals – one cannot say for certain. An examination of their swimming technique explains how they overcome their main obstacle to speed beneath water. During slow and leisurely progression, when the flippers move in an orthodox lateral manner, the braking effect experienced on the anterior stroke is more than compensated for by the thrust of the posterior or drive movement. However, when the animal wishes to increase its speed, it completely changes its action from a lateral to a transverse one; the antero-posterior action soon becomes inadequate, partly because of water-resistance on the recovery stroke (although the flipper is 'feathered') and, more importantly, because the seal simply cannot move its quite considerable flippers fast enough.

The otariids have consequently adopted a 'flying' action similar to that used by penguins under water. With this system there is no wasted effort and minimal drag, but above all it provides, through a change of flipper elevation on the upper (weaker) stroke, at least a certain amount of thrust. It is possible, though it may not have been proved, that they also use the hind limbs to a certain extent, perhaps at higher speeds. Certainly as a result of this adaptation, sealions and their kin obtain a continuous forward propulsion not so far removed from that attained by animals employing body fusiform.

Whatever its ancestry, the walrus is certainly intermediate between the other two families in its mode of swimming, using both pectoral and pelvic appendages. Some authorities believe that it is transitional or, more specifically, a specialized otariid; others that it has evolved from quite separate stock. The solution to this perplexing question may very well lie in the answer to another – do eared and true seals have a common ancestor? This question may never be answered unless fossil evidence becomes more widespread.

The walrus, found only in the waters of the Arctic, has anatomical features similar to those of both its companion families. This could well be the result of convergent evolution, and the fact that there is little conformity tends to support, I believe, the theory of isolation and therefore also the lack of an ancestor common to both the *Phocidae* and *Otariidae*. This, I admit, is pure speculation.

That briefly sums up seal locomotion beneath water – in their most favoured element. On land the situation is reversed, and the phocid seals become extremely inept. One can assume that their aquatic specialization has reached or is reaching a critical stage. The case of the mammoth elephant seals best typifies their situation and the following can apply (with obvious adjustments) to all phocids.

Having gained a length of more than twenty feet and a weight approaching four tons, the elephant seals can only with extreme difficulty and much exertion haul themselves out on to dry land. I once timed an adult cow at one and a half hours before she succeeded in heaving her body clear of the water. At least three-quarters of that time was spent in resting. The performance clearly distressed her.

In needs only a little imagination to foresee a time when the elephant seals will be overspecialized and find themselves unable to leave the sea at all. The Cetacea and Sirenia must presumably have already faced this predicament at some stage in their development and come through satisfactorily. Could the Pinnipedia, or more specifically the *Phocidae*, do the same? Presumably it will be a very long time, even in genealogical terms, before the otariids and walruses find themselves in a similar position, if they ever do.

The most pressing problems for a seal denied the facilities of dry land would relate to the reproductive cycle, the most delicate and important ritual in the life of any species. Could seals equip themselves for mating and parturition afloat, following the example of the whales and sirenians; or would the pups perish? Many seal pups do not swim for at least one month; it is difficult to know whether this is because they cannot or will not. Common Seals, on the other hand, are born with sea-going pelts and swim almost immediately, yet as a species this is possibly the most land-tied of all phocids.

At certain precise times of the year (see *Species Biographies*), many seal species congregate in dense herds at traditional sites; these land-assemblies serve as valuable rendezvous for the species, and ensure their perpetuation. That there are relatively few such sites for each species ensures that enough members will be present, and that they will not be disseminated at random locations in insufficient quantities. This is especially important for species of solitary or nomadic disposition.

If there were not these traditional rendezvous, the chances of sufficient biomasses with correct sex-ratios meeting at the right time in such a featureless world would surely be extremely slim. By no means all seals are polygamous; most true seals, with the exception of the Grey Seal and elephant seals, are, if not monogamous, only loosely socially structured. The problem of social contact would not be so great with these species. The males of the Grey Seal, elephant

A Grey Seal pup, its coat encrusted with snow, shows no apparent signs of discomfort, thanks to the very efficient insulating qualities of its blubber.

seals, otariids and walruses gather round themselves considerable harems of cows during the mating season, when there is much fighting between rival suitors – a process which ensures that only the strongest bulls sire any one season's youngsters.

The Cetacea and Sirenia have surmounted the problems of social organization in various ways – none probably suitable for seals without profound changes. One inevitably wonders whether they could adapt to these changes. The question of the effect on the pelage of an animal of continuous immersion in saline water does not seem to be of such importance. Presumably, if it had an untoward effect, the species could adapt itself accordingly during the normal course of evolution, as did the whales. The Sea Otter (q.v.) has one of the finest pelts in the whole of the animal kingdom, and it is almost exclusively aquatic. Many phocid seals, as it is, spend prolonged periods at sea, and their coats do not appear to suffer as a result.

Certain ectoparasites such as marine lice cannot survive out of water, and for this reason alone the ability to emerge from the sea benefits an aquatic mammal in much the same way as orthodox bathing benefits a terrestrial animal: sun-bathing in its most literal sense, in fact.

For an aquatic mammal covered by nothing other than a naked or rugose hide, the procedure of skin regeneration, or more precisely degeneration, is little changed from that of an elephant or indeed of ourselves. It is a continuous process of dead skin flaking off, and it goes on regardless of the seasons. The gradual moulting of hair on land animals would hardly suit an animal like a seal, which requires its coat to be effective, and therefore totally intact, while it is swimming and diving. A coat which is liable to have some component hairs missing at certain times would quickly become waterlogged, and therefore a possible source of danger. (All the same, though this has never been explained, there are occasions when seals moult at sea.)

Seals (and possibly the Sea Otter) get over this by going through rapid moults or semi-moults while out of the sea – another important

A fur seal from South Georgia demonstrates the use of its powerful flippers for moving over land.

reason why they are tied to land. Indeed the hair comes off elephant seals in large patches still attached to the outer skin. This results, as many photographs show, in an exceedingly moth-eaten and diseased appearance.

Phocid seals have not only dense fur coats but also a layer of sub-cutaneous blubber some three inches thick. In such superb insulation, coupled to a very high metabolism, lies the ability of these seals to thrive in the immensely cold polar seas. But what happens when a seal wishes to dispose of excess heat, for instance when basking in warm sunshine or after periods of furious exertion?

A phocid seal has a large number of highly specialized blood vessels situated all over the body, especially in the limbs, and can lose heat simply by dilating these outer vessels and flushing large quantities of heated blood to the extremities of its body, where it quickly cools. These same blood vessels are also capable, by contracting, of greatly minimizing the flow of blood to the outer surfaces of the body, and so not only insulating but isolating the inner body and vital organs from temperatures often at or below freezing point.

The temperature gradient of a seal swimming in near freezing water (sea water freezes at about $-2°C : 28°F$) climbs from $2°C$ ($36°F$) on the outer surfaces of the body to $37°C$ ($99°F$) only an inch and a half into the blubber. This is an outstanding example of insulation, and from it we can deduce that adult seals in normal circumstances never experience coldness as we know it. One vulnerable part of a seal's body, however, is the flipper – that fragile, exposed and tremendously important organ of direction, momentum and stability. Potentially a great conductor of heat, it would, if supplied with blood in an orthodox manner, cause the animal to lose heat almost as quickly as it could manufacture it.

This problem too is overcome by the positioning of the veins and arteries at the point where the limb leaves the main body wall. The solution is really extraordinarily simple. There is a network of blood vessels entwined in such a way that the arteries (vessels carrying blood *from* the heart) pass very close to the veins (vessels carrying blood *to* the heart), creating a heat-exchange system in which the warm blood entering the flippers loses most of its heat to the cold blood re-entering the body. The animal derives two direct benefits: it does not waste heat and energy in a futile attempt to keep its flippers warm, and because the blood re-entering the body does so at an increased temperature, the internal and vital parts of the body are better protected.

Seals are thus creatures of dual temperatures. Internally, they are more or less conventional warm-blooded animals, while on the outer body surfaces they more closely resemble cold-blooded animals. The likening of a seal to a vacuum flask is extremely accurate, though the seal has the added advantage of generating its own heat from within. The flippers function perfectly at greatly reduced temperatures and at the same time are still supplied with their essential nourishment.

Of all the pinnipeds the fur seals are perhaps the most imposing. They also pose specific questions, the answers to which require more than average deliberation. They are widespread throughout the more southerly waters, with only one species, *Callorhinus*, in the far north. Altogether there are eight species, seven of which belong to the genus *Arctocephalus*.

Fur seals, for reasons still not fully understood, appear to have a heat-conservation system even more efficient than that of the phocids, although they seem not to make fullest use of it. They not only have the usual layer of blubber, but also two coats of fur; the underneath coat, very dense and soft, is guarded by an outer layer of coarser hairs. One must presume that they lack the sophistication of the *Phocidae* in less effective blubber and differences in the vascular system. Unlike the pelage of other seals, which becomes saturated while swimming and provides little extra warmth, the dense undercoat of the fur seals traps within it many tiny bubbles of air which, like blubber, are poor conductors of heat and so help to keep the animal warm.

A further indication of a possibly less well-organized heat-regulation system in the fur seals is found by examining their capacity to lose heat. They seem to suffer more from overheating than other pinnipeds, and can often be seen panting heavily in hot weather and sweating profusely from their flippers, which they wave around in the air in order to increase the airflow over their surfaces.

The single-coated sealions, of which there are five genera and the equivalent number of species, are also predominantly southern in distribution, the notable exception being *Eumetopias* or the Steller's Sealion. It is hard to understand why the fur seals should have an apparently superior insulation to the Steller's Sealion, which belongs to the same family and whose distribution exactly overlaps that of the Northern Fur Seal.

The two races of walruses – the Atlantic and the Pacific – get along admirably with an arrangement similar to that of the cetaceans and sirenians. Their blubber is all important and remarkably effective. Immediately above it is a hide of immense toughness up to two inches thick which, together with a blubber layer of up to five inches, is an extremely successful insulation in itself. The weight of a walrus's hide and blubber makes up about one third of its total weight; and a dead walrus in near freezing water reportedly retains heat within its body for upwards of twelve hours.

An air temperature as low as $-45°C$ ($-49°F$) does not appear to affect a resting walrus at all; at this very low temperature, of course, their hides are frozen solid. In warmer weather conditions, walruses use the same system of vessel dilation to cool their blood as other seals. At such times they are known to glow with quite uncanny pinkness.

There is a lot of uncertainty, for obvious reasons, over such matters as the pinnipeds' dive duration and depth, but of one thing there is no doubt – the sheer mastery of these animals in their adopted under-water world. Most pinnipeds can spend a period of at least twenty minutes below surface, although a span of far less than that is more normal. There are inevitably exceptions to this rule: the Weddell Seal, for instance, has been timed for up to an hour below water and has descended to a depth of at least 1800ft – well into the bathyal zone. This is admittedly exceptional, as the following selection shows:

Species	Max. recorded duration (mins)	Max. recorded depth (feet)
Northern Fur Seal	less than 20	240
S. African Fur Seal	less than 20	150
Walrus	less than 12	about 250
Harp Seal	less than 30	825
Grey Seal	more than 20	about 500
Weddell Seal	60	more than 1800
Hooded Seal	more than 20	more than 1260
Elephant Seal	more than 20	about 2000

It is, however, more than likely that individual performance varies as much in seals as it does in humans.

The walrus in particular seems to be governed to a maximum depth of 250–300ft by an apparent inability to remain submerged for more than twelve minutes. Whether or not it could venture deeper if fitted with an aqualung is debatable. I suspect that its diving performance has never evolved further for lack of necessity; presumably it can find all the clams and other molluscs it needs at that depth.

How then can these animals and the other main groups of marine mammals hold their breath for such long spells? To answer this question, we must first understand the basic mechanisms of normal respiration.

The reflex action of breathing is stimulated in us all by the accumulation of free carbon dioxide in the lungs, which triggers a particularly sensitive area of the brain, known as the respiration centre. In whales, seals and sirenians this triggering mechanism must be overcome. A man can with difficulty hold his breath for about two and a half minutes, but this is a paltry performance compared to a seal's, though the seal has more or less the same equipment as ourselves. How does the seal achieve control?

To begin with, the respiration centre of a seal must be relatively insensitive, more tolerant to a build up of carbon dioxide than a terrestrial animal's. But that on its own would not suffice to make the prolonged dives of these animals feasible. More important is the metabolism and vascular system.

Marine mammals, especially whales and seals, are endowed with very much more blood than terrestrial mammals of equivalent bulk. A figure of up to half as much again is frequently given; this begins to explain why ancient sealers recounting their bloody deeds always made a point of remarking upon the gory state of beaches after a massacre.

The blood of cetaceans and pinnipeds (and sirenians?) has a far greater oxygen storage capacity than 'ordinary' blood; the Weddell Seal is reputed to have a blood oxygen store five times greater than that of a man. In addition, seals can store further supplies in a respiratory pigment (myoglobin, which is akin to haemoglobin and similarly largely constituted from a complex protein called globin) which is found in their muscles. Even so, this is still insufficient oxygen to sustain a long dive, and seals have had to develop still further processes for conserving oxygen. This is done by reducing the rate of metabolism, which in seals is normally much faster than that of other mammals.

An instinctive response, caused when the seal dives and closes its nostrils, reduces the heartbeat from 150 beats per minute to a figure of between four and fifteen, depending upon the depth of submersion – the deeper the dive, the slower the heartbeat. In this way, the blood is still circulated and enough oxygen is conveyed to a few important organs, such as the brain and heart, which require a constant supply. The remaining organs are by-passed by contraction of the vessels, and either function on the oxygen already stored within them or only perform actions which do not require oxygen.

The act of diving and swimming causes the skeletal muscles to distend and contract, thereby breaking down glycogen and forming an organic acid (lactic acid), which by splitting up glucose is essential for the utilization process of energy. This is known as anaerobic respiration, and benefits muscles when deprived of their normal aerobic respiration. Lactic acid is stored within the muscles until the seal surfaces. It is then released back into the blood when the vascular system and metabolism return to normal.

On surfacing a seal will take a few deep breaths in rapid succession,

The Ross Seal inhabits the inner drifting ice zone of Antarctica. It scours the sea floor, using echo-location, for cephalopods and soft-shelled crustaceans. Though shy and clumsy out of water, once swimming it can outpace even the Killer Whale

and in this way rid its body of accumulated carbon dioxide and re-oxygenate it. Some authorities believe that prolonged periods ashore are necessary from time to time, in order to rest and recharge their batteries. If this is so, it provides another reason why seals are tied to the coast, and another problem for them to surmount if they are to relinquish this tie.

The life cycles of seals are of particular interest. In order to breed successfully they first of all have to overcome some complications inherent in their habitat. I have touched on one of these problems in discussing the land assembly question and the reliance of seals on coming ashore. The congregating of seals on land lasts only for rela-tively short periods each year, so the cows not only have to give birth at that time of the year when food is most abundant for their pups to have the best chance of survival (newly born seals are particularly vulnerable to predation), but must also conceive the next season's off-spring at or near the same time. A gestation period of some eleven months is thus a necessity. But this is rather too long for a conven-tional carnivore pregnancy, for it would result in the pup being born while the mother was still out at sea fishing and fattening up for the mating season (cf. gestation of whales). A few types of mammals, seals included, have developed a method of delaying birth by a process known as 'delayed implantation' (see below). Seals, as a rule, only produce a single pup, although twin fetuses have been found.

The reproductive cycle of the Grey Seal (which prefers to breed on undisturbed islets) is a good example. This species is common around the costs of Great Britain (especially Scotland) and widespread over much of the remainder of the east Atlantic, North Sea, Baltic Sea and parts of the west Atlantic Ocean. Before examining the repro-ductive cycle, it is as well to remember that colonies of seals often differ in certain characteristics from area to area as the result of the animals' always returning to the place of their birth – these individual varieties are known as 'clines'. Therefore the following summary, although correct for most British Grey Seals should not be applied to those living in the Baltic or, for that matter, any other locality.

All spring and summer (April to late August) Grey Seals are out at sea fishing. Towards the end of August the seals begin to arrive at their breeding grounds, and from then until the last quarter of September there is a great deal of pre-mating behaviour: territories and hierarchies are established and weak and subordinate bulls, for which there is no room, are banished to the sea for another year. Pregnant cows remain subdued and spend most of their time resting. Pupping in a rookery begins in the early autumn (late September) and goes on for two months, the peak being in October.

Approximately a fortnight after a cow has given birth she is once again receptive and will be mated by her dominant bull. Breeding activity tails off in the first quarter of December and the colony disperses.

The fertilized egg within the female's womb develops normally until it reaches the blastocyst stage, when in normal pregnancy, as the result of repeated cleavage, it becomes implanted in the uterine wall through the trophoblast (the outer sphere) while the inner cell mass becomes the embryo proper.

In mammals such as the pinnipeds which undergo delayed implantation – others include the Stoat (*Mustela erminea*) the Pine Marten (*Martes martes*) and the Greater Horseshoe Bat (*Rhinolophus ferrusequinum*) – the ovum at this stage remains free within the womb in a dormant state for a period of up to three months. Only then does it become implanted and progress in the normal manner.

Delayed implantation, in seals at any rate, seems to perform at least two functions: it gives the cow a respite between the nursing of one youngster and the internal nourishment of another embryo; and it fulfils the more important need to synchronize the actual parturition with the land assembly season.

In mid-January the cows return to land to moult and rest; and at this juncture, gestation resumes with the implantation of the ovum. Soon after the females have completed their moult, in two or three weeks, the males return to land and begin theirs, which is completed by early April.

The choice of this particular time of the year for moulting seems to me to throw up at least one interesting argument in relation to the dependence of seals on dry land. It is perhaps significant that seals emerge from the sea roughly six months after their last prolonged period ashore, and immediately prior to a punishing summer which will be spent at sea fishing, expending much energy and requiring the full extent of all their faculties. Seals would appear not to punctuate their year at sea at this particular time solely for the purpose of moulting, and it seems logical to suppose that the moulting is an incidental event, synchronized to coincide with a few weeks ashore, the real function of which is the resting, recuperation and reoxygenation of the body systems.

If this theory is sound, phocid seals still have much to do before they can adopt the sea as a permanent environment.

Seals are already quite capable of sleeping in a submerged position – they will surface to breath subconsciously; at other times they will either lie on their backs or 'bottle' in a vertical attitude with only their heads above water. Walruses on the other hand have an additional refinement in the form of two pharyngeal pouches, which can be inflated with air from the lungs and which serve as a pair of inbuilt water-wings. These air sacs – the upper limits of the oesophagus – can stretch to huge proportions, especially in the males, and when full of air are sealed by muscular contraction. They probably have other functions as well (see *Species Biography*).

As a result of human persecution walruses and some other seal species have either moved their breeding and resting sites to areas subject to less interference or taken to a more marine existence. Walruses, in particular, appear to have forsaken many of their traditional *uglit* (singular *ugli* – an Eskimo word for the gathering sites) in favour of drifting ice-floes – where they are very much safer. Some authorities believe that walruses have always preferred ice to dry land.

As an order, seals have an abnormally short infancy. There are a few exceptions, as we shall see, but most true seals are reasonably independent after one month. The Ringed Seal (breeding more safely on land-tied ice than many species which breed on drifting ice-floes) has no need of a hasty nursing period and may take as long as three months to become independent. Elephant seals take a similar time, possibly on account of their immense bulk. Fur seals appear to vary between three and eight months. Sealions, because of their warmer habitat, have a more leisurely life which is reflected in lactation periods ranging from six to twelve months.

The walrus is unusual, for its lactation is long by seal standards, sometimes more than two years. The mother/calf bond is very strong, and owing to the slow rate of growth and long immaturity of these animals there is considerable (and necessary) protection afforded within the family 'pod'. One of the more plausible explanations put forward for this relatively long period of mother dependence lies in the walrus's specialized mode of feeding. To be able to excavate its staple diet of clams and other shellfish, a young walrus requires tusks (upper canines) at least three and a half inches long. The rate of dental growth is slow, and such a length is not achieved for about two years.

Seals in general have limited vocabularies. The commonest sound is a loud, hoarse bark of varying pitch, periodicity and intensity. Different species are also known to grunt, sneeze, cough, roar, hiss, snuffle, whistle and bleat. The quieter sounds such as hissing and whining are more frequently used in threat.

Seals are not renowned for their agility out of water. The achievements of phocid seals are unimpressive but the otariids and walruses perform slightly better, thanks to their more tractile hind-quarters.

D. B. MacMillan, in his book *Four Years in the White North* (1918), relates that Etah Eskimoes assured him that walruses frequently travelled nearly a quarter of a mile overland to the freshwater lake Alida near the Foulke Fjord. As far as I know this has never been explained. Walruses have also often been seen scaling cliffs (up to 100ft) and hills. It is difficult to account for these quite prodigious feats.

The Southern Sealion was once believed to travel inland to die; but weak and emaciated specimens found many miles from the sea are more likely to be dying from starvation and exhaustion than from any other cause. Again, however, adequate explanations are completely lacking. Such happenings, including the occasional strandings of whales on beaches, were once attributed to some primitive instinct driving the marine mammals back to the dry land of their forefathers.

The Australian Sealion is reputed to be one of the best movers on land among the pinnipeds, and has frequently been known to venture five or six miles inland. Hooker's Sealion has been credited with similar accomplishments in its native New Zealand.

Californian Sealions, those familiar 'performing seals' of zoos and circuses, are in my personal experience incredibly fleet of foot in case of need. I have embarrassing recollections of a fugitive sealion bowling along at a quite amazing speed whilst I vainly endeavoured to head him off and back into his enclosure. They are not only fast but also agile – this individual regularly made good his escape along a lengthy plank of wood which was used for crossing over to the island in the centre of his enclosure.

Phocid seals progress on dry land by placing their fore limbs on the ground and humping their bulk along like some gigantic looper caterpillar. Even these seals can move with astonishing speed should the situation really demand it.

Little is known about the senses of seals. Eyesight is certainly of prime importance, especially to phocid seals, which apparently pursue much smaller fish than the otariids and at greater depths. It is difficult, if not impossible, to generalize about optical evolution in a group of mammals living in what is fundamentally an 'unnatural' environment which must inevitably demand specialized and idiosyncratic adaptation.

The axes of the eyes, in most species of seals, seem to have evolved in a way which lags somewhat behind the degree of subaquatic specialization to which the species has progressed at any one stage. In other words, before a species has adapted itself to any marked degree, it will retain what is intrinsically a terrestrial eye. As it becomes more at one with its subaquatic habitat the eye will tend to migrate on its axis to a more dorsally orientated direction. This follows in the wake of a feeling of insecurity before the animal has developed the ability to dive deeply, and from a fear (real or imaginary) of land-based predators which would be most likely to attack from above.

The hippopotamuses, with their dorsally protruding eyes, demonstrate how aquatic mammals dependent upon surfacing at frequent intervals are more concerned with possible interference from above water, even though the vast majority of their bulk lies beneath it.

As a species gradually becomes accustomed to inhabiting deeper and deeper pelagic waters, and is able to spend correspondingly extended periods there, so its orbital axis reverts downwards to a forward, lateral or even posterior direction. Phocid seals must now suspect attack primarily from such animals as Killer Whales ($q.v.$) and large sharks – animals frequenting similar depths to themselves in a world which is alien to neither. At the same time, a seal whose survival depends on catching fast-moving small fish in the subdued light of the deep sea surely demands binocular if not stereoscopic vision. Strangely enough, vision, although so important to the true seals, does not always seem to be an indispensable item in their hunting equipment. There are quite a few records of healthy, well-nourished seals being found in a completely blind state; obviously their other senses were well developed.

The eyes of phocid seals, especially of deep sea species, are certainly of a large, receptive, liquid quality and retain a definite dorsal orientation which is rather hard to account for. It is much less pronounced in the otariids and walruses.

Fully stereoscopic eyesight would be most beneficial to seals but there is a necessary compromise between this ideal and a more obliquely angled orbit, since water-friction upon a forward-facing eye would be intolerable. It is not for nothing that the orbits of whales are set at right-angles to the body axis – where they receive the minimum of water-friction and interference.

The refractive index of sea water is different from that of either fresh water or air, so any animal adopting the sea must undergo profound changes in its optical equipment. This aspect of the design of marine mammals is discussed in broader detail in Chapter 4. The lens of a seal's eye is abnormally large, spherical and thick; the rods of the retina are much longer than in other mammals; and nictitating membranes are present as they are in the Sirenia (one would expect them to be invaluable, yet the Cetacea lack them). The eyeball itself is not fixed as it is in the whales, although the extent to which it can be moved is slight. Seals also retain to some extent eyelashes, which have atrophied in whales as they have to a lesser degree in seacows. It is conceivable that eyelashes might serve seals as sense organs in much the same way as do whiskers and eyebrows, locating turbulence and pressure created by visually undetected prey in murky water. Eyelids are perfectly functional in seals, sirenians and some types of whales. There is no lachrymal (tear) duct in marine mammals since this is unnecessary under water. For this reason, seals on land give the

The Northern Fur Seal is the commonest of the fur seals, thanks largely to international protection since 1911. Highly polygamous, the irritable 'beachmasters', the bulls, will gather harems of up to fifty cows.

impression of crying, for tears will run copiously from the eyes and down the face.

According to many observers, the eyesight of seals is poor out of water, but this is nonsense. Seals can realign their focusing rapidly when moving between air and salt water and, as any Polar Bear could confirm, they are exceptionally difficult to approach on dry land without detection. I have witnessed Leopard Seals, on film and in the flesh, peering quickly and repeatedly out of the water in the hope of espying an errant penguin.

One would assume an olfactory sense to be of little use to a fully committed marine mammal, and indeed most whales bear only vestigial traces of one. The Sirenia on the other hand retain, for no apparent reason, quite well-preserved olfactory bulbs, and among the Pinnipedia we come across the most surprising retention of an olfactory sense – only slightly less efficient, it would seem, than that of a terrestrial carnivore. It is hardly likely that an acute sense of smell could be of any use to an animal that hunts its food exclusively beneath water, in conditions where its nostrils would inevitably be closed. The only occasions I can bring to mind where the sense of smell would benefit a seal would be in the recognition of a calf by its mother, and possibly in the sensing of impending danger by a colony resting upon dry land.

Hearing in one form or another, like sight, is of vital importance to any marine mammal. Sound-waves travel better through water than they do through the air, and it would be strange if seals had not found a way in which to exploit this. It must not be assumed that because seals (*Phocidae* and *Odobenidae*) have lost their external pinnae (which are of little use anyway for collecting subaquatic sound-waves) in deference to streamlining, they automatically sacrificed their hearing at the same time. The inner ear of a true seal is strikingly large; it is also highly sensitive, even though the auditory lumen or meatus is closed by muscular action during submersion to prevent flooding. There are various alternative routes through which sound vibrations can be transmitted to the brain. Indeed, the ability to close the ear is one of the first skills learnt by a mammal on the road to becoming aquatic.

Closure of the meatus is achieved in various ways by aquatic mammals but it is more than likely that the reduced pinna of the otariids plays an important role in the ability of these seals to furl the slender cartilage and possibly also to contract the meatus laterally. Phocid seals and walruses have a different system and by the introduction of a valvular plug into the orifice through the auricle muscles, have no need for external pinnae, and this together with the need for streamlining has resulted in their disappearance.

Sounds of an extremely high frequency, similar to those emitted by dolphins, have also been heard from certain species of well-studied seals, and it would be surprising if many more lesser-known species were not found to issue analogous ultrasonics as well. Their development has yet to progress as far as dolphins' and the effective distance over which these sounds travel is still somewhat restricted. This additional faculty must, however, be very useful when hunting in turbid waters, and would assuredly serve a blind seal twofold.

Northern or Alaskan Fur Seal (*Callorhinus ursinus*)

Distribution: Main colonies centred on St George and St Paul islands (Pribilofs) and in the Bering Sea – in excess of $1\frac{1}{2}$ million animals. A further 200,000 are divided between Commander and Robben islands in the Sea of Okhotsk, off north-east Asia.

Description: Males $6\frac{1}{2}$ft and 700lbs. Females $4\frac{1}{2}$ft but only 130lbs – they lack the huge fore-quarters of the males. Males are dark brown with a greyish cape-like mane; females are grey and lighter below. Both sexes have a pale patch on the chest. Tail 2in.; pinna 1–2in.

Habits: Northern Fur Seals are noisy, gregarious animals. They are mostly crepuscular and nocturnal in habits, spending the day asleep. Their main enemies are man and Killer Whales; the stomach of one such whale was found to contain no fewer than twenty-four seals.

In October, adult cows begin to migrate southwards for the winter. They can travel up to about 3000 miles, which takes them to Japan and California. The pups and bulls leave a little later, but the bulls do not travel nearly so far and are usually content to stay in the vicinity of the Aleutian Islands. On migration, the seals usually travel at a distance of some fifty miles offshore but are liable to stray in the pursuit of fish. A reverse migration takes place the following spring, bringing the animals back to their birthplace.

Food: Fish – herrings, sardines, sprats, pollack – also squid. Little is known about exact diets; as with all seals their digestion is extremely rapid, so normal stomach analysis reveals little. However, it is known that these fur seals descend to a depth of at least 240ft, where they have apparently discovered an untapped food source; there appears to be surprisingly little conflict between their interests and those of the fishermen in their path. Ichthyologists have discovered in the stomachs of Northern Fur Seals bones of a fish hitherto unknown to science and never seen alive. This 'seal-fish' has been appropriately named *Bathylagus callorhinus*, and is fairly typical of the group of fish that live off the edge of the continental shelf, in very deep water.

Reproduction: In April and May the bulls emerge from the sea to establish their territories, which are in the order of 250–700sq. ft. The bulls which will eventually become the beachmasters (harem bulls) seldom fight and are content to settle their differences through threat, although subordinate bulls are not tolerated and may be forcibly removed. Once the bulls are sorted out, the cows arrive and soon give birth after a gestation period of 340–50 days which includes a delayed implantation of 14–16 weeks.

Parturition takes place in mid-summer with a head-first delivery of some ten minutes. In less than a week the cows have been mated again. The mother's maternal instinct rapidly wanes and after a couple of weeks she returns to sea, only returning to give occasional suck. The pups are weaned at three to four months, at which time they would be taking about a gallon of milk, rich in fat and protein, at each feed.

Although they are able to swim soon after birth, the pups spend the first month of their lives quietly playing in groups of similar ages within the protection of the rookery. As they grow older they become more adventurous and wander around the periphery of the colony soliciting milk from other cows. They moult their black natal coats at eight weeks.

Males become mature at six years, copulate at eight, but remain in bachelorhood for a further four years – by which time they are eligible to keep harems, and begin working to this end. They can live for more than thirty years. Females are sexually mature at three, but often it is as long again before they carry a pup successfully.

Special features: Northern Fur Seals are interesting for a variety of reasons. Most outstanding is the sheer size of their population concentration in the Pribilofs – the $1\frac{1}{2}$ million animals there form the largest agglomeration of mammals anywhere in the world, far outstripping any herd of big game left in East Africa. Yet towards the end of the last century, through a variety of human motivations (see Chapter 12), they became almost extinct, and only a last-minute change of policy saved them. As the beachmasters retain a harem of some fifty cows, this leaves a large surplus of young bulls, which congregate away from the main herd. From these bachelors an annual quota of 60,000 are harvested. Although this seems, and indeed is, a colossal figure, it has the merit of not affecting the overall long-term population, since the majority of young bulls would never become beachmasters anyway. The revenue from this lucrative trade also helps protect the species from possible attack by the fishing community.

Once the outer guard hairs have been removed, pelts from the Russian islands are sold in the fur trade as 'Copper-island seal', because of the woolly, reddish underfur which fashion decrees must be tinted black or chestnut. Pribilof hides are referred to as 'Alaska seal'.

The physiology of the bulls is of special interest. Marakov, a Russian zoologist, has observed that they remain on their breeding stations for two months without entering the sea or feeding, yet remain extremely active and show no apparent signs of emaciation. This conflicts with the reports of other observers, who describe the

A female Californian Sealion with her one-month-old pup. The pup will already have been swimming well for about two weeks, and will have been fully weaned in a further four or five months.

wretched state of the bulls at the end of the breeding season, noting that many even experience difficulty in reaching the sea.

Californian Sealion (*Zalophus californianus*)

Distribution: There are three subspecies, of which *Z. c. californianus*, with a population of about 50,000 along the Californian coast and on some off-shore islands, is the commonest. Less than half that number of *Z. c. wollebaeki* are located on the Galapagos Islands. A third very rare subspecies, *Z. c. japonicus*, numbering only a few hundred, just survives on parts of the coast of Honshu Island, Japan.

Description: The male can attain a length of more than 6ft and a weight of 500–600lbs. Females are considerably smaller, measuring less than 6ft and weighing only some 200lbs. It is almost impossible to distinguish one subspecies from another by anatomical features; the fur is always dark brown.

Habits: Like other marine mammals, Californian Sealions are very much better studied in captivity than in the wild.

They are intelligent, active and playful animals, especially in their formative years. Sealions are compulsive swallowers of hard, indigestible objects such as stones, presumably for reasons of ballast or perhaps digestion. This habit can cause them much misery; in captivity they will ingest such objects as coins, can-top rings, penknives and even plastic bags, with disastrous consequences. The swallowing of a rubber ball is more than likely to cause fatal impaction, while smaller objects can result in lesions of the aorta, and stomach ulcers. Similar injuries are also found in wild sealions.

Z. c. californianus undertakes seasonal movements up and down the Californian coast, moving north in the winter and south in the spring. It is not known whether the other two subspecies also make seasonal migrations.

Food: Californian Sealions seem to prefer cephalopods but will also consume fish such as hake and herring, shellfish and even seabirds. In captivity only fish is normally offered, and on this diet they can thrive for up to twenty years.

Reproduction: It is surprising that the Californian Sealion, generally, and its reproduction in particular, have not been better studied in the wild. Most of our knowledge about its reproduction stems from observations on captive specimens, of which there are many all over the world. The Galapagos subspecies appears to have been the most fully studied in the wild, though it is unwise to apply these findings to the other subspecies.

Whereas the cows of the nominate race and of the rare Japanese colonies give birth in May and June, those from the Galapagos, owing to their equatorial habit, undergo parturition at the end of the year. Although the species is polygamous, the social structure appears relatively loose: harems comprise about forty cows. Soon after the birth of the pup, the cow is again receptive and is mated. The bulls patrol their territories and the water adjoining them, ready to threaten any intruder. Actual fights seem to be rare and it is usually sufficient deterrent for a bull to rear himself up above his opponent's eye-level. Similarly it has been noticed that a bull only becomes frightened of a man when he stands erect. If he stoops, the sealion shows marked aggression.

A newborn pup measures about 30in. and weighs 13lbs; the mother consumes the placenta. The pup swims freely by the age of two weeks. Weaning is usually completed after five or six months, although pups are able to digest small fish certainly by the age of four months. The milk of the Californian Sealion contains no lactose but includes 36 per cent fat and 14 per cent protein. The chief protein is casein – the principal albuminous ingredient of milk – which is found as a calcium salt.

The maternal instinct is strong, and should a pup enter the water before it is able to support itself, the father also becomes extremely agitated but leaves the actual rescue to the mother.

Gestation takes nearly a year and includes a period of delayed implantation, which suggests that this phenomenon is widespread, and possibly universal, throughout the Pinnipedia.

Bulls mature at three years, and the cows a year sooner, although it may be another year or two before they are capable of carrying a pup successfully.

Special features: Californian Sealions are well known to visitors of zoos and circuses. They have a quite astonishing capacity for learning tricks, which are usually contrived to show off the animals' balancing powers. There is no evidence to suggest that Californian Sealions are better equipped for such displays than other sealions; it is probably more a question of availability and, now, of tradition.

Inevitably, during the early part of the nineteenth century, they were much hunted, mainly for their oil, of which one barrel was procured from the blubber of three sealions. It was a wasteful and cruel process. They were usually shot through the ear but lancing and clubbing were also employed.

Steller's Sealion (*Eumetopias jubatus*)

Distribution: Most northerly of the sealions; found from the Bering Sea, including the Bering Strait and the Pribilof Islands, along the coast of Alaska, south to southern California, where its range overlaps that of the Californian Sealion. It is relatively numerous, with a total population of some 300,000.

Description: The bulls are truly massive. They can attain a weight in excess of 2000lbs and a length of 14ft. Cows, on the other hand, only achieve a length of 8ft and a third of the bull's weight. Coloration is variations of buff, but a wet sealion always appears black. The bulls grow lengthy manes round their muscular necks.

Steller's Sealions do not seem to differ much from their closer relatives, but one aspect of their internal anatomy does warrant attention. All seals have extremely long intestines compared with those of terrestrial carnivores, but those of the Steller's Sealion are indeed phenomenal. The large intestine of one 6ft female measured nearly 10ft (E. T. Engle – 1926), while the small intestine reached the staggering length of 246ft; the total length, then, of the gut was over forty times that of the animal's body! It is still not known why seals should possess such long intestines; presumably the reason is linked to their diet or rapid digestion rate, although how and why is still a mystery.

Habits: The species is rightly wary of man, and except in the breeding season will flee from his approach; its eyesight is particularly acute both in and out of water, and hunters used to experience great difficulty getting within range of it. Nursing mothers, however, will rather pitifully remain to defend their offspring, although a minority escort their pups to the sea and thence to safer localities. Adult bulls usually flee from man, though strangely enough immature males often stand their ground. If the beachmasters are shy of man, they are certainly not reluctant to defend their harems from the attentions of other bulls. The breeding season is a very trying and exhausting time for these master bulls; they spend literally twenty-four hours a day protecting their cows, keeping them in compact units and herding them about the beach in search of peace and quiet. They roar constantly, and by the end of the breeding season are tired and hoarse.

Seasonal movement is variable and quite individual. Steller's Sealions are great wanderers and masters of swimming, but they do occasionally become exhausted and drown, especially in stormy weather – though they usually move shorewards and wait for the storm to blow itself out. The more southerly males (i.e. those of California) migrate northwards in the autumn to return south again in the spring of the following year, whereas the males of Alaska and the Bering Sea travel north in late summer but return as the severe winter sets in. They are naturally busy feeding at this time of the year, as they have an urgent need to replenish their fat and restore their energy in readiness for the forthcoming summer.

Food: The commonest prey is squid. Steller's Sealions have also been shown to consume many different kinds of fish including halibut, herring, cod and lampreys.

Reproduction: The bulls converge on the rookeries in early May, to be followed a few weeks later by the cows, by which time the bulls have established territories of about 500 square yards. The cows are attracted to the bulls already in possession, and these will gather together varying numbers of cows. The strongest can hold as many as eighty, although a more average harem will be ten to twenty individuals. The pups are born very soon after the cows arrive at the rookeries, with the greatest number arriving in early June. The cows are receptive soon afterwards and are mated by the bulls. There then follows the usual period of delayed implantation. It is not until October that the blastocyst begins development.

At birth the single pup measures about 3ft and weighs 40lbs. The first moult takes place at six months; a year or so later the pup will acquire its pale adult coat. After seven weeks the body weight has doubled. A month later the young males (which outnumber the females by about three times) begin to outstrip the young cows. When August arrives many of the pups have already ventured into the sea and begun to catch their own food, although the mothers will continue to give milk for a long time yet, possibly even into the next year.

At twelve months the pups are more or less independent. Cows are sexually mature at three years, and bulls at five.

Steller's or Northern Sealions are highly nervous out of water. At the slightest hint of man's approach they will leap into the water, even deserting the hapless babies by doing so.

Special features: This species underwent the usual persecution by man for commercial reasons. The heyday for hunting Steller's Sealions persisted until early into this century, when it slowly died out. The species is now protected from organized slaughter, although the local Aleuts and Eskimoes still attach importance to various parts of

This fine bull Steller's Sealion was photographed just before it charged the photographer. But aggressive though they appear, their attacks are short-lived and soon turn to flight.

its anatomy: the pelts are used in the making of leggings, and the intestinal membranes are converted into lightweight waterproofs which can be rolled up and carried about in a pocket when not required.

Among their natural peculiarities, these sealions apparently have an aversion to partial immersion in water; they either have to be completely in or completely out. This is also reflected in their mode of leaving the sea – they do not crawl out in the usual way but prefer to leap directly on to some high bluff. Similarly, when entering the sea they dive expertly from a high rock, judging their angle of entry perfectly to suit the depth of the water.

Steller's Sealions have few natural enemies; Killer Whales are presumably the most dangerous. They are seldom seen in captivity, and have a reputation for fierceness.

South American Sealion (*Otaria byronia*)

Distribution: Most numerous of all the sealions. For some reason this species appears to have been overlooked by the sealing industry, and this possibly accounts for its present healthy status (*c.* 800,000). It inhabits the coasts of South America from the Rio de la Plata on the eastern seaboard right round Cape Horn – including the Falkland Islands – and up the western coast to Colombia. The northern-most limit of its range is the equator. The largest concentration of these sealions occurs in the Falklands, where approximately half the total population lives.

Description: When full grown (at six years) the average male measures $7\frac{1}{2}$ft and weighs a colossal 1200lbs, while the female is markedly smaller and lighter at 5½ft and only 300lbs.

Coloration varies considerably amongst individuals, and J. E. Hamilton in the *Discovery Reports* of 1934 and 1939 lists four phases for the bulls and five for the cows. The most prevalent of these (for both sexes) is an overall dark brown with a yellowish tinge underneath; the head and nape is also usually dull yellow. Because of these admittedly highly confusing variations, there used to be much argument about the number of subspecies, but it is now recognized that there is just the one species. It is sometimes called the Southern Sealion.

Habits: Most of our information on this species comes from the above-mentioned *Discovery Reports* – which will well repay investigation by anyone seeking more comprehensive information.

In Hamilton's words, this sealion's character has four principal features: gregariousness, pugnacity, curiosity and timidity. Although the first two of these, and also the last, appear contradictory, they are nevertheless all present. Each animal is a combination of all these qualities; the precise mood and set of conditions at any one time will determine which comes out the strongest. Thus, an aggressive animal one day might be docile the next.

Outside the breeding season, these sealions are happy to congregate together – often to the extent of lying on top of one another (cows and juveniles) and using each other as pillows (bulls). During the breeding season, of course, there is much fighting between bulls and squabbling between cows. Fights are sometimes prolonged and often achieve no decision – both participants becoming exhausted. But more often the battles are short and violent, like savage dog fights, with the bulls aiming to get holds on the muscular necks of their adversaries. The fur is usually matted with blood, but they seem to have a high threshold of pain – anger rather than anguish being the reaction to a deep bite. Hamilton observed that a bull would even abandon coitus in order to engage in a fight. A defeated combatant flees as if for his life, with the victor snapping at his 'heels'.

South American Sealions, like most carnivores are normally highly curious of anything unusual. (See my remarks later on the Leopard Seal.) Hamilton again provides the illustration when he states that he has on more than one occasion been 'embarrassed' by the approach of sealions while sitting on a beach nearby. On the other hand, entire rookeries are known to fly into blind panic on very little provocation; no more than a sudden movement or the appearance of a person above them. It is difficult to explain this panic, which spreads rapidly through a colony, and results in a headlong charge for the sea. Sealions have no terrestrial enemies apart from man and, as I have said, these animals have been virtually ignored by sealers.

Their reactions to humans vary considerably; some will move off timidly, while others resolutely stand their ground and will even

attack, uttering coughs of anger. Men have sometimes been surprised and not a little alarmed at the speed of these seemingly ponderous beasts, which are capable of pursuit for quite exhausting distances over rough terrain.

Sealions, and for that matter all seals, should be observed from a subaquatic viewpoint to appreciate their true and essential character. Once in the water they are transformed from lumbering mock-dogs into sleek and sensual virtuosi – superfish with super-brains. They are very much aware of this transformation, for whereas on land they may be shy and nervous of man, in the water they are bold and playful.

Food: Similar to that of other species, e.g. squid, crustaceans (mainly *Munida*), fish, penguins and possibly also small amounts of seaweed as *Durvillea*. Squid are abundant around the Falklands and are probably the staple diet of sealions in this area.

Nearly all sealions carry a number of stones of varying sizes in their stomachs. Scientists are still not in complete agreement about the function of these stones, some of which can be alarmingly rough. There are four main theories. They may all be correct up to a point; certainly the stones will tend to have the effects suggested in the first two, if only incidentally.

1　That they help to pulp the food in the muscular stomach of the sealion – performing much the same function as the grit in the crop of a bird.

2　That they help to trim the animal while swimming, in the same way as does a human diver's weight-belt. The hind-quarters are very light compared to the front, and it has been noticed that pups, when learning to swim, are 'too heavy forward'.

3　That they help to destroy the nematodes which invariably infest the guts of these animals.

4　That they help to stave off hunger pangs during the fasting period.

Stones weighing collectively as much as 24lbs have been found in one stomach. However, the sealions inhabiting the Falklands are not believed to ingest stones at all – so the question remains unresolved.

Reproduction: Seasonal movements are absent in this species. The bulls arrive at the rookeries directly from their feeding grounds in December, and in the space of a day or two a desolate beach is turned into a bloody arena. That beach will know no more peace until the sealions depart again in February or March. In all this time the bulls will neither eat nor sleep; they will live off their blubber, and be employed constantly in keeping their harems of anything up to twelve cows intact.

Soon after the bulls have become organized, the cows, already very heavy with pup, begin to arrive. They emerge hesitantly from the sea, sampling the air and looking around as if searching for either a particular portion of the beach or an individual bull. While the bulls remain aloof and appear uninterested, the cows select or recognize one and settle down happily.

The pups are born early in the new year. They measure about 30in. and are clad in thick, black fur which gradually fades until the first moult takes place in a year's time. Elaborate courtship succeeds the birth, and mating soon follows. The cows then return for short periods to the sea, returning only to nourish their pups, which, in the meantime, gather together in pods, and spend the time sleeping or playing. Ann and Krov Menuhin observed an actual birth in Argentina recently. It was noticed that the pup is born enveloped in a sac which the mother gently slit open with her teeth – allowing the pup to wriggle free. She then carefully sniffs her offspring, and the individual scent of her pup will unite them throughout the rearing process – one firm reason for the retention of the olfactory sense. Unlike the Californian Sealion, these cows do not consume the placenta, which is cleared up by the hordes of gulls and skuas resident in most seal rookeries.

Once the cows have been served, the harems begin to disband. The mothers concentrate on teaching their pups to get used to the sea. Lactation is completed in about six months, but mortality among the pups is quite high. The heaviest toll is caused (albeit unintentionally) by the fighting bulls – the pups' own fathers or 'stepfathers'.

Special features: There have been occasional attempts to base some kind of industry on these animals, but it has never become economically viable. They are, of course, preyed on by the individual hunter (under licence) in some regions, and in Argentina there is a small industry of sorts.

J. E. Hamilton has unearthed some curious and amusing ancient accounts and descriptions of these animals. One in particular refers to the supposed toxic qualities of sealion liver, and was found in the account of Simon de Alcazaba's expedition to Patagonia in 1535: 'Most of us who ate it suffered from the head to the feet,' and: 'The livers of these seals are so poisonous that they give fevers and headache to everyone who eats them, and presently all the hair on their bodies falls off and some die.'

The species is not seen frequently in zoos, although one specimen did live for over seventeen years at London Zoo. In the 1950s a breeding was recorded at San Diego Zoo.

Walrus (*Odobenus rosmarus*)

Distribution: Nowadays it is accepted that there are two races of walrus – the Atlantic Walrus *Odobenus r. rosmarus* and the Pacific Walrus *O. r. divergens*. Their English names are rather misleading, since the large majority of both forms are only located within the Arctic Circle. It is true that the Atlantic race extends beyond the

Arctic Circle into Hudson Bay and around the south-western coasts of Baffin Island but most of the population is found along the northern coasts of Greenland and in Baffin Bay, with a smaller group centred on and around Novaya Zemlya. The Pacific Walrus inhabits the north-eastern coasts of Siberia, across the Bering Strait and round the north-western extremities of Alaska.

The actual density of the world population is very difficult to estimate, and such estimates differ wildly. Richard Perry reaches some interesting conclusions in his book *The World of the Walrus* (1967). Hundreds of thousands, even millions, of walruses were slaughtered between 1950 and the mid-1950s. Since then, however, the populations have been slowly recovering, and there is now possibly a total population in excess of 100,000. There is, though, no room for complacency: over 12,000 are killed annually in the waters of Alaska and Siberia alone and this is scarcely balanced by the natural reproduction rate of 14 per cent per annum. A single year of overkill or bad reproduction among the walruses could send the whole population into decline.

Walruses used to have very much larger ranges than they do today. Fossil remains have been found as far south as England and Belgium on the east of the Atlantic, and South Carolina on the west.

Description: Walruses are second in size only to the gigantic elephant seals. There is little difference between the two races, although the Pacific animals are on average slightly larger and possess longer tusks which diverge at their tips. Pacific bulls can reach a length of 13ft and a weight 3500lbs, though they are usually slightly smaller; the cows average 10ft and 1760lbs. Atlantic bulls can in extreme cases reach a length of 12ft and a weight of nearly 3000lbs, while the cows average 9ft and 1250lbs. Tusk lengths are very variable, usually about 20in. in an Atlantic bull and 10in. in a cow – exposed tusk, that is; the tusks of Pacific Walruses are about half as long again.

Walruses are virtually hairless apart from their magnificent moustaches, which consist of some 400 stiff yet highly sensitive vibrissae. The main purpose of these bristles is obviously sensory but they also serve to guide food into the mouth.

Habits: Walruses live in mixed herds of up to 100 individuals. They prefer to spend their days asleep, hauled up out of the sea. A certain amount of restlessness, inevitable in any large, closely packed herd of bulky animals, serves to protect them from attack, but they are also known to post a sentinel which remains awake and alert to possible danger. Although walruses are covered by a hide some 2in. thick, they are plagued by the attentions of eighteen different kinds of parasite, including marine lice. The activities of these parasites cause their hosts no little irritation and account for the incessant scratching, and consequent sleeplessness, that characterize walrus behaviour on dry land.

Walruses are extremely vocal creatures. Their utterances have been variously noted and described, most commonly perhaps as bellowing, barking and roaring. They are also known to make sounds that resemble the lowing of cattle and the deep baying of a mastiff; a variety of other sounds includes low whistling, gurgling, grunting and belching. They are probably the noisiest of all Arctic creatures, with the loudest voices.

The primary use of their tusks is the excavation of food, but they also use them as aids to locomotion on land and for hauling themselves out of the water. Indeed, their family name *Odobenidae* means 'those that walk with their teeth'! Tusks also make effective weapons, as many hunters could no doubt testify. I fancy, though, that many of the stories of their attacks on human-beings (however well-deserved they might be) are grossly exaggerated. It is nevertheless quite true that an enraged or wounded walrus can cause dreadful havoc to even a soundly constructed craft, and Eskimoes fear them more than any other Arctic animal. They also have the disconcerting habit of hooking their tusks over the gunwales of boats – an act that has caused many to capsize. It is unlikely that all these instances have been the result of intentional attacks; quite often walruses must mistake small boats for drifting ice floes, or merely want to rest, which they often do by anchoring their tusks to some floating or land-tied object. Nevertheless, many a hunter has been surprised by the speed and agility of a walrus, especially out of the water; thinking himself to be safe, he has been, if not overtaken, at least pursued with as much speed as he himself could muster – a fitting example of the hunter becoming the hunted.

Walruses favour drifting ice floes as lazing grounds presumably on account of the protection and seclusion they afford. Occasionally a great many will pile on to one small floe. Usually the late arrivals have

Dispersal of Walruses

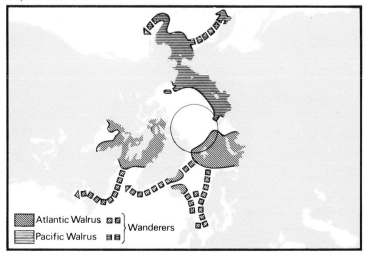

Atlantic Walrus
Pacific Walrus
} Wanderers

to heave themselves on to the top of those individuals already present creating a veritable living mountain and surely much discomfort for those at the bottom. Apart from that, the heat generated by hundreds of walrus bodies can cause the ice to melt; but more often the sheer tonnage will cause the ice to tip up and deposit the whole colony back into the water.

Migration is north in summer, south in winter. It is either during the northwards migration or on the drifting pack-ice (on which they also travel vast distances) that mating takes place.

Food: The staple diet consists of bivalve molluscs such as clams (the most important single food), mussels and cockles, and other invertebrates, including echinoderms (sea-cucumbers, sea-urchins, starfish), gastropods (whelks, sea-snails), crustaceans (shrimps, hermit crabs) and annelids (lugworms, ragworms). The shells of such animals are crushed by the large, pre-molar teeth – walruses possess no molars – and are rejected into the sea, only the soft parts being swallowed.

Many other items have also been recorded in the stomachs of walruses. Vegetable material such as the roots of marine grasses and seaweed is common, too common to have been ingested accidentally. Stones, some as large as a man's fist, are swallowed, as they are by many aquatic mammals and reptiles, including crocodiles. Various theories have been put forward to account for this seemingly strange behaviour in walruses; the three most popular at the present time are for reasons of ballast, aids to digestion or for staving off hunger pangs at times of fasting.

'Rogue' walruses will take readily to catching and eating any large animal they can overtake. Seals are the most usual victims, although walruses can also develop cannibalistic tendencies. Exceptionally old or unbalanced specimens will then refuse all other types of food. Presumably any walrus happening on suitable carrion will consume it; this helps to explain why the flesh of such large creatures as whales is sometimes found in their stomachs.

Reproduction: Some authorities (and Eskimoes) believe walruses to be monogamous, and this theory may well have some substance to it. The truth of the matter is that they are exceptionally difficult animals to study in the wild. Harems are certainly not retained, nor could be, in the almost haphazard, nomadic lives of these animals. Some bulls may make an attempt at controlling such a group of cows but it is difficult to see how they could possibly exercise complete control over them. It is more likely that their entire social structure is rather loose; in fact, one could say that the order of 'first come, first served' is the rule!

Gestation takes about fifty-four weeks. Delayed implantation may or may not be a feature of it; if it is, it must be for only a relatively short period, possibly about ten weeks. The actual time of birth seems to change with the latitude, and can be between March and

August. Newborn calves weigh about 110lbs and are about 3ft long. The weaning period is quite abnormally long. As with all the Pinnipedia, the mothers' milk is very rich, containing about 35 per cent fat and 12 per cent protein. Calves can swim almost immediately, provided they do not have to do so alone.

Cows are mature at four years and the bulls a year later. Walruses can live for more than thirty years if they succeed in avoiding their enemies (apart from man, Polar Bears and Killer Whales also take their toll).

Special features: Walruses have many diagnostic features, many of which have been discussed elsewhere in this book. The strange refinement of the upper regions of the oesophagus (mentioned elsewhere) deserves more attention. These sacs are certainly very important components in their survival kits on extended journeys, when it may be impossible to haul out to rest. This portion of the oesophagus can be dilated to hold as much as ten gallons of fluid – this gives some idea of its size.

Eskimoes, whose observations and deductions are often ignored

Pacific Walrus bulls have longer tusks than their Atlantic cousins. They use their tusks partly as picks to prise molluscs from the sea floor.

by Arctic scientists, need to study the wildlife in their environment in order to survive, and I for one attach much credence to their findings and beliefs. The Eskimoes of Alaska assert that the inflated oesophagus adds resonance to certain of the walrus's calls and to one in particular which is said to resemble the sound of church bells. As if to substantiate this theory, other Eskimoes use these membranes for their drumheads. This explanation has much to commend it, especially when we consider that the pouches are most developed in the bulls.

Another (not Eskimo) theory suggests that the air contained in these sacs helps to provide the diving walrus with additional oxygen. Although rather more flaws can be found in this theory, it cannot be disregarded completely.

For more than 200 years the walrus has been hunted in stupendous numbers, mostly for commercial reasons, and this plundering has more than once brought the species to the very brink of extinction. Only the scarcity of remaining herds, and the consequent lack of economic sense in pursuing them, saved the walrus. During the peak years of exploitation, in the mid-nineteenth century, an annual harvest of 100,000lbs of ivory was normal.

Whalers found walrus-hunting a profitable sideline and were responsible for the death of at least 300,000 walruses in the five years from 1868. This unprecedented massacre netted them some 250,000 barrels of oil, and depleted the walrus population to such an extent that the whalers were forced to return to hunting whales.

The Eskimoes have come in for much attack from conservationists, yet the few thousand walruses they take each year do not affect the total population at all (since there is always a large surplus of bachelor bulls) and each one is of vital importance to them. Furthermore, no part of a walrus carcass is wasted. A close parallel can be seen here in the relationship between the American Indians and the Bison. It is not so much man that despoils our planet as civilized man.

Only in recent years have the problems of maintaining walruses in captivity been conquered, and we should be able to look forward to an increasing amount of successful births in the years to come. It is probably only in this way that we shall solve many of the problems that still confront us in the study of these engaging animals.

Harbour or Common Seal (*Phoca vitulina*)

Distribution: Widespread along the coasts of Arctic and temperate lands bordering the Atlantic and Pacific Oceans. The range extends from north of the Arctic Circle as far south as latitude 30°N. The Harbour Seal is by no means wholly maritime. In the freshwater Seal Lakes and Harrison Lake in northern Quebec, some ninety miles from Hudson Bay, there are thriving colonies of at least 1000 seals. Their ancestors must have been isolated from the main herds as much as 3000 years ago and possibly very much earlier.

Description: Males are about 6ft long and weigh approximately 550lbs; the females weigh less than half that and grow to a length of 5ft.

Coloration varies from dark grey to a dull yellow (darker in North America), liberally speckled with black or brown blotches. The tones are usually lighter on the underside of the body. The Harbour Seal has a more rounded head and a somewhat gentler appearance than the Grey Seal, with which it is often confused.

Habits: The species is not considered to be a great traveller, seldom venturing more than ten miles from its birthplace, although there is at least one record of a young Harbour Seal being captured 470 miles up the River Elbe, near the Czechoslovakian border. Such instances are probably the result of a young seal losing its way and instinctively swimming against the current.

Harbour Seals like nothing more than hauling out on to some smooth, gently inclining beach or sandbank to sleep away their lives, only reluctantly re-entering the sea when hunger overtakes them. They are more land-tied than most other seals, and diurnal in habit, so that I have been able to observe them for many hours and have in the process become very fond of these faintly comical creatures. They are more intelligent and alert than they may at a glance appear, and have an uncanny instinct for predicting danger before it actually becomes imminent, and also for differentiating between those who wish them harm and those who don't. A very large population of some 2000 Harbour Seals is centred on the Wash, England. I have wandered, sometimes accidentally, near to seals basking out on the mud flats, and have been surprised at their comparative indifference towards me. If I have ventured too close, they will invariably sigh heavily and lumber off a few 'paces' to resume their interrupted sleep. On the other hand, I have witnessed them panicking at the mere sight of a wildfowler, and even a person carrying a walking-stick disturbs them.

Food: It is probably fair to assume that most seals will consume just about anything they can catch. Undoubtedly fish forms the bulk of their intake; stomach analysis and the testimony of witnesses have indicated that prey items include cod, herring, whiting, flounders, plaice, dabs, gobies, salmon, various shellfish and even the occasional sea-bird.

Harbour Seals are preyed upon by the Killer Whale and, in the Pacific, by large sharks. Man has killed seals since the Stone Age for reasons of subsistence, sport, commercial gain and (on the part of fishermen) revenge. Nowadays they are also 'controlled' in the name of science.

Reproduction: Breeding varies with the latitude. It begins in early

May in the south and as late as October in the north. Pregnant cows tend to congregate in shallow water, and give birth actually in the water or on a sandbank which will itself be submerged on the next high tide. Consequently baby Harbour Seals have to swim directly and are often born with sea-going pelts; if they are not, they certainly shed their woolly baby-coats in the first few days of their lives. The mothers are especially attentive and protective for the first few weeks, until the babies have gained strength and are able to control their hind-quarters. It takes a pup about three weeks to become fully conversant with its habitat; until then it is unable to haul out of the sea on its own. Lactation lasts only for about a week longer, so the pups very swiftly find themselves on their own. They have the advantage, though, of a substantial layer of fat brought about by the extremely rich milk of the mother, and probably survive, until they have learnt to catch fish, by feeding on less mobile prey such as prawns.

At birth a pup measures about 28in. in length and weighs about 24lbs. Twins are occasionally produced, but if left to the natural mother only one will be reared, the other being ignored. Mothers fast while nursing their calves, but as soon as they have abandoned them they begin on a period of furious activity which includes fattening up again, being served by the bulls and then moulting.

At this time the bulls often engage in mock fights, but these never amount to anything serious; there is no real territorial issue at stake since there are no ritualized land assemblies.

Harbour Seal calves are sexually mature in three years.

Special features: Juvenile seals indulge in 'horseplay' and simulated mating behaviour at the start of the breeding season. Members of the opposite sexes roll over one another in the sea and chase each other, and the young bulls attempt to mount the cows who are themselves by no means reluctant. These games go on for many hours and must be invaluable practice for the time when the seals come of age.

The Harbour Seal, though by no means a common zoo animal, is certainly less uncommon than any other member of the *Phocidae*. Harbour Seals are not very often bred successfully but can, if treated correctly, live for well over 10 years.

Ringed Seal (*Pusa hispida*)

Distribution: There are several subspecies in different parts of the North Polar regions. The species as a whole is circumpolar and in fact occurs throughout the Arctic Circle, extending beyond it into the North Atlantic (around Greenland), the Bering Sea and the Sea of Okhotsk. A relict population (from the Ice Age) lives in the Baltic Sea and the Gulf of Bothnia, which accounts for occasional sightings off Denmark. Other colonies inhabit various freshwater lakes in north-western Europe. The Ringed Seal is by far the commonest seal species in the far north.

Description: The smallest of all seals. There is little, if any, difference between the sexes, which is unusual amongst the Pinnipedia. There are geographical variations in size, but generally Ringed Seals measure between 4ft and 6ft with a maximum weight of 265lbs.

General coloration also varies but there is always the pattern of dark blotches surrounded by the pale rings which give the seal its common name. Background colour can be anything from pale yellow to a very dark olive green.

Habits: The favoured food of this species appears to be fish. It is also known to consume the planktonic crustaceans which abound in polar waters, but it will often ignore these and descend to depths of at least 300ft in its search for small fish.

The distribution of the Ringed Seal is apparently limited by climate rather than food. It prefers to live in the vicinity of land-locked ice. There is thought to be no overall migration, only a general dispersal at the conclusion of every breeding season. It dislikes the open ocean, preferring to stay within a few miles of the coast, although the odd straggler has found its way to British waters.

Food: See *Habits*.

Reproduction: Ringed Seals are particularly interesting in this respect. In the months of April and May the expectant mothers seek out suitable areas of deep snow which has drifted up on the land-locked ice of deep bays. In this snow the cows construct fairly long, narrow and low caves which usually have one end abutting the piled-up ice. At the opposite end there is a hole in the floor which serves as the entrance from the sea. In these cosy, igloo-like lairs, which are totally out of sight, the cows give birth in safety and the pups are pro-tected from the bitter weather.

A newly-born pup is only about 2ft long and weighs little more than 10lbs. Lactation is rather long – about twelve weeks – and this could simply be because of the very safe nature of the breeding site, which does not demand undue haste.

Sexually mature males possess an extremely unpleasant odour, the cause and precise purpose of which is unknown. Cows are mated while still suckling their young. Gestation is about fifty weeks, including a period of delayed implantation.

Special features: Most of the special features of this species have already been mentioned. It has played a fundamental role in Eskimo life since time immemorial and is still a cornerstone in the economy of many tribes.

Several zoos have possessed examples of the Ringed Seal. The London Zoo obtained one in 1905. On New Year's Day 1929 at Skansen Zoo, Stockholm, a Ringed Seal gave birth to a stillborn hybrid calf, sired by a Grey Seal; the cow itself died the same year having lived in that collection for a record fifteen years. Several specimens have been exhibited at the Berlin Zoo and at Hagenbeck's Tierpark, Stellingen, Germany. More recently, a Ringed Seal has been successfully kept at the New York Aquarium, having been brought over from St Lawrence Island in the Bering Sea in 1961.

Baikal Seal (*Pusa sibirica*)

Distribution: This, the only exclusively freshwater seal, is confined to a 400-mile-long lake in central Siberia. Lake Baikal is situated 1250 miles south of the Laptev Sea in the Arctic and 1000 west of the Sea of Okhotsk. It is probably the deepest lake in the world, descending to a depth of about one mile. The Baikal Seal is found mostly in the northernmost part of the lake. Estimates of the population vary between 40,000 and 100,000.

Description: A small seal, rarely exceeding a length of 5ft or a weight of 130lbs, though after a period of heavy feeding it can weigh considerably more. The Baikal Seal is similar in appearance to the Ringed Seal, though it lacks the latter's characteristic rings. It is reasonable to presume that many thousands of years ago, before the colony became isolated in Lake Baikal, the two species were one and the same.

Habits: Much of Lake Baikal is either little known or inaccessible, and knowledge of the Baikal Seal is equally patchy. During the winter the seals tend to converge on Chivyrkui Bay in the north, over which ice forms earlier than it does on the more turbulent open water. The cows emerge from the water, leaving the bulls and immature animals to keep open the breathing holes in the ice. As the winter deepens, the seals find that it is very much warmer in the water than out of it (a difference of as much as 40°C). Presently the cows begin to construct the caves in which they will give birth (see *Reproduction*).

Food: Exclusively fish such as gobies and eels.

Reproduction: The lairs created by the cows are almost identical to those used by the Ringed Seal. The pups are born in March and they too are very similar to those of the Ringed Seal, even to the extent of possessing the same kind of long, white and woolly fetal coats. Gestation lasts for nine months and the pups are born at just about the coldest time of the year.

The pups are weaned in eight weeks and remain in their lairs until the sun gains strength in early June. By this time they will have passed through the most crucial stages of their infancy. When the lairs begin to thaw, the pups emerge to bask in the weak sunshine, but they do not take to the water in earnest until mid-summer. Baikal Seals are sexually mature in four years.

Mating takes place in the spring while the cows are still nursing their young.

Special features: The most important special feature of this species is, of course, its exclusiveness to fresh water.

Hunting these seals is an important part of local Buryat life. As many as 600 people kill annually several thousand seals, mostly in the spring. The seals are killed on the ice by shooting or by trapping in large mesh nets in the water near their breathing holes. The occupation is not particularly lucrative, since the pelts are poor and there is little blubber; let us hope the Buryat people will soon find more profitable work and leave the seals in peace.

Harp Seal (*Pagophilus groenlandicus*)

Distribution: The Ringed Seal, Bearded Seal and this species are the three specialist seals of the Arctic. Other species, notably the Hooded Seal, also occur there, but these are the prima donnas. The Harp Seal (*Pagophilus* means 'ice-lover') is one of the most aquatic of all seals, living in the Arctic and northern reaches of the Atlantic Ocean far out to sea or on drifting pack-ice.

It is found all round Greenland but is, surprisingly, absent from Icelandic waters. That these seals are great travellers is indicated by the fact that occasional specimens are seen in English waters – one in the River Teign in Devonshire. It is a numerous species; the population appears to be divided into three separate breeding groups, which do not intergrade. The following are estimates of their populations: Gulf of St Lawrence 1,500,000–2,000,000; Labrador 1,000,000; and the Greenland Sea 750,000–1,000,000. The grand total could thus be in the region of four million.

Description: Both sexes measure about 6ft and attain a weight of 400lbs. Coloration is generally greyish with black markings.

Habits: As suggested above, the Harp Seal is very gregarious, aquatic and a great traveller. Besides the random travelling, definite seasonal movements are also undertaken. These are northwards after breeding to moult – the rookeries used for this purpose tend to be even larger than the breeding ones – and southwards during the winter to breed.

Food: Fish such as herring, polar cod and pollack, also crustaceans.

Reproduction: The breeding season extends from January to April, most pups being born in the eighth and ninth weeks of the year. This is one species of northern seal which has been well-studied, so we have a wealth of information, particularly about its breeding habits. Cows congregate on drifting pack-ice and give birth within a few yards of each other. To afford their pups greater protection, the

Harp Seal with pup. The fur of young Harp Seals is sold as 'white-coat'. Harp seals are among the most fully committed to an oceanic life.

cows try to avoid the ice-edge, but being extremely cumbersome out of water they contrive to keep open either ice-free 'leads' between the floes, or large holes in the ice itself. If a seal's exit hole should freeze over, it will share another's.

At birth the pups are about 2ft 6in. long and weigh around 24lbs. The yellowish coat turns pure white in a few days and the pups are amongst the most endearing of all, with their black muzzles and melancholy eyes. For a week the mothers are especially attentive, never leaving the sides of their offspring. During the next week the cows occasionally venture into the water, much to the consternation of the frightened pups, who bleat pitifully and 'freeze' in terror should danger (usually in the form of a sealer) appear.

At the end of the second week, the pups have gained a remarkable 44lbs in weight, while the mothers lose almost the same amount. The richness of their milk (42 per cent fat, 11 per cent protein) promotes this rapid growth. There is on record one pup which increased its weight from 17.5lbs at birth to 70.5lbs a fortnight later. Not surprisingly, perhaps, the pups then go without food while they moult. They assume a darker appearance and are known as 'graylings'. When a month old, the young Harp Seals begin to find their own food, which at first consists mostly of crustaceans.

During the first two years of life the calves continue to darken in colour, and the young males eventually show the peculiar saddle-like markings which are characteristic of many adult males. Harp Seals are fairly slow in attaining sexual maturity (cows at six, bulls at eight), but this is compensated for by their longevity, perhaps as much as thirty years.

Special features: A most extraordinary aspect of these animals is their evident ability to withstand a quite remarkable degree of human persecution with little or no long-term ill-effect. It is estimated that the annual kill amounts to some 500,000 seals. Other grisly facts and figures: 687,000 Harp Seals (including 'a few' Hooded Seals) were killed in Newfoundland alone in 1831; since 1720 regular sealing expeditions to Jan Mayen netted a steady 200,000 seals annually, though this century the toll has dropped to a more reasonable 30,000 seals each year; on Novaya Zemlya and Spitzbergen catches increased from 10,000 a year in the last part of the nineteenth century up to an appalling 500,000 in 1925. Two-thirds of the seals killed are pups or graylings; these are slaughtered at the rookeries in March. The remainder are taken a month or so later while moulting. Apart from the value of the pelts, much revenue is also gleaned from rendering the blubber into oil.

Grey Seal (*Halichoerus grypus*)

Distribution: There are three distinct populations of Grey Seal. Over 60 per cent of the total are centred on and around the coasts of Britain; this North Sea population extends along the Norwegian coast (taking in the Faeroes and Scotland) into the Barents Sea. The seals on either side of the Atlantic probably became separated some 100,000 years ago, while those in the east divided into the Atlantic and Baltic groups about 9000 years ago.

The world population can be broken down to the following estimates (after E. A. Smith, 1966): Great Britain and Eire, 37,000; North European mainland, 8000; North West Atlantic, 5000; Iceland and Faeroes, 4000.

The Grey Seal shows a preference for waters between latitudes 45°N and 72°N (which is within the Arctic Circle).

Description: The Grey Seal sometimes occurs in the same areas as the Harbour Seal, with which it is often confused. The Grey Seal is rather larger: the male achieves a length of nearly 10ft and a weight of 630lbs; females seldom exceed 6ft and a weight of 550lbs.

Although coloration varies considerably from area to area, the overall appearance is always noticeably blotched and spotted: males are darker, with pale markings, while with the females the reverse is true. Quite often only the heads of seals can be seen, bobbing in the water offshore. At such times, identification rests with the shape of the skull: the Grey Seal possesses a longer muzzle than that of the Harbour Seal.

Certain Grey Seals may grow small external pinnae – an unknown feature in any other phocid seal. Does this indicate a common ancestry between the *Phocidae* and *Otariidae*?

A fine photograph of a true seal. The Grey Seal has a longer face than the Common or Harbour Seal, a useful 'field mark' when, as is so often the case, only the head can be seen above the water. Note the long claws which help the animal to climb among rocks.

Habits: Social organization only exists in the breeding season. At other times the seals tend to wander aimlessly about, fishing and resting. There seems to be little day/night rhythm – their hours of activity are determined by the seasons, weather and tides.

Food: Grey Seals will eat almost any type of animal food they can catch. This will usually consist of fish, crustaceans and molluscs. The seals are the subject of controversy between fishermen (especially salmon fishermen) and wildlife enthusiasts. Not all fishermen, however, dislike these animals. I know one, in particular, who fished for more than fifty years off the Cornish coast; he regarded the seals as healthy competitors and kindred spirits. In evident admiration, he explained to me how they cruise up and down the nets selecting only the very best fish and ignoring the rest. Occasionally he found a superb fish with claw and teeth marks on its skin while all those around it were unscathed. When I remarked that one could scarcely blame them for learning this trick, he smiled magnanimously. 'No,' he said, 'you just envy 'em.'

Reproduction: Unlike the British animals (see introduction to this chapter), the Grey Seals of the north-west Atlantic and the Baltic give birth in February and March. Breeding rookeries are sometimes very difficult to approach and are often situated in caves or rocky coves.

A newly-born pup, which is clad in long yellowish-white wool, measures about 2ft 6in. and weighs about 35lbs. The milk teeth disappear before birth and the adult teeth come through in a matter of days. In common with most seals, Grey Seal pups put on weight very quickly and in a fortnight weigh between 70lbs and 100lbs. Shortly after the pups have been weaned, they moult and take to the water; they are then deserted.

Females mature at three years, males at six or seven. Their life expectancy and reproductive life is long; cows have been known to give birth at the age of thirty-five, and it is fairly certain that they can live for as long as forty years. The bulls only attain about half that span.

Special features: Grey Seals give the impression of being aquatically more specialized than Harbour Seals. They are certainly less graceful on dry land. They are so much at home in the sea that they sometimes even sleep at the bottom of shallow water – automatically ascending to breathe before submerging again.

They have been hunted for centuries, and on more than one occasion almost exterminated. As it is, their numbers are severely reduced in certain localities, especially in the Danish waters of the Baltic and in the Gulf of St Lawrence. Sixty years ago the species was dangerously close to extinction in Britain – its main stronghold – and only two Acts of Parliament in 1914 and 1932, establishing an adequate close-season, saved them. Now, particularly in the Farne Islands, an annual cull of seal pups is considered necessary in order to keep their population down to a manageable level. Fishermen in the Faeroes and Iceland consider these seals 'good sport' and take rifles on their fishing trips. In days gone by, these unfortunate animals were at least utilized; nowadays their bodies are ignored and left to rot.

The Grey Seal is commoner in captivity in northern Europe than it is in America, possibly owing to the remoteness of the western Atlantic breeding areas. Breeding in zoos is steady if not spectacular. More often they have to deal with a flow of 'orphaned' pups which, though messy and time-consuming, are not difficult to rear. One noteworthy specimen, christened 'Jacob', arrived at Skansen in Sweden in 1901 at an estimated two years of age, and died in 1942.

Crabeater Seal (*Lobodon carcinophagus*)

Distribution: The commonest of all seals – perhaps as many as five million exist (one estimate says fifty million). They are widespread round the Antarctic continent both on the shoreline and on drifting pack-ice. Great travellers – individuals being found as far away as Australia, New Zealand and north of Buenos Aires.

Description: One of the most distinctive of all seals, often referred to as the 'white seal' because of its extremely pale coloration, gradually achieved (through fading) after the moult. The sexes are virtually the same size: the maximum length is 9ft; weight 510lbs.

Habits: Despite its abundance the Crabeater Seal is comparatively little studied. It is not thought to be migratory in the strictest sense of the word. The seasonal movements which it does undertake are simply calculated to keep in touch with its food, which moves north

Young Crabeater Seal.
Crabeaters are unusually fast
over the Antarctic snow,
reputedly reaching speeds
of 15mph.

in winter. As the ice frontier retreats again in spring, so the seals travel with it. It is among the fastest of the phocid seals over ice or dry land, attaining speeds of up to 15mph.

Food: Exclusively Krill – a type of crustacean for which its teeth are specially adapted and refined (see *Special Features*). Such specialization means that it does not compete with other seals, and could account for its abundance.

Reproduction: Owing to the inaccessibility of its habitat, little is known about this aspect of its life. Pups are born in October (the Antarctic spring) on drifting pack-ice. Mating is believed to take place in November or December. Pups are a lengthy 4ft at birth and are clad in thick, brown fur.

Female sexual maturity is achieved in two years, males take a year longer. Lactation probably takes about three weeks, and the pups' first moult follows it.

Special features: The most singular fact about these animals is their diet and their adaptations to it. Their teeth are unique: the molars have up to five projecting cusps on the top jaw, and when the mouth is closed the lower teeth are so positioned that they fill the spaces in the upper teeth and so form an efficient straining system through which the water is rejected and the Krill retained.

Fortunately the pelts of Crabeater Seals are usually scarred, either through fighting amongst themselves or from attacks by Killer Whales, and so are of little commercial value. As the pups are virtually unobtainable, they also escape; this could help to account for the present large numbers.

Leopard Seal (*Hydrurga leptonyx*)

Distribution: The range of this species is similar to that of the Crabeater Seal, except that the Leopard Seal ranges further afield

The sleek, somewhat reptilian Leopard Seal is an efficient killer of fish, penguins and young seals, and is the only pinniped which habitually feeds on warm-blooded animals.

and is a frequent visitor to the waters of Australia, New Zealand, Cape Horn and Patagonia. A winter population of about 1000 congregates on Heard Island in the Indian Ocean but otherwise it is a very solitary animal. Total population has been put at 200,000. They do not seem to venture farther north than 30°S.

Description: Very large: males up to 10ft; the females are unique amongst seals in being up to 18in. longer. Weight 660–960lbs, the latter a male specimen at Stellungen Zoo, which died in 1939. Apart from this there is little sexual dimorphism. Coloration is predominantly grey with pale spots on the upperparts grading down to an opposite situation on the underparts. Leopard Seals are exceptionally sleek and agile with very large, powerful, reptilian heads.

Habits: Leopard Seals are animals of lonely and fearsome ways. They are the pinniped counterparts of the Killer Whale and will eat anything from fish and cephalopods to the rotting carcass of a great whale.

There is no set migration, since the species is of a nomadic disposition and seems more or less to go where fancy takes it. Leopard Seals are expert swimmers, but somewhat helpless out of the water, and appear not to use their limbs at all for progression. In order to leave the water they have been known to 'take a run' at the ice and shoot out of the water on to it in the way many penguins do.

Leopard Seals, like all carnivores, are very intelligent and inquisitive and have been seen to take a keen interest in the curious ways of man. I have a soft spot for this much maligned creature of the southern polar seas, though it has been known to show aggression towards man. On the occasions on which one has been disturbed while asleep, the only sounds it has been recorded as having uttered are a few low whistles and a quiet chuckling! There are a few records of a Leopard Seal chasing a man, and of underwater attacks.

Food: As stated in the preceding section, they will consume almost anything. Their staple diet, however, is penguins, of which they take large amounts. Over the years they have evolved crafty ways of catching these birds when they are at their most vulnerable, i.e. when out of the water or when entering or leaving it. The seals lie in wait near the ice-edge; on occasion they will even leap clear of the water to land right in the middle of a group. Sometimes they will chase penguins through the water, where they are a match for the evasive birds, who porpoise shorewards in a frantic attempt to reach safety.

These animals also prey on the smaller members of the their own family, especially pups. The Leopard Seal's only enemy is the ubiquitous Killer Whale, and of this it shares a dread in common with all other large oceanic animals.

Reproduction: Little is known about its breeding habits; presumably they follow a similar pattern to those of the Crabeater Seal.

Few pups have ever been seen. Observations suggest that they are long and thin at birth with large heads, like miniature adults. They progress from small, relatively inactive food such as crustaceans to their adult diet. At birth pups are probably at least $4\frac{1}{2}$ft in length and weigh about 60lbs; they are believed to undergo their first moult while still being suckled. At this time their general colour changes from light grey to a pattern closer to the adults. Sexual maturity is attained at three years in the female and four in the male.

Special features: The Leopard Seal is a very important member of the Antarctic fauna. It is the greatest predator of the penguin and probably also serves as a stabilizer in the populations of many other animals, including other seals such as the Crabeater, Weddell, Ross and the Kerguelen Fur Seal.

The poor quality of pelt renders the Leopard Seal of little commercial value, and their solitary habits mean that orthodox hunting is out of the question. A few are killed every year in South Georgia, but these are only incidental to the killing of the Southern Elephant Seal which still continues under licence.

The species is little kept in captivity, perhaps more for reasons of unavailability than because of any serious problem in its management. I have seen extremely contented Leopard Seals at Duisburg Zoo in Germany; they have a disconcerting and hypnotic way of looking at you, almost as though they were sizing you up. They are eager through the water and continually rear up to search for victims. The old-fashioned name of 'Sea-leopard' suits them better.

Weddell Seal (*Leptonychotes weddelli*)

Distribution: As a species, seldom strays out of sight of the Antarctic ice-fields and is found all round the permanent ice. Occasional specimens have been noticed near South Australia, the Falklands and

even as far north as Juan Fernandez (33°S). The species is relatively numerous, with a world population estimated at between 200,000 and 500,000.

Description: The Weddell Seal is a large rotund animal, averaging 10ft in length and weighing as much as 900lbs. Coloration is dark grey above and lighter grey below; the entire body is covered with pale blotches. The head is disproportionately small and the brown eyes are large and liquid.

Habits: This species is non-migratory – its movements depend on its shifting food supply. The Weddell Seal is renowned for its marathon diving exploits, and it is indeed a highly aquatic species, especially in winter, when the sea is by far the warmest place for an Antarctic seal to be. These hardy animals spend the entire winter beneath the ice, keeping breathing holes open or using the natural 'bubbles' of air which exist underneath the ice-layer.

As the ice recedes in the spring the seals follow it southwards, always keeping in contact with the main ice-cap. During the summer, when the atmospheric temperature is warmer, the seals spend much time basking out of the water. They are known to sleep very soundly, a man having to shout and make a great deal of commotion in order to wake one up. When awakened they show no fear of man, merely gazing at him with a vacant expression. If bothered to any great extent, the seal will move off across the ice towards the nearest breathing hole (from which it is never far). Its terrestrial movements are remarkably serpentine, and it appears not to use its forelimbs at all (as is the case with the Leopard Seal). It may show disgust at being disturbed by emitting a few low hisses, groans and whines.

Weddell Seals, like many other seals, cut their breathing holes by embedding their lower incisors in the ice and revolving the upper incisors and canines until a hole is cut. The method of cutting is similar to that of a tin-opener and puts great strain on the teeth, which, in elderly specimens, are very worn. A widespread phenomenon in the Pinnipedia is the retirement instinct. Many old, sick or injured specimens (one hesitates to say all) display the urge to put as much distance as possible between themselves and their more energetic companions. There have been cases of bodies being found up the sides of glaciers, as much as 3000ft above sea level and as far as thirty-five miles from the sea.

Food: Squids, and other cephalopods, crustaceans and bottom-living fish. Food is obtained from very great depths (see *Special features*).

Reproduction: Pupping takes place from early September to November after a gestation period of ten to eleven months. The new-born pup measures about 4ft and weighs about 60lbs. It is coated in a thick, reddish-grey fur, which is shed after a fortnight while the pup is still being suckled. Lactation takes six or seven weeks. Immediately it ceases, a remarkable change overtakes the mother, from her initial and intensive parental care she displays a lack of interest and begins to neglect her pup. Sometimes this phase begins even before lactation finishes.

It is really an astonishing turnabout, for in the early days the mother will defend her pup aggressively and, should it die, remain by the body for many days. It is not merely the neglect which is surprising – this is all part of preparing the pup for independence – but the fact that this neglect often turns into antagonism against the pup itself. As many as 50 per cent may die before they reach the age of independence. Some are killed by their own mothers who turn on them while trying to drive off another adult. The mothers seem to be consumed by blind anger like that of a rabid dog.

The bulls arrive to mate the cows while they are still nursing their pups and fasting. At this time fighting between rival bulls is quite common. By the time the cows are receptive – six to seven weeks after birth – the pups will have gained about 190lbs in weight and be large enough to retain their own heat.

Special features: The Weddell Seal has extraordinary diving capabilities, which appear even more miraculous when we consider its moderate size. The Elephant Seal is just able to surpass the Weddell Seal's maximum depth (believed to be 1800ft), but it is far larger – as much as 7000lbs heavier than the Weddell Seal.

Until recently the Weddell Seal has been virtually ignored by man. It seems too much to hope that this situation will continue; as commercial sealing in the Antarctic becomes more likely to undergo a resurgence after a period of about 100 years, the Weddell Seal (together with the Leopard Seal and Crabeater Seal) is right in the firing line. The nations most likely to begin Antarctic sealing are the Soviet Union, Japan and Norway, and they, together with the other nine representatives of the Antarctic Treaty, have signed an agreement to undertake sealing only along guidelines set down by conservationists rather than commercial principles. Annual catch limits have been set at 5000 Weddell Seals, 12,000 Leopard Seals and 175,000 Crabeater Seals. The very rarely seen Ross Seal is totally protected, as are the Southern Fur Seals, which suffered great persecution in the nineteenth century.

Mediterranean Monk Seal (*Monachus monachus*)

Distribution: An exceptionally rare species in grave danger of rapid extinction. The total population is probably about 500.

Its range includes all the shores of the Black Sea, the Mediterranean,

The Mediterranean Monk Seal belongs to the rarest and possibly the most primitive pinniped genus. It is also the only genus to live permanently in warm waters.

the coasts of North-west Africa, south to Cape Blanc, and the Madeira and Canary Islands. In the whole of this range there are probably no more than 20–30 small colonies.

Description: Adult males are very dark grey with pale or yellowish underparts. Females and immatures are much paler above. All monk seals have very small nails on their hind-flippers, and large ones on the fore-flippers. They measure about 9ft and weigh up to 700lbs.

Habits: Little is known about the habits of monk seals. The Mediterranean Monk Seal is not a great traveller, and is known to be very faithful to its home. It has sometimes been forced in these days of intense persecution to live a solitary life. Its vocalizations have been recorded as yelps, barks, grunts, howls, sneezes and a repetition of 'o' and 'ah' sounds.

The species shows a preference for small beaches and the shelter afforded by rocks and caves.

Food: Probably most flatfish, reef fish and octopuses. By pinniped standards, monk seals have extremely short alimentary canals, about eight times the body length.

Reproduction: Pups, which at birth measure about 3ft and weigh 45lbs, are born on land in September and October after a gestation of some eleven months. Lactation takes six to seven weeks but the pup stays with its mother for three years; it is sexually mature a year later.

Although mating takes place after pupping, ovulation does not occur in recently-pupped cows as it does in the majority of pinnipeds, so that cows can only bear pups every other year. (This is also true of the Bearded Seal.) The slow rate of reproduction aggravates its present rarity and makes conservation extremely difficult.

Special features: Monk Seals have for a long time been too rare and scattered for large-scale hunting. But evidently in the past – as far back as the ancient Greek civilization – these seals have been the subject of much attention, superstition and hunting. The *Red Data Book* states, in its characteristic matter-of-fact way, that the reasons for its decline are an unceasing pursuit by fishermen and disturbance of its last remaining refuges (caves with submarine entrances) by skin-divers.

The Monk Seal is legally protected in many countries, but enforcement is extremely difficult. The establishment of nature reserves is imperative.

V. Ziswiler writing *Extinct and Vanishing Animals* (1967) puts the population between 1000 and 5000. (It is almost certainly now much lower.) Regarding the other monk seals: Ziswiler estimates 1500 Hawaiian Monk Seals and 'a few individual' Caribbean Monk Seals; other authorities believe the latter to be already extinet.

Part of a large colony of Elephant Seals. Packed in this way they are often mistaken for boulders. At the end of the breeding season they return to the sea to catch squid and build up their strength.

right Another use for the
hind flippers. This Californian
Sealion demonstrates the
extreme flexibility of its body.

below The extremely rare
Hawaiian Monk Seal.

far right Hooker's or New
Zealand Sealion bull.

Hooded or Bladdernosed Seal (*Cystophora cristata*)

Distribution: Frequents the north Atlantic Ocean and the Arctic Ocean east to the Barents Sea, west to Baffin Bay and south to Newfoundland. It is very rarely encountered on the main ice-cap or dry land, preferring drifting ice floes and the deep seas. It is therefore almost impossible accurately to estimate numbers but it is probably fairly abundant – between 300,000 and 500,000.

Description: The largest true seal to be found in the Arctic regions. Cows are only a little shorter than the bulls, which measure some 10ft, but weigh much less, averaging 550lbs, compared to the bulls' 880lbs. Colouring is once more variable. (This inconsistency seems to be more prevalent in marine mammals than it is in terrestrial ones.) Bulls are generally bluish-grey above and paler below; some specimens are covered in either light or dark markings. Cows are paler overall than the bulls and also have less distinct markings.

A remarkable feature of both sexes is the black 'hood', which gives the species its common English name. This hood, which extends from above the eyes down to the muzzle, is in reality an enlargement of the muscular and elastic nasal cavity. As with the elephant seals, this proboscis can be inflated to quite large proportions, and the inter-nasal septum can be forced out of the left nostril to appear as a striking red bladder. It is thought that the display of this adornment indicates either fear or anger, or possibly both.

Habits: Hooded seals are extremely accomplished swimmers and spend much time in open water, diving deeply. The animals spend most of the year in widely scattered areas, converging at their breeding grounds (Jan Mayen and north of Newfoundland) in February and March. The Hooded Seal shares its rookeries with the Harp Seal but is otherwise a solitary species. After breeding, the seals tend to disperse in a northerly direction.

Food: The Hooded Seal gathers its food both from the lower and upper levels. It descends to over 1200ft to hunt such items as echinoderms, which live on the sea bed, while nearer the surface fish and cephalopods (especially squid and cuttlefish) are collected. Unfortunately, since these seals are usually only hunted whilst fasting, either at the breeding rookeries or during the moult (when they sometimes bunch together), it is very difficult to gauge their food consumption and preferences accurately.

Reproduction: Pups are born soon after the cows haul out of the sea on to the floes. A new-born pup is about 3ft long and weighs 28–30lbs; after a week's feeding it will have doubled its weight. The pup is known as a 'grayback' or 'blueback' on account of its silvery-blue-upperparts, which contrast sharply with its almost white belly. Lactation is concluded in three weeks and the pup is then deserted;

Conspicuously suffused by a pink glow from the dilation of blood vessels in their skins, large herds of Walruses, such as this, suggest a thriving population. In fact, the Walrus is a seriously endangered genus.

within the next three weeks it will also take to the sea and follow the adults. For the next three or four years, until sexually mature, it will live a mostly solitary life. If Hooded Seals do congregate outside the breeding season or while moulting and immature, it is almost certainly in sexually segregated groups.

Special features: Greenland hunters kill between 2000 and 3000 Hooded Seal pups annually. The adults of both the Harp and Hooded Seals suffer at the same time. The Harp Seal pelt is superior but the flesh of the Hooded Seal is regarded as a delicacy by the Eskimoes. Fortunately, there are close-seasons operating; the Hooded Seal should, in fact, only be hunted between 10 June and 10 July. Man is their greatest enemy, but Polar Bears and Killer Whales also take their share.

Southern Elephant Seal (*Mirounga leonina*)

Distribution: The species is now widespread and recovering its numbers following terrific pressure of hunting in the nineteenth century. It has a circumpolar distribution and is found on most islands of the southern oceans and also, more rarely, on the Antarctic mainland, although it prefers ice-free habitats. The largest aggregation (some 300,000 seals) is centred on South Georgia; other islands supporting large colonies are Macquarie, Kerguelen and the Falklands.

Description: The giant among pinnipeds – roughly three times as large as the biggest walrus. Bulls measure 17–19ft and weigh up to 8800lbs; cows 10ft and an estimated 2000–2200lbs. The coat of the bull varies from light brown to grey and is paler below; cows and

immature animals are a more uniform grey.

It is not surprising that elephant seals should have been so christened. The weight of a bull is only slightly less than that of an elephant, and he also possesses an extraordinary trunk-like proboscis which, in an adult specimen of eight years, can be inflated during the rut to a length of well over 2ft, at which time it overhangs and curves into the mouth. Inflation is occasioned by muscular action and blood pressure. The function of this curious appendage is now generally agreed to be that of a resonating chamber, increasing the effectiveness of the bull's roar.

Elephant seals have few teeth, and these, except the canines, are probably non-functional. They also differ from other seals in respect of their nails. Seals, albeit for rather obscure reasons, retain well-developed nails; the elephant seals, however, have markedly reduced ones on the fore limbs and none at all on their pedes. The most obvious function of a seal's nails is to facilitate scratching – an activity which is almost an occupation to many. They also enable the animals to climb among rocks. The first and fifth digits of the elephant seal's pedes are greatly elongated.

Habits: On land, elephant seals progress only with much difficulty, although they do seem to employ their forelimbs more than other phocids. They show misplaced trust in man, allowing him to approach as closely as he wishes. In spite of the difficulty experienced in leaving the sea, they seem to enjoy basking in the sunshine and will lie for hours with scarcely a visible movement. These animals also enjoy flicking sand over themselves with their forelimbs, probably as a cooling mechanism or for easing irritation caused by parasites and dry skin.

Elephant seals have remarkably supple spinal cords, and they can

The Hooded or Bladdernosed Seal lives in or near the drifting pack ice of the north Atlantic and Arctic, only occasionally visiting dry land. The curious 'hood', seen here in stages of inflation, is thought to be used solely to intimidate adversaries. The species is closely related to the Elephant Seal.

Elephant Seals are sometimes known as 'sea elephants'. The bulls are the largest of all pinnipeds and indulge (below) in fierce battle during the breeding season, raking their opponents' necks with their long upper canines, and leaving permanent scars.

with ease bend their bodies into 'U' shapes – a posture usually adopted in threat – and are even able to touch muzzle to hindquarters.

In water the elephant seal excels. It can be found more than twenty miles from the coast, but often gives the impression of being lazy, especially in calm water where it will quietly lie with only head and hindlimbs exposed.

Apart from the two periods each year when elephant seals habitually come ashore for lengthy spells, i.e. when moulting and breeding, they are largely solitary. There is no migration in the strictest sense of the word. The animals simply move north and south as the ice frontier moves. In and around January they haul out of the sea in order to complete their moult, which takes about forty days. At this time, with the dead epidermis coming off in strips and patches, the animals look incredibly dilapidated, almost as if they were coming apart at the seams. It is, in truth, an extremely trying time for them, since they cannot feed and have to remain out of the water; they often take to mud wallows and occasionally these are so deep that the animals become trapped there and perish.

Food: In order to reach its food, which is principally deep sea animals such as cephalopods (especially squid and cuttlefish) and fish (skate and sharks, etc.) the Southern Elephant Seal descends to considerable depths where there is very little light. In order to make fullest use of

what is available, its eyes are very large and sensitive.

Reproduction: Polygamous. The majority of bulls come ashore in September; this heralds a period of violent activity. The beaches erupt into a mass of roaring, fighting and blood-smeared beasts, but out of the general confusion a pattern develops, and by the time the cows arrive a few weeks later the majority of territories have been established. Despite the violence of the in-fighting, the bulls seem not to mind or even notice the deep wounds they suffer, and fatalities are rare.

The dominant bulls collect as many cows as they can reasonably expect to hold, usually between ten and twenty though 30–50 is not uncommon. The younger and less successful bulls patrol the adjacent sea and colony boundaries on the look out for immature or unattached females. When severely frustrated they will endeavour to steal a beachmaster's cow, and usually suffer in consequence.

The single pup is born about a week after the cow arrives, and soon afterwards she is mated by the bull, so beginning another cycle. The new-born pup measures about 3ft and weighs approximately 80lbs; it is clad in thick, black, woolly fur which is moulted about a month later. Lactation takes three weeks. After a similar period spent in fasting, the pup is weaned, moults and is ready to take to the sea. During this very short suckling period – the Northern Elephant

The cow Elephant Seal protesting at the camera could easily be mistaken for a young animal, so great is the disparity in size between her and the huge bull behind.

Seal's is much longer owing to the milder climate – the pup's weight increases by about 20lbs every twenty-four hours, and the mother loses roughly one third of her body weight. The milk of the Southern Elephant Seal is reputed to be the richest in the world, containing about 80 per cent fat.

Mortality is high in the first year of life, perhaps as high as 50 per cent, the principal reasons being starvation (orphaned and lost pups), accidents caused by the trampling of fighting bulls, or sinking into melting snow and becoming trapped when it re-freezes. As soon as the pups brave the sea, many become prey for the Killer Whale and Leopard Seal. Those that survive achieve sexual maturity in two to five years, depending on their environment; herds which suffer from regular persecution tend to mature earlier than those living a more natural life on islands such as Macquarie and the Falklands.

Special features: Owing to the sheer bulk of these animals, it is not at all surprising that elephant seals have been the victims of intense hunting pressure. After the fur seals had been practically extermi-'nated in the mid-nineteenth century, the sealers turned their attention to the elephant seals. By 1900 very few remained, and legislation in 1910 came only just in time to save them.

A bull over 10ft in length yields about 720 pints of oil, and at present about 6000 are killed annually, mostly on South Georgia. The slaughter of these seals is an exceptionally bloody and revolting business; apart from the fact that they are very difficult to kill (there are astonishing reports of mutilated and skinned bodies suddenly lurching to life, and making off down the beach), each body contains well over 800 pints of blood.

There are quite a few Southern Elephant Seals in captivity around the world; but under no circumstances can they be regarded in captivity as successful. To date, there has not been, to my knowledge, a successful captive breeding, although several stillborn pups have been produced, notably at the St Louis Zoological Park, Missouri. Maximum documented longevities have been as long as fifteen years for the female and twenty-four years for the male.

In America the majority of captive experience has been gained with the Northern Elephant Seal. The first record of any elephant seal in captivity was as long ago as 1882, when six young specimens of the northern species were taken to San Francisco, but it is only in recent years that their lives have been prolonged for more than a few years at the most.

Dugong & Manatees

The Sirenia

Peace be to those whose graves are made
Beneath the bright and silver sea!
Peace, that their relics there were laid
With no vain pride and pageantry

from 'The Sea Diver' by Henry Longfellow

By virtue of inhabiting an ecological sanctuary, four species of sirenians have managed to survive to the present day. Whether they can withstand the onslaught of man remains to be seen, and there seems little doubt at the present time that their days are numbered.

The extinction of the harmless sirenians would be a crushing indictment of man's ruthlessness. Already one species, the Steller's Sea-cow (*Hydromalis*), has been exterminated (see below). Sirenians are animals of tremendous scientific and aesthetic interest, second only to the Cetacea in marine specialization. Like the whales they never venture on to dry land, and have lost all visible traces of their hindlimbs. They are large animals, typically measuring about 8ft and weighing over 440lbs; vaguely reminiscent of a seal, perhaps, but with almost hairless, rugose hides. Their forelimbs are blunt and paddle-like, and are sometimes used in the gathering of food, being fairly mobile. Instead of hindlimbs, the tail is broadened horizontally, but it lacks the fine perfection of a whale's especially in the three manatees (*Trichechus*), where it is merely a rounded spatulate fluke, though obviously quite adequate for propulsive purposes. The Dugong (*Dugong*) has a deeply notched tail, more like that of a whale, as had the extinct *Hydromalis*. The head, too, is strange, with very small eyes furnished with nictitating membranes, no external pinnae, and in the manatees very thick cleft lips, either side of which can be moved independently to facilitate feeding; there are also tough bristles which help in the ingestion of food. The muzzle is large with elevated valve-like nostrils.

I find it remarkable that these far from beautiful animals should have been named after the voluptuous sirens or sea-nymphs that so tempted Ulysses; 'sea-cows' suits them so much better! Presumably the great length of early voyages was enough to allow confusion to creep into the minds of lonely sailors. The mythological sirens lured their victims by their songs, and although members of this order can utter whistling calls, these could only with great imagination be described as alluring. It is more likely that their habit of reclining in an upright posture to nurse and suckle their young reminded the early sailors of mermaids.

The pair of mammae is unusually situated in an axillar position (as is the case in the elephants – see below), with the teats practically upon the posterior edge of the forelimbs. Those of the cetaceans and pinnipeds are sited in the usual inguinal position.

Sirenians are exclusively herbivorous and largely nocturnal, spending the day asleep with only their nostrils showing above the water. During the night they feed on a wide variety of marine plants such as seaweed, and have even been known to rise head and shoulders out of the water to take low-growing vegetation.

A curious and significant feature of these animals is their dental structure. The manatees have no incisors, but male Dugongs have two in the upper jaws which project downwards into small tusks; in females these are non-protruding. The Steller's Sea-cow had no teeth whatsoever, their place having been taken by horny ridges more suitable for the mulching of the marine algae on which they fed. In both families the front molars drop out as they wear down and are continually replaced from the rear. All this is significant because something almost identical takes place in the elephants which, with the hydraxes, are their closest relatives. Fossil sirenians found in Africa also reveal skeletal similarities with the early proboscideans, proving quite definitely that these animals were derived from plant-eating ungulates, whereas the whales' and seals' ancestral stock was carnivorous. The rugose texture of the hide suggests that they may well have been almost naked even before opting for an aquatic life.

All the bones, especially the ribs, are very dense, hard and heavy, perhaps to compensate for the otherwise light body. There are only six cervical vertebrae in the manatees (seven in the Dugong), resulting in the shortened neck characteristic of most totally aquatic mammals. Small rudimentary nails are present in *Trichechus manatus* and *T. senegalensis* but are lacking in the others.

Sirenians are shy, sluggish and placid beasts, confined to coastal regions in the tropics – two species in the New and two in the Old World. They favour shallow lagoons and estuaries, and some regularly travel far up rivers and may be found living in salt, brackish or even fresh water.

Their brain is small despite a large skull. Hearing is reputedly acute, although the actual orifice is little bigger than a pore, but their eyesight is weak. Being defenceless they only survive today by inhabiting waters that are too shallow for the Killer Whale and large sharks,

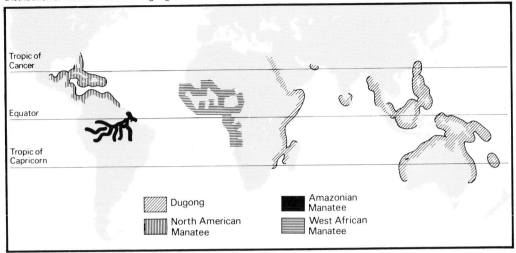

Tropic of Cancer

Equator

Tropic of Capricorn

Dugong

North American Manatee

Amazonian Manatee

West African Manatee

and too saline for freshwater crocodiles. Unfortunately man prizes them, especially for their fat and flesh, and so kills any he encounters; this continues even now in spite of legal protection. Other threats to their survival are set out in the *Species Biographies*.

One species which did not survive was the Steller's Sea-cow – the giant among sirenians – measuring nearly 30ft and weighing 3t. It was discovered by Bering in the North Pacific in 1741, but within thirty years most of the population of a few thousand had been wiped out by Russian whalers and sealers. It is possible that some small pockets persisted into the nineteenth century but not beyond. This species at least had evidently overcome the problems of leaving the tropics. It lived mostly on marine algae.

Dugong (*Dugong dugon*)

Distribution: Extremely far-ranging but scarce. From the Red Sea south to Madagascar; the coasts of the Indian Ocean to the Pacific as far east as the Solomon Islands and New Caledonia. Found only between the 30° parallel – north to the Ryukyu Islands, and south to Perth in Western Australia.

Status: Rare and declining everywhere with the possible exception of Australia – where the species is protected. This area together with New Guinea could be its last stronghold.

Description: 8–10ft; about 384lbs. Females a little smaller than males. Blue-grey above, paler below. The prehensile muzzle is a flat disc of strong yet pliable bristly skin with a vertical cleft underneath giving the animal a strange profile. There is a thick layer of blubber which does not seem to serve it well as an insulator.

A North American Manatee resting in a typically somnambulistic attitude. The entire sirenian order (four species) is typified by a sluggish, peaceful and vegetarian nature.

Habits and food: Dugongs graze on the sea-bed, sometimes pulling out whole plants and shaking them vigorously to rid them of mud and sand. It is this grazing that earned them the apt title of sea-cows. They used to congregate in large herds of many hundreds but nowadays their numbers are greatly reduced. This species is believed never to enter fresh water willingly, remaining constantly in coastal shallows. It is reputedly capable of staying submerged for 16 minutes, but a shorter dive is more usual.

Reproduction: Very little reliable information available. Females bear a single calf every year, and gestation is thought to be about six months. The birth probably takes place just beneath the surface, with the calf being taken up for its first breath. Mothers have been seen teaching their calves to swim by holding them and slowly submerging until they learn the necessary breathing rhythm.

Special features: The flesh of the Dugong is eagerly sought, and in some regions (notably Malaya) aphrodisiac properties are attributed to various parts of its anatomy. The blubber yields about 50 pints of oil, and the tusks and hide are also valuable.

The species is protected in many parts of its range, but enforcement is not easy. Hunting is usually carried out by spearing or netting, and the replacement of the old cotton and hemp nets by nylon means that the animals' chances of breaking free once caught are greatly reduced.

In captivity the Dugong lives quite contentedly but breeding prospects are poor. It consumes about 20lbs of vegetable food daily.

North American Manatee (*Trichechus manatus*)

Distribution: Coasts and coastal rivers of south-eastern North America (principally Florida), the Caribbean, south to north-eastern South America, particularly the Orinoco River. Summer extensions as far north as Texas. Those living in St John's River move to the warm water springs for the winter, at which time they generally fast.

The rotund shape of the Dugong (and most other marine mammals) is caused by large deposits of blubber. Like Manatees, the Dugong is rarer and its future is threatened largely by man's depredations.

Status: Sometimes considered to be two subspecies: the West Indian Manatee (*T. m. manatus*) and the Florida Manatee (*T. m. latirostris*). If so, the West Indian race is the more numerous, and the Florida race better protected. *T. m. manatus* is reported to be still plentiful in British Honduras but heavily persecuted (despite legislation) in Guyana, Cuba, Surinam and Cayenne. *T. m. latirostris* has been virtually exterminated on the Florida Peninsular, but since the Everglades National Park was enlarged in 1950 the species has been sensibly protected in this area at least, with stiff penalties meted out to offenders. Hopefully, enough manatees remain to replenish their numbers, if given time. Inevitably, though, they are still dying – either intentionally slaughtered for food, accidentally killed by outboard motors or killed more naturally by sudden drops in temperature, which they appear unable to withstand.

Description: Up to 10ft (average about 6ft); weight up to 550lbs (average about 440 lbs). Uniformly dull grey. See also main text.

Habits and food: A docile animal inhabiting warm, turbid bays and muddy estuaries, where it browses on the luxuriant pastures of water hyacinths and lilies. Manatees will browse or sleep submerged for upwards of ten minutes before surfacing. They live in small groups or families, as many as thirty-five having been seen together. Their preference for turbid water is probably due to the protection it affords.

Reproduction: Parturition occurs at any time of the year after a gestation period of about six months. At birth the calf weighs 40lbs and has no milk teeth. Its few small incisors are absorbed before maturity, leaving just the replaceable molars. The calf spends the first hour of its life at the surface on its mother's back; over the next two hours she submerges gradually until the baby is free-swimming.

Special features: The flesh is said to be very tasty and correspondingly valuable. The hide, oil and bones are also prized for a variety of reasons. Apart from direct predation, which goes on in Central and South America almost unabated, much damage is also done by outboard propellers, which either injure or scare the animals away from their feeding grounds. Various schemes are in hand to help the species, including its removal to reserves and canals – which it is hoped it will keep free of weeds. However, it does not take kindly to transportation and many individuals die; nor does it seem inclined to breed in its new surroundings, so its future is still in jeopardy.

Fossilized and blackened manatee bones are not uncommon on Florida beaches, and are worth looking out for in this area.

The species can live for long periods in captivity if looked after correctly. It prefers warm water (*c.* 20°C : 68°F), and it is interesting to note that at Duisburg Zoo in Germany a manatee of this species suffered severe skin diseases before being introduced to salt water.

South American Manatee (*Trichechus inunguis*)

Distribution: *Restricted to fresh water.* The lower reaches of the Amazon and its tributaries. Prefers sluggish or still waters and avoids foaming rapids or 'white water'.

Status: Extremely rare and continuing to decline alarmingly. Protected officially but protection not enforced.

Description: Up to 6ft; weight *c.* 440lbs. The smallest of all sirenians, characterized by white breast patch and elongated flippers.

Habits and food: Apart from their localization, similar to other sirenians.

Reproduction: Presumably similar to other sirenians.

Special features: Hunted remorselessly by spear, and now also by rifle and from powerboats. Easy to kill when the waters are low. Thousands are slaughtered every year mainly for their flesh, fat and hides, but the sporting element cannot be overlooked.

West African Manatee (*Trichechus senegalensis*)

Distribution: Tropical west Africa; from Senegal in the north to Angola in the south. Not restricted to the coast, and will venture far up rivers, sometimes hundreds of miles.

Status: Rare and steadily decreasing but there may be some areas where it remains quite plentiful.

Description, habits and food: Very similar to North American Manatee.

Reproduction: Presumably similar to other sirenians.

Special features: Afforded half-hearted protection in some areas, but this does not prevent the widespread, uncontrolled killing by local people which is the main threat to its future. The meat is exceedingly valuable, and some manatees are also killed in the name of crop protection, as they are attracted to the swamps where rice is cultivated.

9 Polar Bear & Sea Otters

My way is on the bright blue sea,
My sleep upon its rocking tide;
And many an eye has followed me
Where billows clasp the worn seaside.

from 'The Sea Diver' by Henry Longfellow

Although not coming within the main scope of this book, there are a few important animals which cannot be ignored, or relegated to a dutiful mention in the appendices. Three species in particular demand a fairly detailed treatment. The Sea Otter *Enhydra lutris* of the North Pacific, a member of the *Mustelidae*, and the Polar Bear *Thalarctos maritimus* from the family *Ursidae*, are two of these; both form individual genera in the order Carnivora, and are the best known. The third member of the trio is the Marine Otter or Chingungo *Lutra felina*, a rare South American 'cousin' of the Sea Otter.

These three species are almost wholly dependent upon the sea, only seldom venturing on to dry land. Of course, the fundamental difference between these 're-entrants' and the whales, seals and sirenians was their *independent* motivation towards the sea. In so progressing they have provided a fine example of adaptive radiation, showing that even when well along an evolutionary limb a new branch may sprout in order to explore an ecologically open door. If for no other reason, these animals occupy a position of importance and significance. The three specialist orders inclined towards a marine existence at an early stage in their development, and very soon adopted it unreservedly, so that their transformation progressed in a more general direction.

Apart from the otters and Polar Bear, there is also a quantity of assorted species from various orders which either make direct use of the sea from time to time or else find themselves there through an ulterior motive (e.g. via swimming to an island) or even accidentally. These can only be mentioned in passing; they are really outside the range of this book. (See appendices.)

Polar Bear (*Thalarctos maritimus*)

The Polar Bear spends most of its time on pack-ice when not actually swimming. Some animals migrate south in the winter, and others move into the interior of such countries as Iceland, Norway, Canada, Alaska and the Soviet Union. Occasionally they are encountered on the tundra further south. The species' distribution is circumpolar, and its disposition nomadic – not surprisingly, considering its ever-changing habitat of ice that is constantly melting, re-freezing and drifting. It occurs in the Arctic seas of Europe, North America and Asia but in fewer numbers now than earlier this century. Over 1000 are slaughtered every year by a variety of people for a variety of reasons. The local Eskimoes, in my opinion, are the only people now with sufficient cause to continue the hunting. The exact population is impossible to estimate accurately but probably does not exceed 18,000–20,000.

This popular inhabitant of zoos is a familiar animal, and should need no superficial introduction from me, its distinctive creamy-white and dense fur being immediately recognizable. Additional characteristics are its relatively long neck, small head and external ears, and hairy paws. It is large and carnivorous, weighing as much as 1100lbs when adult. One specimen weighed 1600lbs, but that was exceptional. Females are smaller and weigh a little less. Height at the shoulder approaches 4ft 6 in., and the length over 7ft; the tail is insignificant.

Polar Bears live a solitary existence, ranging far to find food. They walk with a shambling gait, the head swaying from side to side, and can maintain it for many hours, even days, without fatigue; but once forced to gallop, perhaps by hunters with dogs, they soon tire. Out of water they are surprisingly agile, climbing steep bluffs and leaping easily across wide creeks. Swimming is accomplished by the fore-limbs, the hind ones serving as a rudder, but they are not as proficient as is often stated. They are capable rather than spectacular swimmers; they have evolved none of the refinements to be expected in con-firmed aquatic mammals, barring a certain sleekness of form and broadening of the soles – which are also covered in thick fur, pre-sumably as a protection from the striking cold of the ice.

Though they have been seen on occasions many miles from land and swimming strongly, it remains true that they are more terrestrial in inclination than aquatic. Seals are their main prey, and their chances of catching these animals in water are nil. They are therefore effectively tied to the ice. From sheer necessity, though, they have to swim and would not survive for long were they unable to do so, for one of the Polar Bear's main hunting techniques is to swim in amongst the ice-floes and approach a seal from the water, effectively cutting off its retreat. Alternatively, a bear may lie patiently by a breathing hole in the ice, after blocking up the others in the vicinity, waiting for a seal to appear; it kills it deftly with one tremendous blow of its forepaw, and hauls it through the ice hole with such force that it can crush the seal's pelvis.

When stalking prey over ice the Polar Bear shows a great deal of cunning and resourcefulness. It makes full use of its white camouflage and any available cover or undulations in the ice, pressing itself flat like a huge cat or sliding noiselessly in and out of the water. This is also the technique employed when approaching humans, which it sometimes does, more from curiosity than with malicious intent. There are remarkably few confirmed cases of Polar Bears following and actually attacking a man, although they are certainly dangerous animals of uncertain temper.

The Ringed Seal (q.v.) is the favourite prey, but this diet is varied with fish, sea birds, carrion, etc.; anything edible will be tackled, even mosses, lichens and seaweeds should they present themselves. If the bears come across the appropriate bushes in the summer they will gorge themselves on berries.

Like their swimming abilities, their ability to dive has frequently been exaggerated. In fact the Polar Bear seldom descends below 6ft and usually only a matter of inches; nor can it stay submerged for more than a couple of minutes.

Males and barren females den up during the coldest spells of the winter but punctuate these with periods of activity. On the other hand, a pregnant female (or one with young) constructs a long burrow in the hard-packed snow, the entrance to which is subsequently sealed by drifting snow, and remains there in a dormant or comatose state for up to 140 days, until her offspring, usually twins, are produced early in the New Year. At birth the cubs are blind and naked and scarcely larger than rats; they weigh only about 1½lbs each. The warmth of the mother's fur and of the 'igloo' itself insulates them from an average external temperature of as low as $-10°C$ ($14°F$). Living off accumulated fat, the mother retains her cubs inside, feeding them off milk formed from her rich blubber, until the winter wanes. Shen then breaks out and has the entire summer ahead in which to teach them to hunt. At this time the cubs are extremely playful, inventing all manner of games, but watched over constantly by their assiduous mother.

Mating occurs in the spring, the males sometimes fighting savagely, but implantation of the fertilized egg is probably delayed for four or five months, ensuring that parturition takes place in mid-winter. The reproductive rate is slow, which further inhibits the recovery of depleted populations, and in the normal course of events a female only brings forth cubs every third year. If she loses her previous offspring prematurely, she will be mated again sooner.

During their second summer the cubs are abandoned, and for the ensuing few months and following winter they will experience many dangers and hardships, from hunters with rifles to the very winter

Polar Bears, despite their more or less terrestrial shape, are as much mammals of the sea as seals, depending on it entirely for their living.

overleaf Polar Bears are sure-footed and deceptively fast over ice or dry land.

The Sea Otter is one of the
few animals to use tools.
Stones from the sea bed are
used to smash clams, which
the otters rest on their chests
as they float on their backs.
Curiously, off the western
coasts of North America,
Sea Otters have found
discarded beer cans etc.
positively beneficial, for
within this evidence of
human pollution octopuses
have found a useful shelter,
and Sea Otters exploit this
fact to their own satisfaction.

160

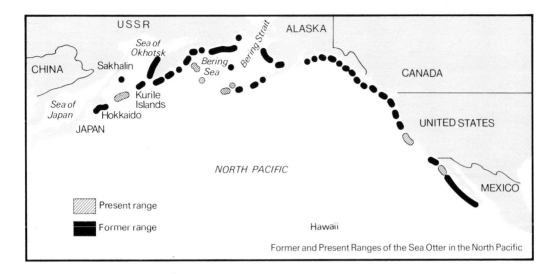

Former and Present Ranges of the Sea Otter in the North Pacific

itself. In the first few months of life the cubs put on weight and a layer of blubber-fat which is retained throughout life as an aid to insulation.

The Polar Bear's sense of smell is its main faculty. Eyesight and hearing are less effective but adequate. The brain, surprisingly, is smaller than that of any other species of bear.

Sea Otter (*Enhydra lutris*)

Various species of otters make use of the sea at times. I know some families of European Otters (*Lutra lutra*) in Scotland which habitually live on the coast, and appear to get a very good living from the sea, but only the Sea Otter (*Enhydra lutra*) and Chingungo (*Lutra felina*) are entirely marine. The Sea Otter, once thought to be extinct, was 'rediscovered' in 1938. Many thousands were taken every year. The principal cause was the demand for its exquisite fur (known in the trade as Kamchatka Beaver), although the Abalone fishermen of western America accused them of threatening their livelihoods and even today, despite vigorous protection, they still try to stir up hostility towards them.

The northern race (*E. l. lutris*) occurs from Kamchatka to the western Aleutian Islands and south to the coast of British Colombia. The kelp beds off the western North American coast are the favoured haunts of the southern race (*E. l. nereis*) It is found locally from the Canadian border south to Baja California; southern limit about 30°N. Its numbers are slowly recovering following the terrible destruction it suffered. Today the Killer Whale and sharks must rate as its worst enemies.

The Sea Otter is the smallest marine mammal, with the exception of the Chingungo, although it is one of the largest otters, second only to the Giant River Otter *Pteronura brasiliensis*, which is just, on

161

average, a little larger. The Sea Otter male measures about 4ft 6in. including the tail (which is less than a quarter of the total and markedly shorter than that of river otters) and weighs some 80lbs; females about 4ft and 70lbs. It is very unlike the freshwater animal, differing in structure, appearance, food and habits. The teeth are not those of a fish-eater, and indeed it lives almost exclusively off sea-urchins, molluscs, crabs and possibly a few small fish, for which it will dive to considerable depths, sometimes as much as 300ft although 60–120ft is more usual – but it is capable of diving as deeply as necessary. The duration of a dive does not normally exceed five minutes. As a rule, the Sea Otter will not stray far from shore, preferring to remain within sight of land, but there are exceptional reports of Sea Otters being encountered as far out as thirty miles. Large fin-like hind feet provide the swimming impulsion; by comparison the fore feet are very small and cushion-like, and at a glance appear to be deficient in toes. The claws are in fact retractile.

The fine pelt of the Sea Otter and the layer of air it traps within it protect the animal even from polar conditions without the assistance of the blubber found in so many marine mammals. It lives in mixed herds of varying sizes, sometimes comprising well over 100 individuals, and indulges in many fascinating antics and habits. For instance, it is one of a very select group of tool-using animals. After foraging on the seabed for shellfish, it will frequently also bring to the surface a smooth stone. The otter turns on its back (a favourite position), lays the stone on its chest and proceeds to hammer the mollusc on it, or vice versa, until the shell is broken open; the edible interior is then scooped out and consumed. It might well be that this was a trick learnt to overcome the problem of severe tooth decay that sometimes afflicts these animals.

A supine posture is obviously very relaxing to these otters, since they invariably assume it when they do not need to forage or move speedily. At dusk they are known to enter the kelp beds, and twist round in such a way as to become entangled, so that they do not drift away from their companions overnight. There are a few reliable reports of animals hauling out on to a rock or isolated shore in order to rest or sleep; but they are indeed exceedingly clumsy and awkward on dry land, and the activity is confined to a few individual groups living in secluded northern areas or as a way of sheltering from exceptionally stormy weather.

The teeth are not only fewer than in a river otter (the dental formula being 3/2, 1/1, 3/3, 1/2 or a total of thirty-two teeth compared to a river otter's 3/3, 1/1, 4/3, 1/2 or a total of thirty-six teeth – the first upper premolar on either side is missing, as are two lower incisors), they also give the misleading impression of being worn down. In fact the molars are flattened and rounded for crushing shells, and possess no cutting cusps.

Grooming or preening is a matter of the utmost importance as to

Sea Otters rarely venture on dry land, and then only to rest at the water's edge, like this specimen, photographed on one of the Aleutian islands.

an aquatic furred animal. On no account must the fur be allowed to become unkempt, and much time and effort is spent on its care. Judging by the fine quality of the Sea Otter's fur, the effort is justified; some experts consider it to be unrivalled. It is glossy, dense and thick, so thick in fact that it is almost impossible to see the skin beneath, even when tweezers are used to separate the hairs. Longer, white-tipped guard hairs are sprinkled all over and add to its visual beauty.

There is no precise mating or breeding season but there are peaks of activity. The rut begins in March and continues for a few months. Gestation is estimated to take 12–13 months, and according to recent work includes a delayed implantation period of 7–8 months. Usually a single well-developed pup is born every second year. It is born at sea, and is furred, with open eyes. The mother is extremely attentive, cradling the pup as she swims or floats on her back, and rarely allowing it to stray far away, although the pup is well able to do so, being capable of swimming well from birth and having the playful and mischievous nature of all young carnivores. The pup is looked after for over a year, and often those of different years are seen together with the same mother.

Marine Otter (*Lutra felina*)

The Marine Otter or Chingungo is a rather small animal, measuring in all about 3ft (the tail being responsible for a third) and weighing only $6\frac{1}{2}$–11lbs. The appearance is somewhat grizzled and the fur, being semi-erect, is rather harsh to the touch – most un-otterlike. It is uniformly dark with pale-tipped guard hairs.

Its range includes almost the entire length of the Pacific coast of South America from the Ecuador/Peru border in the north to Tierra del Fuego in the south. In spite of this extensive range, numbers are greatly reduced, mainly through the reprisals (justified or not) of fishermen and casual persecution by hunters who use them as target practice. The freshwater prawn *Criphiops caementarius* attracts the Chingungo to rivers and estuaries, and it occasionally penetrates far up them in search of this delicacy. Otherwise, crabs and even cuttle-fish feature in its diet. There is very little reliable information available on this species, and the interested reader is advised to consult a standard work on the *Lutrinae*. A certain amount of general matter can no doubt be applied to the Chingungo.

Relations with Prey & Non-prey Species

Merrily, merrily goes the bark,
Before the gale she bounds;
So darts the dolphin from the shark,
Or the deer before the hounds.

from 'The Lord of the Isles' by Sir Walter Scott

The majority of whales, seals and sirenians are sociable creatures, gathering together in groups or schools, and often associating with members of different species. Whales are renowned for their friendly, playful and gentle natures, even the Killer Whale (providing it has a full stomach, and is not unduly surprised) having a great capacity for companionship. This statement will probably be treated with scepticism by those who have neither studied or known these animals. It has to be remembered, though, that these are *mammals*, and as such are reasonably intelligent. The basic difference between a Killer Whale and, say, a Great White Shark – both rapacious killers – is the latter's cold-bloodedness. It lives within narrow guidelines, motivated by blind instincts and urges, most of which are only concerned with the acquisition of enough food to satisfy its voracity.

It is easy enough, by means of good food and treatment, to 'get through' to and win the confidence of a Killer Whale. The dangers arise through carelessness or when liberties are taken, and when the whale perhaps loses its inhibitions and begins to play increasingly roughly. A wild Killer Whale is quite obviously another matter, and it is doubtful whether it plays in the same manner.

For an idea of a Killer Whale's appetite see species description. It must be realized that this species hunts in packs and usually shares its prey, so the animals listed are not complete specimens but parts thereof. As a species, it plays an important role in maintaining the healthiness of the sea and other populations. Just as herds of ungulates need the attentions of carnivores such as lions, leopards and wolves, so do those of seals and dolphins. Some humans are frequently upset and revolted by the sight of a lion pulling down a gazelle, but they do not usually notice the total equanimity displayed by the other gazelles. They know themselves to be safe and that there is one pride of lions at least which will not be bothering them for a while.

Under the boundless sea, hidden from our sight, many fights and struggles take place. We know little of these conflicts and can only picture what takes place from the shreds of evidence presented to us – the flight and panic of smaller mammals such as dolphins, seals and sealions when confronted by the Killer Whale; or the dumb agony of a great leviathan badly mauled by that same animal; or panic-stricken penguins fleeing from the Leopard Seal as their own hunger forces them to enter the water. But most awe-inspiring must be the terrible duels contested in the depths between the huge Sperm Whale and the comparably large and fearsome cephalopod, the Giant Squid *Architeuthis*.

The cephalopods are the largest and most mobile of all the invertebrates. They have a highly developed nervous system and can surprisingly be taught elementary 'tricks', if indeed they may be so termed. They have certain anticipatory powers and react intelligently to quite complex stimuli. One hesitates to use the word 'intelligent' in connection with animals; our vanity prevents us from admitting that an invertebrate could have some degree of intelligence. But under controlled conditions, octopuses have learnt remarkably quickly to recognize a coloured probe that issues some reward from another, differently marked, that discharges a very slight but uncomfortable electric shock.

Architeuthis by any standards is an immense and formidable animal. It grows to a length of 50ft (possibly much more), including the ten suckered tentacles which are used in the acquisition of food and for progress along the seabed (not for swimming); one specialized tentacle serves as a reproductive organ. The suckers of even a small octopus are extremely powerful, and one fastened to a rock is almost impossible to remove by force without injuring it, so the strength of an *Architeuthis* can be imagined.

Sperm Whales have frequently been caught with skin heavily scarred by the powerful toothed suckers of Giant Squids. Presumably these whales were the victors, as they lived to tell the tale, but victory can by no means be a foregone conclusion. There is no way of accurately gauging the size to which a Giant Squid *could* grow, for one larger than 50ft would be a match for any Sperm Whale, and the only way we have of gathering information is from the remains in whale stomachs. A Sperm Whale engaged in a struggle hundreds of fathoms down would need to surface more frequently to breathe than it would if merely foraging, and here of course the squid has the advantage. Unable to surface, the whale, for all its bulk and strength, would rapidly tire and subsequently drown. On a few occasions such a fight has been observed in progress at the surface, the whale presumably having forced its way up. But there is no doubt that squid hunting in the deep sea is a dangerous occupation. No wonder the whales usually concentrate on the smaller varieties.

Apart from large squids and sharks there are few sea animals capable of preying on the mammals; there is therefore much inter-order predation between the whales and seals. The Polar Bear's preferred food is the little Ringed Seal, and walruses (usually rogues) may develop a taste for other pinnipeds and even their own kind.

The spoils and discarded items from whaling vessels have benefited various oceanic carnivores, including the Killer Whale. These resourceful animals, regarded as pests by whalers, quickly learn of the vessels' presence and either follow in their wake with the skuas, petrels and shearwaters (which incidentally have been seen consuming the excreta of marine mammals) or attack any carcass that is being towed.

I have already stressed the importance of decaying carcasses to the marine ecology. Inevitably many do not get the chance to decompose slowly through bacterial action, and are devoured by higher forms of life such as walruses and of course the ubiquitous Killer Whale. The Polar Bear is attracted from many miles by the presence of a dead great whale, the prime attraction being the guts and blubber. A healthy Polar Bear hunting at an optimum level usually only consumes these parts of a seal, leaving the remainder to the Arctic Foxes and other scavengers.

The inter-relationship between the planktonic animals (and plants) and the great whales is a most absorbing subject. The baleen whales are predators on an enormous scale; in other words, the swarms of Krill, etc. through which they slowly sail must appear like so much thick mist, while the Krill for its part is obviously insensitive to the presence of such gigantic killers in their midst, and indeed to their own extreme importance. Thus we have one of nature's most intriguing paradoxes. The baleen whale feeds by drifting through the plankton, and lowering its lower jaw – which flaps down and acts as a scoop, allowing the water and food to flow into the mouth and out at either side through the baleen plates, while the residual organisms are retained on the fringes and swallowed.

A right whale has a cavernous mouth with steeply arched upper jaws from which the large quantity of long baleen rods or plates is suspended. The tongue is relatively large and muscular, and is lifted in order to expel the water from the mouth through the baleen when the whale wishes to swallow whatever food has accumulated. A finbacked whale has a smaller mouth, correspondingly shorter baleen and a comparatively small, non-functional tongue. In addition, the throat contains many longitudinal furrows or pleats which compensate for the oral deficiencies in the following way: as the whale progresses, the water flows into the mouth and distends the throat into a considerably larger pouch which, when filled, can be contracted by means of special muscles to force out the water, thus achieving the same result as the tongue of the right whale. These latter species, then, are known as 'skimmers', and the finbacked whales as 'gulpers'.

Pilot Whales are well known for their close-knit communities and cooperative habits. However, this is not always to their advantage, for in shallow or murky water large numbers can cause confusion in the echo-location equipment, leaving the animals stranded, as in the illustration.

Not so long ago the baleen whales were thought to live exclusively on plankton. Recent findings, however, confirm that they also eat other foods, apparently always preferring the smallest available. The Sei Whale is known in Japanese waters as the 'Sardine Whale' because of the large quantities of that fish which it consumes. Likewise the Humpback and Fin Whales frequently ingest small fish, a fact which has earned the latter the names of 'Herring-whale' and 'Herring-hog' in the North Atlantic. Occasionally such unlikely items as seabirds have been found in the stomachs of great whales – these presumably having been taken accidentally.

The Odontoceti have a more varied diet than the Mysticeti, and while the latter feed somewhat indiscriminately, their feeding mechanisms dictating what kind of food will be sought, the toothed whales pursue individual food items, and therefore have a wider choice available to them. So although they work a great deal harder to catch their prey, once caught it is more satisfying. There is no doubt though – and their bulk rather proves the point – that the baleen whales have the easier life.

If we estimate that the average baleen whale consumes 2–3 tons of plankton (five million Krill) every day (and this is probably an under-estimate), we can put the amount of plankton consumed by the entire whale population *before their destruction by whalers* in one Antarctic summer at 150 million tons. I raise the obvious but unanswerable question: what is happening to the surplus now that the whales have gone, and what effect is it having on the Antarctic environment? It is reasonable to assume that plankton feeders such as fish, penguins and other seabirds are undergoing population explosions, and this may well be happening, although it is virtually impossible to be sure that the increases so far recorded are due to a surfeit of plankton, and not to climatic or other related factors. The Leopard Seal and Killer

Whale, the two most important predators of warm-blooded prey in these waters, should also be indirectly benefiting from an over-abundance of plankton, but once again the nature of the Antarctic wilderness makes accurate surveying impossible.

Not all the relationships encountered in the sea between the mammals, or between mammals and other forms of life, are of such a violent nature as those we have been discussing. I have already remarked on the friendliness of dolphins in particular, and they are certainly extraordinary carnivores, probably the most extraordinary of all. In captivity, a dolphin will consume about 40lbs of fish daily, although it will obviously have to work very hard to catch that amount in the wild. Nevertheless, wild dolphins appear to have plenty of time at their disposal for leisure. Entire schools will abandon fishing to sport in the pressure-field immediately ahead of vessels, and have often been seen playing with turtles and even such inanimate buoyant objects as planks of wood and lumps of cork.

Many whales undertake long migrations to and from their feeding and breeding areas, and often do so in the company of other species. Whether they have met up fortuitously *en route* or at a preordained embarkation point is impossible to say, but there is no doubt that by travelling in large herds they are safer from the attacks of Killer Whales and sharks. This trait has been especially noticed with the smaller species, and great herds of Gill's Bottlenosed and Pacific White-sided Dolphins have been seen in company with the aptly-named Pilot Whales. Sometimes a herd numbering over a thousand individuals is led by a solitary old bull Pilot Whale. Blackfish, as these whales are also known, are expert navigators, using the sonar equipment found in probably all cetaceans, and possibly follow distinctive features of the seabed close to shore. They can, however, at times be confused by gradually shelving beaches and become stranded. Owing to their habit of following one another blindly, such strandings often include many individuals.

There are several instances of symbiotic pairings between marine mammals and other species, especially the parasitic lice which cause profound irritation to many seals, sealions and great whales. The pinnipeds in particular have problems in keeping their dense fur clean and free of sessile growth and parasites. They spend much of their time when on land grooming, and even those species with naked and rugose hides suffer from the attentions of similar parasites which live in the numerous folds and creases, especially those near the neck and 'armpits'. A more commensal relationship exists between certain great whales and crustaceans such as barnacles, which attach themselves to the beasts just as they do to the hulls of ships. One Humpback was discovered to have over 990lbs of barnacles adhering to it. The whales certainly resent this association; the effect of so many barnacles impairs their natural streamlining and therefore causes much energy to be wasted. Humpbacks migrating along the west coast of Africa

Bottlenosed Dolphins are quite capable of repelling the attack of a shark (above) by painfully torpedoing it with the 'beak'. The photograph shows how remarkably similar the streamlining of fish and dolphin is.

are said to congregate at the mouth of the Congo River where the decreased salinity kills off or at least removes the barnacles.

Apart from a host of chance meetings and short-term partnerships which must inevitably crop up from time to time, there are many recurring seasonal relationships. The land assemblages of breeding pinnipeds attract many scavengers; especially skuas and gulls, which are tolerated, if not welcomed, by the seals. In fact the skuas provide a worthwhile service and help to ensure the successful functioning of the summer rendezvous, whatever the reason for their presence. Different species of seals sometimes share the same breeding grounds but usually keep strictly apart from each other, although Californian Sealions and Northern Elephant Seals enjoy lying amongst each other.

A seething mass of copepods cluster round an old wound on the body of a Narwhal. Many marine mammals are plagued by lice, crustaceans and barnacles.

Relations
with Man

11

In the year 1690 some persons were on a high hill observing the whales spouting and sporting with each other, when one observed: there – pointing to the sea – is a green pasture where our children's grandchildren will go for bread.

from *History of Nantucket* by Obed Macy

There can be few more depressing stories in the entire history of man's exploitation of nature than the destruction of the unfortunate great whales. The whales have not only suffered untold cruelty but now face total extermination. Already entire populations have been wiped out, and the only reason why no species has yet been finished off is due to the vastness and inaccessibility of the oceans; a pocket or two somewhere has always managed to escape. How ironic if biological extinction were to complete the job.

The basic rule of extinction is very simple: it occurs when a species' mortality is continually greater than its recruitment. There are though, some very special additional factors in the case of whales.

Man does not actually have to kill the last whales of a species with his own hands, as it were, to cause its disappearance. Biological extinction will quickly follow the end of commercial whaling, should that end be due to a shortage of raw material, i.e. of whales. Whalers have long sought to defend their wretched trade by insisting that whales are automatically protected: as soon as they become rare, and therefore uneconomic to pursue, man will have no choice but to stop the hunting. That is a very nice theory, but it is the theory of an accountant and not of a biologist; only an accountant could apply commercial economics to complex biological systems. The reasons for its absurdity are many and varied. In the case of whaling it can be summed up in the following way. When the stock has been reduced below a critical level, a natural, possibly unstoppable downward spiral begins because of three main factors. First, the animals lucky enough to survive the slaughter will be too scattered to locate one another owing to the vastness of the oceans. Secondly, whales being sociable animals probably need the stimulus of sizeable gatherings to induce reproductive behaviour (which has social inferences as well as sexual).

It is quite likely that two individuals meeting through chance will not be compatible. (They can hardly be expected to be aware of their own rarity or to realize any need for adjusting their natural inclinations.) This is especially so with polygamous species like the Sperm Whale. Thirdly, and perhaps most important in the long term, even allowing that the whales might still be able to band together in socially acceptable groups (thanks to their undeniably excellent communicative systems), there is a real danger, possibly even a probability, that the whales' gene pools would by then have sunk so low as to be biologically unviable. That is to say, the characteristics possessed by the original population *in toto* would be whittled down to those characters possessed by only the few remaining individuals. The result of such a biological calamity is inbreeding, less ability to adapt to new conditions, and less individual variety. Three words can sum it up: *protracted biological extinction*. The future 'hopes' of these animals are further discussed in the final chapter.

A detailed history of whaling has little claim in a book dedicated to the glory of the animals themselves and not to those who have set out methodically to destroy them. There have already been enough works published which concern themselves with the mechanics and history of whaling, and which revel in the gory details and excitement of a whale hunt. However, lest I am accused of idealism, sentimentalism or some other similar folly, a few fundamental observations should be made.

In all fairness, it has to be stated at the outset that men have hunted whales since before recorded history. We know little about whaling in those days, and indeed even up to the eighteenth century it was a subject generally ignored by historians, who evidently regarded whaling as just another industry. In fact it was very much more than that, and the revenue derived from whale-oil and baleen was of vital importance to the economies of many nations.

One cannot blame primitive people for hunting whales nor can one censure too harshly the methods they employed, since they knew no other way; and whichever way you set about it, whaling is a nasty, cruel and bloody business. I am sure that even some of the early commercial whalers, although they probably would not have admitted it, did not much care for their job – but at least it was a job, and the wages earned on a successful trip could not be equalled in any other trade.

The roots of the industry were small, tenuous and widely scattered. They sprang up spontaneously where and when the need and opportunity arose, as described in the extract from the *History of Nantucket* which headed the chapter.

Before the days of commercial whaling, whales (and seals) had been caught as desired by such people as the Eskimoes and Faeroese. The entire animal was utilized, the meat, hide and bones being the most important prizes. They were hunted and regarded in just the same way as any other game animal. And because of the relatively small

demand – one whale goes a long way in a small community – this type of hunting had little, if any, significant effect on the overall populations. In those days whales were easier to catch than might be imagined. They were abundant, flocked together and preferred to remain inshore, nor did they have much fear of man. Commercial whaling was the inevitable sequel to subsistence whaling, and it was with this progression that the rot set in. From the mid-eighteenth century to the first half of the nineteenth, whaling flourished. From methods developed between the tenth and sixteenth centuries by the medieval Basques – generally considered to be the Fathers of Whaling – all latter-day techniques sprang.

There is no doubting the excitement of a whale hunt or the rewards at the end of it, and the thirst for blood and killing seemingly inherent in so many men must have made the prospect irresistible. The chaotic slaughter and dismembering procedure which followed were revelled in by entire villages, including the women and children. It is difficult to imagine modern communities entering into this revolting butchering with so much zeal; they prefer it to go on out of sight, either on the

A Humpback Whale ends its days alongside a New Zealand tug in the Tory Channel. In the Antarctic part of their range, Humpback numbers fell from c. 22,000 in 1930 to c. 3,000 in 1965.

These porpoises were spotted by Japanese hunters more than ten miles from land. Stampeded shorewards, they eventually struck dry land, where they were clubbed or knifed to death.

These porpoises were spotted by Japanese hunters more than ten miles from land. Stampeded shorewards, they eventually struck dry land, where they were clubbed or knifed to death.

high seas or in remote outposts.

Nowadays, even though only two nations – the Soviet Union and Japan – are concerned on a large scale, whaling is still a high-powered business. As the world's whale stocks (which belong to no-one, or everyone) become increasingly rare, so the catching techniques are improved. And, like a dog chasing its own tail, we have the ridiculous inflationary spiral of better and better vessels, built along the lines of floating factories, chasing fewer and fewer whales. There can be only one result. Modern whaling methods and those aspects of it which affect the future of whales are further discussed in Chapter 13.

Man has not always viewed cetaceans only through mercenary and bloodthirsty eyes. They have been the subject of enthusiastic narratives and fables, accorded God-like powers, and revered for their beauty, grace and friendliness. The ancient Greeks and Romans realized that although they lived in the sea and had the form of fishes, there was something faintly humanoid about them, although they may not have been able to pinpoint exactly what.

Greek mythology abounds in legends about dolphins as man's friend and rescuer. Dolphins were stringently protected, and dolphin-killing was the equal of homicide.

Dionysus – the god of wine – was said to have created dolphins when he discovered, during a voyage from Icaria to Naxos, that he was being abducted by pirates. Calling upon his magical powers, he changed the oars into snakes and filled the boat with plants and the sound of flutes. The pirates, thinking they were going mad, jumped

Porpoises enjoy riding in the pressure field ahead of ships. It is ironic that they should be here escorting a US gunboat, when the US Navy has exploited them for a wide range of dangerous and cruel duties.

overboard and were immediately changed into dolphins so that they could do no more harm.

Odysseus had a shield and ring struck bearing a dolphin motif after a dolphin saved his son, Telemachus, from drowning. And Arion, a singer and musician, was rescued after having been thrown overboard by pirates by a dolphin that had been enchanted by his last song. There is, as a matter of fact, up-to-date evidence proving that dolphins

do indeed enjoy the sound of music.

Dolphins have been a source of much pleasure to many people. There are many dependable and fascinating accounts of dolphins having become almost over-friendly with human bathers, and also of dolphins co-operating with primitive fishermen – most commonly, of dolphins driving such fish as mullet into nets placed in shallow lagoons. Some such commensal activities are carried on today, and it is unfortunately not possible to discuss them here in the detail they deserve. Suffice it to say that usually these partnerships, built up over generations, are pure mutualism. The fishermen undoubtedly derive great benefit from the shepherding influence of the dolphins, while the animals, for their part, find the panic-stricken fish easy to capture.

More recent dolphin/man relationships are not always so mutualistic. Chapter 12 deals with some of their lives in captivity, from the research specimens (which have yielded much valuable information) to those animals induced to perform tricks in return for either a good life in some establishments or a diabolical one in others. The

An infuriated Polar Bear is about to tackle its antagonist, an Eskimo sled dog. In this instance, the Eskimoes managed to keep the bear at bay.

even more disturbing subject of navy-trained offensive and defensive whales is summarized in Chapter 13.

Man the killer, hunter and progressive is a powerful force, and the romantics have always been overshadowed by his activities. There are at last, though, some welcome signs that more and more 'ordinary' people are becoming less satisfied with his disastrous and cruel ways. The study, or more precisely observation, of natural history – once the preserve of 'cranks' and 'eccentrics' – has never been more widely followed.

Many volumes have been written on the relationships between man and marine animals. Every country fortunate enough to have some coastline has its own heroes and histories to recount, and there are many variations on the theme of man versus the sea and its occupants.

Sealing obviously followed a similar pattern to whaling, due regard being paid to the seals' dependence on land for certain periods of the year. Certainly seals were preyed on by man in the Middle Stone Age (c. 10,000 years ago), and probably even in the Old Stone Age. In more recent times the capture of seals was treated as a diversion from commercial whaling or as a profitable sideline. When the whaling vessels began to penetrate the Arctic and Antarctic seas following the depletion of temperate whale stocks, the enormous populations of true seals, fur seals and walruses could hardly be overlooked. Some whalers abandoned whaling altogether for a while and set out to kill as many pinnipeds as they could find. The booming fur industry, then centred in Canton, encouraged them, for here was a product that even the multifarious whales couldn't provide.

Once again, before briefly examining the sealing industry, we must take care to differentiate between the motivation of people such as the Eskimoes, whose lives were inexorably linked to their wildlife, particularly seals, and who depended entirely upon them for the provision of meat, oil, clothing, footwear, harpoon lines, dog traces, pouches, tools and knives etc., and the mass slaughters entirely promoted by commercial interests from distant lands. As with whaling, no-one can deny or condone the cruelty involved in the primitive methods of hunting. The seals are harpooned and 'played' in the same manner as an angler lands a large fish. But it is a cruelty forced out of necessity, and the brutality of the commercial sealers makes it shrink into insignificance.

Briefly, then, it was but a short step from the times when individual seals were taken on voyages of discovery in the seventeenth century to help eke out boring rations and provide valuable vitamins, to the time when their commercial value was appreciated. Realization of that appreciation followed swiftly, and before long expeditions set out with only one aim in mind – to collect as many seals as possible.

The seals, in their innocence, must have viewed their approaching executioners with mild curiosity, for they were tame and made no attempt to escape. The crews of sealers had just endured an arduous and prolonged voyage, they were working against time, and the ships' officers were hard men who purposefully whipped the crews up into a state of frenzy, when all considerations and standards of humanity were lost. An orgy of killing followed, so brutal it almost defies description.

The helpless seals were clubbed, lanced or simply skinned alive; their companions watching with apparent unconcern. Such a blood-bath was beyond their realm of experience, and man, till then, was an unknown figure. They could not have equated what they saw with death, injury or pain until it was too late.

Towards the end of the eighteenth century and during the nineteenth, mercantile sealing enjoyed (if that is the word) its heyday. Expeditions set sail to exploit this new-found source of wealth. They were costly affairs even in those days, and sponsors demanded and generally got high profits. Populations of seals, which a few years before had been healthy and large, visibly shrank and disappeared. The expeditions travelled farther afield and discovered more species and fresh populations, and soon these too were ravaged. As the numbers of seals dwindled, the sealers were forced to become less selective and even more ruthless. The plight of the seals moved them not at jot; their ever-increasing scarcity was frustrating, and the sealers vented their bitterness on the poor seals, as if blaming *them* for their insufficient numbers.

A few quite horrifying figures help to indicate how serious the posi-

If provoked, Elephant Seals can move at alarming speeds, and even a well-disposed scientist has to be on his toes.

tion was, and indeed still is – many species and populations have been unable to recover from the type of slaughter that is indicated by the few examples set out below. Seals are gregarious animals, as are whales and ungulates, and as such are the most susceptible to critical population levels. Their social life has more than sexual relevance: it plays an important role in the location of food and feeding grounds, defence against natural predators, and the raising of young. The relict populations to which many seals have been reduced are hardly viable units.

The case of the Juan Fernandez Fur Seal (a race of the Guadalupe Fur Seal) is a fitting example. Its population in 1792 was estimated at three million, although it had already been suffering persecution. Between 1778 and 1805, more than three million pelts were marketed in Canton. On Mas Afuera Island (in the Juan Fernandez archipelago) there were, at the same time, no fewer than 1797 sealers from fourteen ships all killing seals. By 1807 there were only 300 seals left; today about fifty exist.

Between 1908 and 1910 Japanese hunters slaughtered nearly four million Northern Fur Seals on the Pribilof Islands.

The Pacific Walrus is another seal threatened by commerce. Eskimoes equipped with rifles have been destroying about 10,000 annually for their tusks, which are carved and sold to the many soldiers stationed in the Arctic. As the walruses only produce about half that amount of young each year, the population suffers a yearly deficit of 5000, not counting natural fatalities. Between 1868 and 1873 whalers took at least 60,000 walruses each year as a diversion, then returned to whaling as the stocks ran out. Exclusive hunters of the walrus accounted for a steady 20,000 annually.

Mercifully common sense began to prevail, even if only as a result of economic fear, and seals started to receive at least some degree of protection. The remaining large colonies were culled (as opposed to indiscriminately slaughtered), and certain species protected by law or cropped according to quotas.

Seals still have their problems, of course, quite apart from those species which are on the brink of extinction. The emotive question of seal-culling which both perplexes the conservationist and angers the nature-lover (the two are not always the same animal) is summarized in Chapter 13.

The sirenians, though few in number, provide possibly the best example of the havoc unrestrained man is capable of causing. There are those who suggest that Sirenia is a dying order anyway, ecologically and biologically. I would dispute this assertion. They may not be familiar figures to most people, nor have they spectacular ways, but they were destined for a long and peaceful existence, if only because they occupy a natural sanctuary.

If the remaining four species are now on the threshold of extinction, it is through no fault of theirs or nature's; man alone is to blame. When, as happened in 1958, two traders are discovered with ten tons of dried Amazonian Manatee meat (equal to 220 adult animals) in their possession, the future of these harmless animals is indeed bleak. (See also Chapters 8 and 13.)

The fine pelt of the Sea Otter, already mentioned in Chapter 9, certainly brought about the near annihilation of the species. It is recorded that in 1856 118,000 Sea Otter pelts were sold by the American-Russian Company; in 1885 only 8000 were sold, and by 1910 the figure had dropped to 400. At that time a single pelt fetched an exorbitant price. Protection came only just in time, in 1911, to save the species. An estimated 500–1000 had survived the slaughter.

The story of the destruction, which began in 1741 following Steller's discovery of Alaska, is a ghastly one. Continuous slaughter throughout the year, day and night, was maintained with parties of hunters relieving each other. During the 126 years of Russian occupation of Alaska, the total number of Sea Otters killed probably exceeded 800,000, and most of these in a few decades. Although the Russians were the main culprits, traders from America, Japan, England, Spain, France and Portugal also scoured the North Pacific in search of them. None were spared, not even mothers with young. That was the penalty the animal paid for possessing the rarest and finest of all precious furs.

12

Marine Mammals in Captivity

Oh, the rare old Whale, mid storm and gale,
In his ocean home will be
A giant in might, where might is right,
And King of the boundless sea.

Ancient Whale Song

Lee S. Crandall, writing the Introduction to his authoritative *The Management of Wild Mammals in Captivity* (1964), says '. . . and some groups such as the Cetacea have been omitted entirely (from the book) as not usually considered as proper zoological-garden subjects'. In the case of the great whales this is still true and probably always will be – one cannot envisage any way in which adults of these giants could be accommodated in artificial enclosures. Apart from successful captures and confinements in America of young Californian Grey Whales, which of course later had to be released, I know of no other experiments of this kind, successful or not. The largest cetaceans to be regularly and satisfactorily kept are Pilot Whales, the Killer Whale and the Beluga – all toothed whales.

What is significant about the above extract from Crandall's book is that there is no mention of dolphins. It shows just how recent is the upsurge of interest in these animals as captives and performers.

We need not go too deeply into the ethics of encouraging dolphins (or any other animal) to perform 'tricks' in return for their 'daily bread'. My own view is that, as long as the housing and veterinary facilities and food are perfect, the pool is screened from the extraneous noises of pumping machinery, etc. that cause distress, the staff are dedicated, sympathetic and knowledgeable, the workload of the animals is neither too hard nor so light as to induce boredom, the animals are not made to work should they be off-colour, overtired or bored with a stereotyped routine, and ample provision is made for their social (and hopefully reproductive) lives, there cannot be too many objections to their presence in dolphinariums. The trouble is that *all* these provisos are seldom if every complied with.

Dolphinariums could do good services to the conservation of all whales if they planned their shows along more serious and scientific lines. But commentaries are usually infantile, the stock tricks are trivial, and the educational facilities of most establishments are non-existent. One must also consider the question of capture from the wild; only an insignificant number is as yet born in captivity. The advocate of dolphinariums counters very reasonably by pointing out that some 400,000 dolphins are killed commercially every year, over half of them 'accidentally' drowned in the nets of tuna fishermen.

The expensive and complicated water-treating and filtering equipment needed to maintain dolphins successfully should, in theory, prevent any but the best-suited establishments from doing so. But this is a complex subject. I am not so much concerned here with the correct captive management of marine mammals but with the ethics and effects of the subject. In common with most naturalists, I have a healthy aversion to animals being made to perform tricks for the gratification of pleasure-seeking humans. (I use the word 'made' purposefully.)

The best that can be said about performing sealions is that they accept their lot with glorious equanimity and appear not to mind being made to perform belittling antics. I am much more concerned about the training methods that have been used, but accept that, these days, zoos seldom resort to physical cruelty. Circuses will always worry me; they set out unashamedly to exploit animals and are staffed, or so it seems, exclusively by showmen without a sign of a zoologist anywhere in sight. Californian Sealions, the species invariably used, are fortunately tough characters and can tolerate a great deal of abuse.

Dolphins are an entirely different proposition. The Bottlenosed species, living naturally in more coastal waters, is by far the commonest in captivity, responding readily to good treatment. The majority of research on live cetaceans is carried out on this species. The Common Dolphin is more oceanic and less disposed to a pool existence. Other species are occasionally encountered, especially in America, where dolphinariums were pioneered, and Japan. Breedings are still not commonplace even in these two countries, but in most years some Bottlenosed are produced and, in Japan, successes have been recorded with the Common, Gill's Bottlenosed and Risso's Dolphins. Pilot Whales and the Pacific White-sided Dolphin are popular in both America and Japan.

Compared to the pinnipeds (phocid seals are kept regularly and reasonably successfully in zoos), dolphins are delicate creatures requiring much complicated machinery and apparatus, together with great care and husbandry. Careful regard must be taken of their prodigious intelligence and sensitivity, and to treat them as mere animals is not only dangerous but is to do them a great injustice. The performing routine which might be a chore to a sealion is a necessary part of dolphin management, provided of course that it is neither overdone nor allowed to become stereotyped. When I say 'a neces-

A female Killer Whale leaps 20 feet out of the water while performing in an oceanarium. In captivity, these much feared creatures have shown themselves adaptable and well disposed towards human beings.

Although a spectacle such as this somewhat degrades a wild animal and is regarded by many to be in bad taste, it does, to those with eyes to see it, demonstrate the magnificence of form, sense of balance and touch of the Californian Sealion. Moreover, they do seem to enjoy performing.

sary part of their management', perhaps it would be more accurate to say that it fulfils a useful function for which, I might add, it was not designed. If dolphins are not occupied with learning and performing tricks they might become bored and listless in the absence of other diversions.

Leaving aside the performing dolphins, which are only of incidental importance, the considerable scientific work done on research specimens has added tremendously to our understanding of how these animals function and behave. Dr John Lilly, who instigated research on live dolphins, began his work with a dolphin called 'Flippy' caught in 1947 off the Florida coast. He decided to study dolphin vocalization when he noticed, during work on the motivational systems of the monkey brain, the extraordinary correlations between the brain of the dolphin and man. Lilly thought it likely that dolphins could be taught a language (if indeed they did not already have one of their own) and embarked on a long programme of difficult research – so difficult, in fact, that he gave it up in 1968 when he experienced serious misgivings about the strains he was imposing on his dolphin 'friends'. It is a pity more scientists do not display such humanity. Before disbanding his laboratory he had made some considerable advances. Too often this type of research is approached from too human an angle, with many basic assumptions based on human and not animal linguistics. However, there were some amazing breakthroughs, and new developments continue to be made today by other workers.

Most of all, the dolphins' incredible powers of communication – indispensable in the wild – have been demonstrated in a variety of often spectacular ways. Two dolphins – 'A' and 'B' – completely visually isolated in separate pools, were able to communicate with each other and even relay information. Dolphin 'A' was able to *tell* dolphin 'B' the correct lever to manipulate in order to obtain a reward of fish after this information had been given by the experimenter only to dolphin 'A'. Many tasks and variations on this theme were accomplished by the dolphins with so much assurance that it was obvious they did indeed have a language of sorts. Communication calls are a variety of whistling sounds – the higher range of which is beyond human sensitivity. It is calls of this type by which wounded or elderly animals elicit aid, and which serve to unite mother and young.

The sonar emissions are entirely different and are comprised of a staccato, machine-gun-like series of ultrasonic clicks, as described elsewhere. Another American researcher, W. N. Kellogg, after discovering the uncanny powers this arrangement offered the dolphins, vainly endeavoured in various ways to upset or jam it. Despite sending sound waves through the water and re-broadcasting previous calls by the same animal, in a maze-like pool, the dolphin was totally unimpressed. Every type of sound tried by the experimenters proved completely ineffectual. It is apparent that dolphins are not only able to distinguish fine degrees of form but also of texture. A fish induces instantaneous response and approach, while an identical plastic 'fish' achieves only sound response. A metal bar also stimulates sound response.

A blindfold dolphin can approach a fish thrown in the water (the 'plop' of a fish hitting the water brings immediate reaction) at the opposite end of a sound-jamed pool *at full speed*, successfully evading many nets, bars and other obstacles. Such is the power of their sonar; and yet in spite of the reduced role vision plays, this too is by no means useless. A performing dolphin can leap high out of the water to take a small portion of fish directly from the trainer's hand; this not only indicates good stereoscopic vision but also exceptionally quick and accurate realignment between water and air.

Our technological sonar is by no means as efficient as a dolphin's. It is composed of constant unvarying sounds whereas dolphins can vary the frequency and volume of theirs. In short, they have FM sonar. The variation and rapidity of the emissions coupled to their respective echoes appreciably simplifies the judgement of distance. We are unable to differentiate a wooden hull from a metal one or, for that matter, a whale from a submarine. But in total darkness a dolphin can tell one species of fish from another and will always go for the favoured one.

The sonar of dolphins (and of course all cetaceans) has not been so remarkably perfected without good reason. Just as the communicative calls are invaluable in murky and dark conditions, so too is the sonar. Dolphins for some reason tend to coastal waters often near rivermouths, where conditions are frequently turbid, and unless they were able to detect obstacles in good time they would be in constant danger of serious injury. So obviously eyesight alone cannot be relied upon.

Lilly carried out considerable research on the imitative abilities of dolphins, and discovered some interesting facts. He classified the imitations in four categories. First, a laughing sound – heard shortly

One of the most popular animals in the world, the Bottlenosed Dolphin also seems to enjoy performing for its 'captors'.

after a woman has laughed. Secondly, whistling – although natural to a dolphin, certain sequences were reminiscent of the whistling of humans and of electrical equipment. Thirdly, various imitations of contrived human sounds. Fourthly, and most surprisingly, the imitation of human words. He has heard and recorded a wide range of words, some closely copied, 'others less clear but verging so closely on human rhythm, enunciation, and phonetic quality as to be eerie'. In addition he found that dolphins had a profound dislike of acoustic deprivation (absolute silence in solitude). In such a condition a dolphin would enormously appreciate the only sounds it heard (those of its keeper) and quickly learn to imitate them. The human sounds played to the dolphin whenever it 'spoke' were intended as a reward and evidently regarded as such by the dolphin, which increased its own output in order to get the reward more often. As a development from this experiment the dolphin was allowed to hear, by means of a loud-speaker, the general everyday conversation of his keepers. At the same time a hydrophone relayed from the pool to the laboratory any sounds the dolphin made, and very quickly it began to respond with imitations. It should be borne in mind that the difference in vocal equipment between man and dolphin ensures a rather rough-sounding imitation and so high-pitched as to be almost outside our unaided range.

Once Lilly abandoned his project on humanitarian grounds, it might have been hoped that other less prominent workers would have been influenced by his decision. This sadly did not happen. If anything, the number of laboratory dolphins increased, and another even more ominous aspect of research began to gather momentum – soldier dolphins. It is a sinister reflection on man's attitude to a perhaps comparable form of intelligence that he should so abuse it. He professes to be enthralled by its beauty and charm yet inflicts upon it every conceivable type of injury and insult. Large and small dolphins (and now even sealions) are trained to undertake complex and often dangerous (sometimes suicidal) military tasks. A man-to-dolphin translator is used which converts several hundred four-syllable words into high-frequency whistles which are easily assimilated by the dolphins. Anyone who has marvelled at working sheepdogs has perhaps a hazy impression of what a highly-trained dolphin is capable of accomplishing. Some of the jobs are of a simple fetching and carrying nature, such as the transporting of mail to the Sealab crews, but others are more difficult and dangerous. These include the recovery of lost torpedoes, detection of enemy submarines and the planting of mines. Perhaps most revolting of all is the employment of dolphins as aggressors and defenders. Not being naturally warlike, aggressive behaviour has to be conditioned into the brain by electrical and chemical stimulants. In Vietnam, bases like the one at Cam Ranh Bay, defended by Pentagon-trained 'dolphin patrols', were virtually

Morgan, a Pilot Whale at the US Naval Undersea Research and Development Center's Hawaii laboratory, prepares to fasten a grabber claw to a torpedo. This operation is part of the Deep Operations Recovery System, which provides ocean recoveries from depths of 1000 feet.

untouched by saboteurs, while neighbouring ones suffered heavy damage. A human frogman is no match for a single-minded brain-washed school of dolphins, especially if they are equipped with hollow daggers attached to their snouts, daggers which incorporate a CO_2 cartridge.

Such repulsive human behaviour can be given no more space. I hope I have said enough already to give some idea of the atrocities 'civilized' man is capable of inflicting upon innocent creatures of great intelligence. As Jacques Cousteau once said, 'No sooner does man discover intelligence, than he tries to involve it in his own stupidity.'

The sirenians are not zoo-subjects either (in fact only comparatively few species of pinnipeds are), but they are encountered in several of the better zoos, especially in Europe and America. Longevity can be reasonable but breeding prospects are not good, and in any case sirenians hardly make ideal exhibits, having as much inclination to put on a show as a well-fed crocodile, while lacking that animal's *je ne sais quoi*. Most casual zoo visitors in my experience regard them only as dim-witted seals anyway! Nevertheless, I would have no hesitation in encouraging their appearance in more zoos if only they could be induced to breed. They badly need all the protection and as many sanctuaries as they can get. Manatees have been bred in confinement, though not in a zoo as such. Some kept in the grounds of George-town's Botanical Garden in Guyana, which are fed every morning on lawn cuttings, have produced calves. Almost certainly the best place to attempt to establish protected herds is in the animals' native countries, and in environments as similar as possible to their natural ones.

Polar Bears now frequently reproduce in captivity and are always great crowd pullers. These cubs were born in Copenhagen Zoo. Mothers display pronounced maternal enthusiasm, sometimes too much for the cub!

The Polar Bear is an old zoo-favourite, and in spite of being invariably housed in shocking enclosures which quite often closely resemble a cell in one of the seedier prisons, it is a species which can achieve satisfactory longevity. In recent years, thanks to improved standards of husbandry and knowledge, Polar Bear cubs have become a more and more frequent attraction in some of the better zoos.

(The *Species Biographies* at the end of Chapters 6, 7 and 8 often include references to the animals in captivity, and these should be referred to as well.)

The Future

13

Whether owing to the almost omniscient lookouts at the mastheads of the whale ships, now penetrating even through Behring's Strait, and into the remotest secret drawers and lockers of the world; and the thousand harpoons and lances darted along all continental coasts; the moot point is, whether Leviathan can long endure so wide a chase, and so remorseless a havoc.

from *Moby Dick* by Herman Melville

No one can reasonably predict a bright future for the whale. Herman Melville's prognostications in Chapter 104 of *Moby Dick* (1851) were understandable for the time in which it was written. He optimistically predicted that: 'the whale-bone whales can at last resort to their Polar citadels, and diving under the ultimate glassy barriers and walls there, come up among icy fields and floes; and in a charmed circle of ever-lasting December, bid defiance to all pursuit from man,' and 'we account the whale immortal in his species, however perishable in his individuality,' and 'in Noah's flood he despised Noah's Ark; and if the world is ever to be flooded again . . . then the eternal whale will still survive, and rearing upon the topmost crest of the equatorial flood, spout his frothed defiance to the skies.' These quotations un-fortunately owe more to poetry than fact. It is easy to wax poetical about whales. What is amazing is that the hard-headed governments of a few nations still dole out the selfsame platitudes in a desperate attempt to defend the indefensible.

It is fashionable in a minority of scientific circles to categorize the growing worldwide alarm for the future welfare of the great whales as sentimental claptrap. But those of us who care must be concerned. Can we not weep for the death of a species? If our worst fears, in the course of time, are proved groundless then we will rejoice – for it is not in anyone's interest, least of all the whalers, to exterminate a single species. In the meantime, our concern is not so much for the name of a species, but for the plight of those individuals that comprise the species.

It is not to our credit to kill hundreds of thousands of warm-blooded, highly sensitive animals every year in one of the cruellest ways ever concocted by man. The old-fashioned method of spearing with harpoons from open boats was bad enough but at least it had some semblance of hand-to-hand encounter, with man putting himself in considerable danger and giving the whale, if unintentionally, some chance of escape. Modern man has no need to put himself in such danger.

The present-day set-up is a horrific affair. Whole schools are pursued over the oceans. Modern whaling fleets include spotter helicopters, radar and sonar, and supply, factory and hospital ships, apart from the actual killer boats, ensuring that all whales sighted can be caught; even the fastest swimming varieties such as the Minke and Sei Whales have little chance of avoiding the slaughter. The harpoon, fired from a cannon, has at its head an explosive grenade which bursts within the whale's stomach causing a protracted death over a period of an hour or more. The point (just behind the mammal's head) which would produce instantaneous death can seldom be hit in a rough sea, so the harpooner waits until the moment of sounding and then aims at the hump of the spine as it breaks surface.

Once a whale is killed it is inflated with air, and left to float while more are chased. A radio beacon, radar reflector and marker flag left in the carcass enables the fleet to re-locate it when hunting is finished. All the whales are then collected and either processed one by one on the factory ship or towed to the land base.

One hopes that it is not already too late for the Blue Whale and the Greenland Right Whale; only time will tell. Other species might survive if protected from over-exploitation and excessive pollution in the crucial years to come. We have no way of knowing of the damage already done to the gene pools of those drastically reduced populations, nor do we even know how many whales still exist. There is too much guesswork about population levels at the moment. The truth is, with the possible exception of Fin Whales in the Antarctic, our knowledge is insufficient and patchy. The estimates which are often quoted usually refer to a maximum figure and not the minimum. We may still be unaware of the rarity of some species. Until we know accurately the stock levels, we should not juggle with the future of these wonderful and important animals. The present degree of protection, in spite of recent improvements, still allows the whaling fleets to sail too close to the wind.

Before going any further, we must consider a basic, two-pronged question. First, can the hunting of whales be undertaken at the present time without endangering their survival? And arising out of this question, or rather its answer, another considerably more difficult one appears: should whales be hunted at all? I put these questions to Dr Ray Gambell, late of the Whale Research Unit of the National Institute of Oceanography in London. Dr Gambell is now Scientific Adviser to the International Commission on Whaling (IWC). Here is his response: 'Controlled harvesting of whales is scientifically acceptable, but the IUCN (International Union for Conservation of Nature and Natural Resources) has this year (1973) changed its whale policy on largely aesthetic grounds. These two factors are the major points which figure in discussion of whaling today. Whilst the first can be answered logically, the second is based on personal opinions – hence much of the muddled thinking which is prevalent.'

The Sea Otter, unfortunately, has one of the finest of all pelts, a possession which has almost brought about its extinction through relentless human persecution.

In this book, man has been portrayed mainly as a plunderer, and while I am convinced that the mass slaughter of whales and seals in such barbarous ways is the most degrading of all human pursuits (including the wars we wage upon each other), it cannot be denied that, if certain safeguards are taken, whales and seals could represent an important natural resource. Whether we consider exploitation of that resource socially acceptable or not is a matter for the individual and his conscience to decide.

As I have mentioned elsewhere, whales could be said to represent by far the safest, and in the long term most economical, method of harvesting plankton, although personally I would like to think that the plankton was one 'resource' we could do without.

Most people will accept man against animal in a personal context as a fact of life. It is the extermination of entire populations that have taken hundreds of millions of years to evolve, for such trivial reasons as those set out in Table 2, that is unacceptable. For these and all other whale by-products there are already adequate substitutes; there is no longer any social or moral justification in continuing the hunting on such a mammoth scale.

Japan, the greatest danger to whales now that the Soviet Union has hinted at the running down of its own industry, seeks to defend her policies by accusing the anti-whalers of being sentimentalists, and by pointing to her own reliance on whalemeat as human fodder. In fact, Japan, the world's third most powerful economy, is not reduced to subsisting on whalemeat (which accounts for less than one per cent of the national protein intake); fish and vegetables are her main foods, while she *exports* much whalemeat.

If we are to continue hunting whales on any scale, for whatever reasons, one of the first problems to be solved, quite apart from the principles of conservation, is that of cruelty. If we do not consider this aspect we are placing the name of a species above the individuals, and thereby fall into the same trap as so many conservationists who lose all sight of what they are trying to save and of their original motivations. This is tantamount to electing ourselves to a position of superiority where an ideal becomes the most important consideration. We no longer torture convicts to death, not because we fear for the future of our species but because we do not consider it to be the sort of thing in which a civilized race indulges. It could be argued that animals do not care for their species, merely for themselves. If we look after the animals, the species will take care of itself.

Besides being warm-blooded with a complex nervous system, like ourselves, a whale has a very low tolerance of pain. On being harpooned, a whale experiences more pain than for example a soldier does when injured on the battlefield. Research indicates that while the soldier experiences 'wound-shock', rendering him insensitive to pain until much later, the whale does not. So when the harpoon is plunged in and thrust about or when the grenade explodes, the whale experiences the most terrible agonies for possibly more than an hour before finally succumbing to the mercy of death.

The International Commission on Whaling, founded on 2 December 1946 in Washington to safeguard the future of whales (and therefore whaling), has by now a history of ineffective regulations. It is almost as toothless as the great whales themselves. The Commission sets out at the same time to protect and exploit whales – a task which would be hard enough for even a powerful body. Some of its rules, while well-intentioned, are naive, and the wording of the Convention itself almost invites contempt. There is no real way in which a member can be bound by a rule or amendment to the Schedule; the two major whaling nations refuse time after time to abide by the majority rulings of the other member nations.

It is not to this Commission or like bodies that we must look for effective whale protection, but to legislation by sympathetic countries prohibiting the import of whale derivatives. Already some powerful nations have done this, and it may be the best way in which pressure can be brought to bear on those irresponsible nations which insist on endangering the greatest animals ever to have lived. As the finbacked and right whales became rare, attention was naturally focused on the smaller species, and now even the position of the dolphins has to be viewed warily.

Besides the direct exploitation, the ever-increasing pollution of the oceans has also to be considered. High concentrations in the tissues of whales of pesticides and polychlorinated biphenyls, together with heavy metals such as mercury and tetraethyl lead, are causing damage to the brain, nervous system, liver and other organs. The place of the odontocetes (and pinnipeds) at the apex of a fairly complicated food pyramid further increases their susceptibility. The sea is becoming more heavily polluted every day, but even if all new pollution were miraculously stopped forthwith, the build-up already present would remain for an indefinite period. A dolphin or seal, on consuming a fish, introduces into its body-system elements from a very wide area of the ocean. Baleen whales, although feeding mostly on the relatively inactive plankton, travel vast distances to obtain this food, and so are liable to the same influences in spite of being at the head of only a short food chain.

As I have described in Chapter 11, seals have suffered almost as much as the whales, but their outlook is a little brighter. This is not to say that they are no longer exploited. They are, but the direct killing does not threaten nearly so many species. There is no need to discuss the sealing industry in more detail, but the question of culling has to be mentioned as this, when done in the name of science, is often said to be in the animals' own interest. It is a subject which perplexes the conservationist and greatly angers the nature-lover. I must confess to being both perplexed and angry. I have no wish to see scientists becoming demi-gods, and yet the arguments in favour of a cull of some populations are very convincing.

There are two diametrically opposed reasons for operating a cull: one is anti-seal, the other pro-seal. The anti-seal lobby points to the seals' diet of fish (which man sees as his property), the damage they do to his nets, and the fish in them which they do not consume. Grey Seals in particular also form a link in the life-cycle of a nematode roundworm which lives in the flesh of cod and salmon, harming the fillets which might otherwise be produced. There is no doubt that seals *can* present an expensive problem to a human fishing community.

The conservationists who advocate culling certain seal colonies do so because of the evidence that in certain areas the seals are grossly overpopulated, causing themselves much self-inflicted misery and indeed threatening their own survival chances. Once again, do we play God or do we allow seals to sort out their own problems in their own way? This latter solution would not offend our consciences so much, but there are dangers involved which we do not as yet fully appreciate. Overcrowding to the extent that has occurred in some areas, like the Farne Islands, is not a natural phenomenon, and might well have been induced by human agency, in which case it may be necessary for us to take some action in order to redress the balance.

There is no spectacle more distasteful than that of a man beating the brains out of an endearing, helpless and trusting seal pup. But this is a favourite method of culling. There are certainly problems in the alternatives. As many bulls are polygamous, shooting them will not affect the long-term population, and it has been found in practice unfeasible to shoot cows, either with or without calves. Of course, as it is impossible to tell a male pup from a female, and as between 50 and 60 per cent of pups are believed to die in their first year anyway, many seals are killed needlessly – although I expect the anti-seal people would dispute this.

That some species of fur seals are as seriously endangered as many whales can be deduced from Table 3. Some of these are utterly dependent on perhaps a solitary island stronghold, and are therefore in an extremely vulnerable position, at the mercy of a small number of unaware people. And there are few ways in which outside interests can influence events in these remote places. The sirenians are in a similar predicament; they have not even the advantages of the vast and inaccessible territories of the whales. It is surprising that so many have clung on for so long. Laws which cannot be enforced are hardly worth the paper on which they are written down, yet this is the only protection many species get.

Only an internationally approved plan of ocean management can satisfactorily safeguard the mother sea and those who live in it – an intelligent ecologically orientated Law of the Sea, in fact. The current rule that to take continually more than the maximum sustainable yield overwhelming ecological disaster the earth could face.

There can be no comparison between mammals and fish, which lay millions of eggs and can withstand even quite severe overfishing. The mammals reproductive rate is extremely slow; and it is an elementary rule that to take continually more than the maximum sustainable yield (MSY) of any hunted animal is not only a catastrophic policy but also bad economics. Many populations of commercially valuable whales have been reduced to such pitiful remnants that they are uneconomic to pursue. The only way of allowing these species to rebuild their status is to leave them in peace for at least twenty-five years. A moratorium along these lines was recommended by the United Nations conference on the human environment in Stockholm in 1972, but rejected a few weeks later by the IWC, although only six member nations voted against it. (Four voted for the moratorium, and four abstained.)

The IWC's Scientific Committee, though it often disagrees internally, asserts that even a ten-year moratorium cannot be justified, and that the present system of quotas and international observers already satisfactorily protects whales. Other scientists believe that such complacency is based on very shaky fishery data, which has little or no relevance to mammals such as the whales. And as the Friends of the Earth point out: 'The idea that the Russians and Japanese observe the quotas anyway is fanciful.'

Walrus bones lie strewn round the remains of an old Eskimo hut on Coats Island, Hudson's Bay. This mammal is of great importance to the Eskimoes, a good reason for them to conserve it, but at the current rate of slaughter the Walrus's future looks doubtful.

Appendix I

CLASSIFICATION AND CHECKLIST OF CETACEANS, PINNIPEDS AND SIRENIANS

Order *CETACEA:* WHALES

Suborder *ODONTOCETI:* Toothed Whales

Superfamily *Platanistoidea*

RIVER DOLPHINS

Family *Platanistidae*

Subfamily *Platanistinae*

GANGETIC DOLPHIN *Platanista gangetica c.* 8ft. The rivers Ganges, Indus and Brahmaputra, and their tributaries. Local

Subfamily *Iniinae*

GEOFFROY'S DOLPHIN *Inia geoffrensis c.* 8ft. The Amazon and its tributaries. Local
CHINESE RIVER DOLPHIN *Lipotes vexillifer c.* 8ft. The Yangtze Kiang and Tung Ting Hu (lake). Local

Subfamily *Stenodelphininae*

LA PLATA DOLPHIN *Stenodelphis blainvillei c.* 8ft. The Rio de la Plata and its tributaries. Local

Superfamily *Physeteroidea*

Family *Ziphiidae*

BEAKED WHALES
SOWERBY'S WHALE *Mesoploden bidens* 12-21 ft. North Atlantic and European waters
GERVAIS' BEAKED WHALE *M. gervaisi* 12-21 ft. North Atlantic
TRUE'S BEAKED WHALE *M. mirus* 12-21 ft. North Atlantic
GRAY'S BEAKED WHALE *M. grayi* 12-21 ft. South Pacific
BLAINVILLE'S BEAKED WHALE *M. densirostris* 12-21 ft. Universal
STEJNEGER'S BEAKED WHALE *M. stejnegeri* 12-21 ft. North Pacific
STRAP-TOOTHED WHALE *M. layardi* 12-21 ft. South American, South African, Australian and New Zealand waters
LONGMAN'S BEAKED WHALE *M. pacificus* 12-21 ft. Australian waters
CUVIER'S BEAKED WHALE *Ziphius cavirostris* 17-28 ft. Universal
NEW ZEALAND BEAKED WHALE *Tasmacetus shepherdi c.* 19 ft. South Pacific
BAIRD'S BEAKED WHALE *Berardius bairdi* 28-40 ft. North Pacific, not common
ARNOUX'S BEAKED WHALE *B. arnouxi* 28-40 ft. South Pacific
BOTTLENOSE WHALE *Hyperoodon ampullatus* 20-30 ft; snout up to 18 in. long. Northern hemisphere waters
SOUTHERN BOTTLENOSE WHALE *H. planifrons* 19-30 ft. Southern hemisphere waters

Family *Physeteridae*

SPERM WHALES

Subfamily *Physeterinae*

SPERM WHALE *Physeter catodon* 28-66 ft. Universal

Subfamily *Kogiinae*

PYGMY SPERM WHALE *Kogia breviceps* 7-13 ft. Universal. Rare

Superfamily *Monodontoidea*

Family *Monodontidae*

WHITE WHALE or BELUGA *Delphinapterus leucas* 11-17 ft. Arctic and Northern waters

NARWHAL *Monodon monoceros* 13-19ft including tusk – usually one (up to 7ft); females lack tusk. Arctic and northern waters

Superfamily *Delphinoidea*

Family *Stenidae* ROUGH-TOOTHED DOLPHIN *Steno bredanensis c.* 8ft. Universal, warmer waters
CHINESE WHITE DOLPHIN *Sousa sinensis c.* 8ft. Coasts of South Asia
PLUMBEOUS DOLPHIN *S. plumbea c.* 8ft. Indian Ocean
MALAYSIAN DOLPHIN *S. borneensis c.* 8ft. Malaysian waters
SPECKLED DOLPHIN *S. lentiginosa c.* 8ft. Indian Ocean and Australian waters
WEST AFRICAN WHITE DOLPHIN *S. teuszii c.* 8ft. West African waters
AMAZONIAN WHITE DOLPHIN *Sotalia fluviatilis* 5-8ft. Amazon River and its tributaries. Local
GUYANA WHITE DOLPHIN *S. guianensis* 5-8ft. North-eastern coast of South America

Family *Delphinidae* TYPICAL DOLPHINS

Subfamily *Delphininae* MALAY DOLPHIN *Stenella malayana* 5-8ft. Indian Ocean and South Pacific
BRIDLED DOLPHIN *S. frontalis* 5-8ft. Atlantic and Indian Oceans
BLUE-WHITE DOLPHIN *S. caeruleoalbus* 5-8ft. South American and Japanese waters
EUPHROSYNE DOLPHIN *S. styx* 5-8ft. North Pacific and Atlantic
CEYLON DOLPHIN *S. alope* 5-8ft. Ceylonese waters
NARROW-SNOUTED DOLPHIN *S. attenuata* 5-8ft. Pacific
LONG-BEAKED DOLPHIN *S. longirostris* 5-8ft. Pacific
GRAFFMAN'S DOLPHIN *S. graffmani* 5-8ft. Pacific
SMALL-HEADED DOLPHIN *S. microps* 5-8ft. Pacific
SPOTTED DOLPHIN *S. plagiodon* 5-8ft. Atlantic
TORRES STRAIT DOLPHIN *S. roseiventris* 5-8ft. Torres Strait
COMMON DOLPHIN *Delphinus delphis* 6-8ft. Universal
CAPE DOLPHIN *D. capensis* 5-8ft. South African and Japanese waters
PACIFIC DOLPHIN *D. bairdi* 5-8ft. Pacific
BORY'S DOLPHIN *D. boryi* 5-8ft. Australian waters
RISSO'S DOLPHIN *Grampus griseus* 5-10ft. Universal
BOTTLENOSED DOLPHIN *Tursiops truncatus* 9-13ft. Universal
RED SEA BOTTLENOSED DOLPHIN *T. aduncus* 8-13ft(?). Red Sea, Indian and Pacific Oceans
GILL'S BOTTLENOSED DOLPHIN *T. gilli* 8-13ft(?). Pacific
PACIFIC BOTTLENOSED DOLPHIN *T. nuuana* 8-13ft(?). Pacific
TASMANIAN BOTTLENOSED DOLPHIN *T. maugeanus* 8-13ft(?). Tasmania
WHITE-SIDED DOLPHIN *Lagenorhynchus acutus* 5-10ft. North Atlantic
WHITE-BEAKED DOLPHIN *L. albirostris* 5-10ft. North Atlantic and European waters
INDIAN BROAD-BEAKED DOLPHIN *L. electra* 5-10ft. Indian, Atlantic and Pacific Oceans
PACIFIC WHITE-SIDED DOLPHIN *L. obliquidens* 5-10ft. North Pacific
GRAY'S WHITE-SIDED DOLPHIN *L. thicolea* 5-10ft. Pacific
GRAY'S DOLPHIN *L. obscurus* 5-10ft. Southern hemisphere waters
PEALE'S DOLPHIN *L. australis* 5-10ft. Southern hemisphere waters
CRUCIGER DOLPHIN *L. cruciger* 5-10ft. Southern hemisphere waters
BORNEAN DOLPHIN *Lagenodelphis hosei c.* 8ft. Bornean waters

Subfamily *Cephalorhynchinae* COMMERSON'S DOLPHIN *Cephalorhynchus commersoni* 3-6ft. South American waters
BLACK DOLPHIN *C. eutrophia* 3-6ft. South American waters
TONINE or HECTOR'S DOLPHIN *C. heavisidei* 3-6ft. South Pacific and Cape Seas

Subfamily *Orcinae* KILLER WHALE *Orcinus orca* 20-30ft. Universal
FALSE KILLER *Pseudorca crassidens c.* 16ft. Universal
IRRAWADDY DOLPHIN *Orcaella brevirostris* 6-7ft; short snout (12-19 teeth in each ramus of jaw). Very small dorsal fin. Coasts and estuaries of south-east Asia
PILOT WHALE *Globicephala melaena* 13-27ft. Pacific, Atlantic and European waters
INDIAN PILOT WHALE *G. macrorhyncha c.* 25ft. Pacific, Atlantic and Indian Oceans

PACIFIC PILOT WHALE *G. scammoni c.* 25ft. Pacific
SOUTHERN PILOT WHALE *G. edwardi c.* 25ft. South African seas
PYGMY KILLER *Feresa attenuata c.* 8ft. Atlantic and South Pacific (tropics)

Subfamily *Lissodelphinae*

SOUTHERN RIGHT WHALE DOLPHIN *Lissodelphis peroni* 5-8ft. South Pacific
NORTHERN RIGHT WHALE DOLPHIN *L. borealis* 5-8ft. North Pacific

Family *Phocaenidae*

PORPOISES
COMMON PORPOISE *Phocaena phocaena* 4-6ft. Northern hemisphere waters
PACIFIC HARBOUR PORPOISE *P. vomerina c.* 5ft. Pacific
BI-COLOURED PORPOISE *P. dioptrica c.* 5ft. South American waters
BURMEISTER'S PORPOISE *P. spinipinnis c.* 5ft. South American waters
DALL'S PORPOISE *Phocaenoides dalli c.* 5-6ft. North Pacific
TRUE'S PORPOISE *P. truei c.* 5-6ft. Japanese waters
FINLESS BLACK PORPOISE *Neomeris phocaenoides* 4ft. Pacific and Indian Oceans

Suborder *MYSTICETI*: Baleen Whales

Family *Eschrichtidae*

CALIFORNIAN GREY WHALE *Eschrichtius glaucus* 40-52ft. Pacific. Rare

Family *Balaenopteridae*

LESSER RORQUAL or MINKE *Balaenoptera acutorostrata* 25-33ft. Universal. Declining
SEI WHALE *B. borealis* 40-60ft. Universal. Declining
COMMON RORQUAL or FIN WHALE *B. physalus* 60-80ft. Universal. Becoming rarer
BLUE WHALE *B. musculus* 90-108ft. Universal. Extremely rare
(PYGMY BLUE WHALE *B. m. brevicauda c.* 65-72ft. Southerns seas)
BRYDE'S WHALE *B. brydei c.* 33ft. South African waters. Rare
HUMPBACK WHALE *Megaptera novaeangliae* 36-50ft. Universal. Rare

Family *Balaenidae*

GREENLAND RIGHT WHALE or BOWHEAD *Balaena mysticetus* 48-70ft. Arctic waters. Extremely rare
NORTH ATLANTIC, BLACK or BISCAYAN RIGHT WHALE *Eubalaena glacialis* 45-57ft. Rare
PACIFIC RIGHT WHALE *E. sieboldi c.* 65ft. North Pacific. Rare
SOUTHERN RIGHT WHALE *E. australis c.* 65ft. Southern hemisphere waters. Rare
PYGMY RIGHT WHALE *Caperea marginata c.* 20ft. Southern waters. Extremely rare and little known

Order *PINNIPEDIA*: SEALS

Family *Otariidae*

EARED SEALS
SOUTH AFRICAN FUR SEAL *Arctocephalus pusillus* 5-9ft. South-west Africa and Cape Province. Common
SOUTH AMERICAN FUR SEAL *A. australis* 4-6ft. South America, Falkland and Galapagos Islands. Common
AUSTRALIAN FUR SEAL *A. doriferus* 5-6ft. South and southern Western Australia. Local, little known
TASMANIAN FUR SEAL *A. tasmanicus* 5-8ft. Tasmania, neighbouring islands and the mainland east to Sydney. Local
NEW ZEALAND FUR SEAL *A. forsteri* 5-7ft. New Zealand and neighbouring islands. Increasing (*c.* 100,000)
KERGUELEN FUR SEAL *A. tropicalis* 4-6ft. Antarctic and subantarctic islands. Local
GUADALUPE FUR SEAL *A. philippii* 5-6ft. Guadalupe (off California). Rare and little known, persecuted
NORTHERN, ALASKAN or PRIBILOF FUR SEAL *Callorhinus ursinus* 5-7ft. North Pacific

islands, Bering Sea. Widespread
CALIFORNIAN SEALION *Zalophus californianus* 6-7ft. Californian and Japanese coasts, Galapagos Islands. Local. Japanese subspecies *Z.c. japonicus* probably extinct
STELLER'S SEALION *Eumetopias jubatus* 7-10ft. North Pacific, Bering and Beaufort Seas. Common
SOUTH AMERICAN or SOUTHERN SEALION *Otaria byronia* 6-8ft. South America and Falklands. Widespread
AUSTRALIAN SEALION *Neophoca cinerea* 7-12ft. Great Australian Bight and the Houtmans Abrolhos. Rare
NEW ZEALAND or HOOKER'S SEALION *Phocarctos hookeri* 6-10ft. Southern New Zealand and neighbouring islands. Local

Family *Odobenidae*	WALRUSES

ATLANTIC WALRUS *Odobenus rosmarus rosmarus* 8-12ft. Arctic regions (see map). Rare
PACIFIC WALRUS *O. r. divergens* 10-13ft. Arctic regions (see map). Declining

Family *Phocidae*	TRUE SEALS

Subfamily *Phocinae*	NORTHERN SEALS

HARBOUR or COMMON SEAL *Phoca vitulina* 4-6ft. North America, north Europe and north-east Asia. Widespread
KURILE HARBOUR SEAL *P. kurilensis c.* 5ft. Northern Hokkaido and neighbouring islands. Discovered in early 1960s. Rare
RINGED SEAL *Pusa hispida c.* 5ft. Arctic, North Atlantic and Baltic Sea. Common
BAIKAL SEAL *P. sibirica* 4ft. Lake Baikal. Local
CASPIAN SEAL *P. caspica* 4-5ft. Caspian Sea. Common
RIBBON or BANDED SEAL *Histriophoca fasciata* 5-6ft. Sea of Okhotsk and west of Bering Sea. Local, little known
HARP SEAL *Pagophilus groenlandicus c.* 6ft. Arctic and the western North Atlantic. Widespread
GREY SEAL *Halichoerus grypus* 6-10ft. Northern Europe and north-eastern North America. Stable
BEARDED SEAL *Erignathus barbatus* 7-10ft. Arctic and northern waters. Scattered

Subfamily *Lobodontinae*	SOUTHERN SEALS

CRABEATER SEAL *Lobodon carcinophagus* 8-9ft. Antarctic. Very abdundant
ROSS SEAL *Ommatophoca rossi* 8-10ft. Antarctic. Rare, solitary and little known
LEOPARD SEAL *Hydrurga leptonyx* 7-11ft. Antarctic and subantarctic regions. Nomadic and widespread
WEDDELL SEAL *Leptonychotes weddelli* 9-10ft. Antarctic. Numerous

Subfamily *Monachinae*	MONK SEALS

MEDITERRANEAN MONK SEAL *Monachus monachus* 8-10ft. Mediterranean Sea and north-west Africa. Extremely rare
CARIBBEAN MONK SEAL *M. tropicalis* 6-8ft. Jamaica. Probably extinct
HAWAIIAN or LAYSAN MONK SEAL *M. schauinsland* 6-7ft. Western Hawaiian Islands. Rare but stable (1400-1800)

Subfamily *Cystophorinae*	PROBOSCIS SEALS

HOODED or BLADDERNOSED SEAL *Cystophora cristata* 8-11ft. Arctic and north-eastern North America. Widespread
SOUTHERN ELEPHANT SEAL *Mirounga leonina* 10-20ft. Subantarctic islands and southern South America. Widespread and recovering
NORTHERN ELEPHANT SEAL *M. angustirostris* 8-16ft. Islands off southern California and Baja California. Recovering, but not common. Local

Order *SIRENIA:* **SIRENIANS**

Family *Dugongidae*   DUGONG *Dugong dugon* 8-10ft. Far ranging in warmer waters (see map). Rare, threatened with extinction

Family *Trichechidae*   MANATEES
NORTH AMERICAN MANATEE *Trichechus manatus* 6-11ft. South-eastern North America, Caribbean and north-eastern South America. Rare
SOUTH AMERICAN MANATEE *T. inunguis* 5-6ft. The Amazon River and its tributaries. Extremely rare and threatened with extinction
WEST AFRICAN MANATEE *T. senegalensis* 6-10ft. Tropical west Africa. Rare

Appendix II   OTHER SPECIES WHICH VISIT THE SEA

Order *PRIMATES:* **PRIMATES**

Family *Cercopithecidae*

Subfamily *Colobinae*   PROBOSCIS MONKEY *Nasalis larvatus* The tropical forests and mangrove swamps of Borneo. An expert swimmer and capable diver – occasionally seen swimming out to sea

Order *CARNIVORA:* **CARNIVORES**

Family *Mustelidae*

Subfamily *Lutrinae*   Many species, especially the:
EURASIAN OTTER *Lutra lutra* Europe, Asia, Java, Sumatra and northern Africa. Principally a freshwater animal but groups living near the coast will frequently adopt the sea as their home

Order *ARTIODACTYLA:* **EVEN-TOED UNGULATES**

Family *Hippopotamidae*   HIPPOPOTAMUS *Hippopotamus amphibius* African rivers and estuaries
PYGMY HIPPOPOTAMUS *Choeropsis liberiensis* The coastal region of central west Africa

Both these species have been witnessed in the brackish water of estuary mouths, and individuals must occasionally venture into shallow coastal water

ENDANGERED SPECIES

CALIFORNIAN GREY WHALE: Rare but now protected

COMMON RORQUAL or FIN WHALE: Very rare, protected, but future uncertain

BLUE WHALE: Extremely rare, could be declining towards extinction

PYGMY BLUE WHALE(?): Rare, needs further research

BRYDE'S WHALE: Rare, needs further research

HUMPBACK WHALE: Rare but protected. Stable in the north Atlantic, but
dangerously rare in the Pacific

GREENLAND RIGHT WHALE: Greatly depleted, could be beyond recovery

NORTH ATLANTIC RIGHT WHALE: Depleted and rare

PACIFIC RIGHT WHALE: Greatly depleted, could be beyond recovery

SOUTHERN RIGHT WHALE: Greatly depleted, could be beyond recovery

PYGMY RIGHT WHALE: Rare, needs further research

POLAR BEAR (*Thalarctos maritimus*): Local. Could stabilize/increase/decrease –
dependent on man

MARINE OTTER (*Lutra felina*): Apparently in danger, needs further research

SEA OTTER (*Enhydra lutris*): Rare. As for Polar Bear

GALAPAGOS FUR SEAL (*Arctocephalus australis galapagoensis*): Subspecies of South
American Fur Seal. Once believed extinct; depleted but could survive

GUADALUPE FUR SEAL (*A. philippii townsendi*): Once believed extinct, but may now
be recovering

JUAN FERNANDEZ FUR SEAL (*A. p. philippii*): Once believed extinct, now confirmed
to exist but extremely rare

JAPANESE SEALION (*Zalophus californianus japonicus*): Probably extinct

ATLANTIC WALRUS: Local; probably declining to rare

KURILE HARBOUR SEAL: Presumed rare, needs further research

SAIMAA SEAL (*Phoca hispida saimensis*): Subspecies of the Ringed Seal. Confined to
the Lake Saimaa system – a relict population, some 8000 years old. Rare but
protected to some degree; hopefully stable

ROSS SEAL: Very local, confined to the Antarctic seas

MEDITERRANEAN MONK SEAL: Desperately rare and gravely threatened. Perhaps only
300-500 exist. Protected

CARIBBEAN MONK SEAL: Probably beyond recovery if not already extinct

HAWAIIAN MONK SEAL: Very rare. Could stabilise/increase/decrease – dependent
on man

DUGONG: Rare and likely to be generally declining

NORTH AMERICAN (WEST INDIAN) MANATEE (*Trichechus m. manatus*): Depleted,
likely to be declining. Protected in some areas

NORTH AMERICAN (FLORIDA) MANATEE (*T. m. latirostris*): Depleted. Could stabilize/
increase/decrease. Protected but very restricted range

SOUTH AMERICAN or AMAZONIAN MANATEE: Desperately rare and gravely
threatened. It is afforded paper protection. Almost certainly declining

WEST AFRICAN MANATEE: Presumed rare, needs further research, but almost
certainly declining

N.B. Besides the Japanese Sealion and Caribbean Monk Seal – which may both
already be extinct – the Steller's Sea-cow (*q.v.*) and Sea Mink have become extinct
in recent times, the latter in the nineteenth century off the north-eastern coast of
America, where it was slaughtered for its valuable hide.

Appendix IV GLOSSARY

Definitions are relevant to the context of this book and are not full expositions

abyssal: The deepest *pelagic* zone – below *c.* 6000ft
asymmetrical: Lacking symmetry
axillar: At or near the armpit

baleen: The horny, triangular plates suspended from either side of the roof of a
    baleen whale's mouth, the frayed inner edges of which act as a filter – see main text
bathyal: the intermediate *pelagic* zone between *c.* 700ft and *c.* 6000ft
benthic: Pertaining to the flora and fauna of the seabed
biserial: Arranged in two series or parts
blastocyst: A spherical *blastula* formed by repeated cleavage of the fertilized ovum;
    the inner cell-mass becomes the embryo proper
blastula: A stage of embryonic development – usually a hollow ball of cells. See
    blastocyst
blow: A whale's *spout*
blowhole(s): A cetacean's nostril(s)

cephalic: Pertaining to the head
cephalopods: A class of molluscs including squids, octopuses, nautiluses and
    cuttlefish
chitin: The horny, protective covering forming the cuticle of insects etc. Adj.
    chitinous
circumpolar: Ranging round either the North or South Pole
cochlea: The spiral part of the inner-ear, concerned in registering the reception
    and pitch of sound
commensalism: Members of different species associating for unequal benefit – see
    mutualism and *symbiosis*
copepods: Minute crustaceans with oarlike feet
cull: A selective killing
cusp: The cutting projection on a tooth

dorsal: Pertaining to the back

ectoparasite: A parasite living on the outside of another organism
echinoderms: A more or less radially symmetrical group of marine invertebrates,
    including starfish, etc.
embryo: A young animal in its earliest stages of development
epiglottis: A cartilaginous flap protecting the *glottis* during swallowing
euphotic: The sunlit upper zone of the sea – between the surface and *c.* 700ft

follicle: A deep pit surrounding the root of a hair (hair-follicle)

glottis: The opening of the *trachea* into the pharynx

hydrosphere: The globe's water-mass

inguinal: Pertaining to the groin
internasal septum: A partition dividing the left and right nasal passages

krill: Originally a whaler's name for *Euphausia superba* – a shrimplike crustacean
    consumed in large quantities by baleen whales. See main text

lactation: The suckling period or production of milk
littoral: Pertaining to the seashore or the shallow water near the shore

maxilla: A large tooth-bearing bone of the upper jaw. Sometimes used for the
    whole of the upper jaw
meatus: A passage or canal
monogamous: Taking a single mate
mutualism: Members of different species associating for mutual benefit – see
    commensalism and *symbiosis*

nares: The nostrils of vertebrates
nasals: Nasal bones – a pair of membrane-bones over and protecting the nasal cavity
nictitating membrane: A third, usually transparent, eyelid

oesophagus: That part of the gut leading from the *pharynx* to the stomach
orbit: The eye cavity or depression in a skull

palatine: A bone forming the posterior part of the hard palate. The anterior part is formed by the *maxilla* and *premaxilla*
parturition: The act of giving birth
pectoral: Relating to the breast
pedes: Feet
pelagic: Pertaining to the *marine hydrosphere* or oceans
pelvic girdle: The skeletal support for the hind-limbs
periotic: Pertaining to the inner-ear
pharynx: That part of the gut between the mouth and the *oesophagus*
photosynthesis: Synthesis by green plants of organic compounds by use of energy absorbed from sunlight
phytoplankton: The plant varieties of *plankton*
pinna(e): Outer ear flap(s)
plankton: Mostly microscopic free-floating or drifting aquatic organisms – capable of only minimal self-propulsion, usually in a vertical direction
pod: A social unit or *school* of whales or seals, especially walruses
polygamous: Taking a number of mates at the same time (see *monogamous*)
premaxilla: The front incisor-bearing bone of the upper jaw
proboscis: A trunk or prolongation of the nose

ramus: A projecting part or process of a bone
rookery: A traditional assembly site of seals and various other animals
rostral: Pertaining to the forehead
rugose: Wrinkled

sclerotic membrane: The firm outer coat of the eyeball; the cornea in front of the eye
school: A family or social group of aquatic animals
sebaceous: Tallowy
spout: The explosive exhalation of a whale on surfacing, appearing as a fine mist – see main text
squamosal: A paired membrane-bone of the skull assisting in the articulation of the lower jaw
symbiosis: Members of different species living in close association – see *commensalism* and *mutualism*

tail-fluke: The flattened *sebaceous* tip to the tail of a whale or sirenian
temporal: Pertaining to the temple
tetrapod: Any four-limbed vertebrate higher than the fishes
trachea: The windpipe

ugli(t): Eskimo word for gathering site(s) of walruses
upwelling: The upward progression of nutrient-rich water from the *abyssal* zone, prompted by the removal of surface waters through currents

vascular system: The circulatory system
vestigial: Reduced to a trace or remains of an organ or appendage
vibrissae: Sensitive whiskers, usually projecting from the face

whale-bone: See *baleen*

zooplankton: The animal varieties of *plankton*
zygomatic arch: Cheek-bone, formed by the processes of the cheek and *temporal* bone

Appendix V

Food preference of whales caught in Japanese waters

Species	Krill	Squid	Sardine	Octopus
Sperm Whale	2	1,513	4	19
*Sei Whale	367	145	168	2
Fin Whale	410	2	1	0
Blue Whale	50	1	1	0

Note: The figures indicate the number of stomachs found to contain each item, and not necessarily exclusive diets. (Adapted from Mizue)
*The Sei Whale is then both a 'skimmer' and 'gulper'.

The Commercial Uses of Whales

BY-PRODUCT	COMMERCIAL USE
Ambergris	Fixative for perfume Used in high quality soap
Baleen	Whips and riding crops Brooms and brushes
Blood	Used in plywood manufacture Fertilisers
Chemical salts	Creatine used in soups
Collagens = gelatine (present in bone, skin and tendons)	Used in photographic film, edible jellies and confectionery

Endocrine glands = hormones	Medicines and pharmaceutics
Liver	Vitamin A
Pituitary glands	ACTH (cortisone derivative) used in treatment of rheumatoid arthritis
Skin	Leather for bicycle saddles and handbags
Sperm oil *(unrefined)*	Mixed with mineral oil Dressing hides in leather industry
(refined & filtered) *Spermaceti*	Used in ceremonial candles, cold cream, lipsticks, brushless shaving cream and ointments
(filtered)	Lubricating oil for light machinery
(hydrolysed – sulphated *sperm oil)*	Used in emulsification of mineral oils, cutting oils, textile lubricants, and for dressing hides
(saponified – sperm oil alcohols)	Cetyl alcohol used as a superfatting agent in creams; also used on water-holes in Australia to prevent evaporation
do	Oleyl alcohols: hair oils, creams, lotions, dye-solvents, lipstick lubricants
do	Free alcohols: textile finishing, dressing light leathers, dye-solubilising and blending agents in printing inks, plasticiser bases for carbon papers and stencils
do	Oleyl and acetyl alcohols converted to sodium salts of their sulphate esters: powders, pastes and detergents
do	Halogenated oleyl and acetyl alcohols: yield eg. Cetyl pyridinium bromide – valuable for cationic surface-active agents and germicides
do	Synthetic esters of cetyl and oleyl alcohols produced for plasticising, synthetic resins and emulsification
Tendons	Tennis racket strings Surgical stitches
Whale bone	Bone meal for fertilizers Shoe horns, chess sets and toys
Whale meat	Food for poultry, pets, zoo animals and fur farm mink Meat meal (mixed with bone meal) Culture medium for screw-worm flys etc. Soups and gravies Cooked and mixed with wheat bran – fed to domestic animals and cows etc.
Whale oil *(Glyceridic oil of the baleen* *whales is used in the* *production of glycerine,* *margarine and soaps)*	Saponified: yields glycerine for dynamite, curing tobacco, medicines, and stearates for soap Polymerised: yields varnishes, oil cloth and linoleum, drying oil in the manufacture of paints, and printing ink Hydrogenated: yields margarine, cooking fat compounds, lard and shortening
Fin Whale oil (hardened)	Used in candles and crayons
Whale teeth	Ivory for carving and souvenirs Piano keys

Selected Bibliography

An asterisk (*) indicates a work specially recommended for the general reader

ALLEN, GLOVER M. 'Extinct and vanishing mammals of the western hemisphere with the marine species of all the oceans' *Spec. Publ. Amer. Comm. Int. Wildlife Protection* No. 11, 620pp (1942)

ALPERS, ANTHONY A.* *A book of dolphins* John Murray, London 1960
Dolphins Houghton Mifflin, Boston 1961; John Murray, London 1963

BERTRAM, COLIN *In search of mermaids. The manatees of Guiana* Peter Davies, London 1963

& BERTRAM, RICARDO 'Manatees of Guiana' *Nature* London 196 (4861): 1329 (1962)

'The status of manatees in the Guianas' *Oryx* 7 (2/3): 90-3 (1963)

'Manatees in the Guianas' *Zoologica* New York 49(2): 115-20 (1964)

BOOLOOTIAN, RICHARD A. 'Distribution of the California Sea Otter' *Calif. Fish Game*, 47(3):287-92 (1961)

BUDKER, P. *Whales and whaling* George G. Harrap, London 1958

BUREAU OF SPORT FISHERIES AND WILDLIFE, *Rare and endangered fish and wildlife of the United States* Washington DC 1966

BURTON, MAURICE *Systematic dictionary of the mammals of the world* Museum Press, London 1962; Apollo Editions, New York 1968

BURTON, ROBERT* *The life and death of whales* André Deutsch, London 1973; Universe Books, New York 1973

CARRINGTON, RICHARD* *Mermaids and mastodons* Chatto & Windus, London 1957

CARSON, RACHEL (1951)* *The sea around us* New American Library New York 1954; Penguin Books, London 1961

CLARKE, ROBERT 'Southern Right Whales on the coast of Chile' *Norsk Hvalfangsttid* 54(6):121-8 (1965)

CRANDALL, LEE S. *The management of wild mammals in captivity* The University of Chicago Press, Chicago & London 1964

CROMPTON, JOHN* *The living sea* Collins, London 1958

DORST, J. & DANDELOT, P. *A field guide to the larger mammals of Africa* Collins, London; Houghton Mifflin, Boston 1970

ENGEL, LEONARD *Sea* (Life Nature Library) Time-Life International 1961

FRIENDS OF THE EARTH (FOE) Various publications, London

GOODWIN, GEORGE G. 'Mammals of the Honduras' *Bull. Amer. Mus. Nat. Hist.* 79(2):107-95 (1942)

GRAVEN, J.* *Nonhuman thought* Arlington, London 1968

HALL, E. R. & KELSON, K. R. *The mammals of North America* (2 vols) Ronald Press, New York 1959

HAMILTON, J. E. 'The Southern Sealion' *Discovery Reports* 8:269-318. University Press, Cambridge 1934

'The Leopard Seal' *Discovery Reports* 18:239-64. University Press, Cambridge 1939

'A second report on the Southern Sealion' *Discovery Reports* 19:121-64. University Press, Cambridge 1939

HARDY, ALISTER C. *The open sea* Collins, London 1956; Houghton Mifflin, Boston 1971

HARMER, S. F. 'The history of whaling' *Proc. Linn. Soc. London* 1927-28:51-95 (1928)

HARRINGTON, C. R. 'Polar Bears and their present status' *Canadian Audubon* 26(1):4-11 (1964)

HARRIS, C. J. *Otters, a study of the recent Lutrinae* (The World Naturalist Series) Weidenfeld & Nicolson, London 1968

HARVEY, H. W. *The chemistry and fertility of sea waters* University Press, Cambridge 1966 (reprinted)

HEWER, H. R. *Grey Seals* Sunday Times Publications, London 1962

HICKLING, GRACE *Grey Seals and the Farne Islands* Routledge & Kegan Paul, London 1962

HOOKE, NINA W.* *The seal summer* Arthur Barker, London 1964

HORSFIELD, BRENDA & STONE, PETER B. *The great ocean business* Hodder & Stoughton, London 1972; Coward McCann, New York 1972

HOUSBY, TREVOR* *The hand of God – whaling in the Azores* Abelard-Schuman, London, New York, Toronto 1971

HOWELL, A. BRAZIER *Aquatic mammals.* Charles C. Thomas. Reprinted by Dover, New York 1970; Remploy, Newcastle-under-Lyme, Staffordshire, England 1971

HURRELL, H. G.* *Atlanta, my seal* William Kimber, London 1963

HVASS, HANS *Alverdens Pattedyr* Politikens Forlag, Copenhagen 1956 (English translation: *Mammals of the World.* Methuen, London 1961)

INTERNATIONAL UNION FOR CONSERVATION OF NATURE AND NATURAL RESOURCES (IUCN) Various publications. Morges, Switzerland. See also SIMON, NOEL

INTERNATIONAL COMMISSION ON WHALING Annual Reports, London

JACOBS, JAKE* *Marineland diver* Dodd, Mead, New York 1960

KELLOGG, R. 'The history of whales – their adaptation to life in the water' *Quart. Rev. Biol.* 3:29-76, 174-208 (1928)

KELLOGG, W. N. *Porpoises and sonar* University of Chicago Press, Chicago 1961

KENYON, K. W. 'The Sea Otter' *Oryx* 4(3):153-8 (1957)

    'Recovery of a fur-bearer; coveted pelt caused Sea Otter decimation' *Nat. Hist. New York* 72(9):12-21 (1963)

    & RICE, D. W. 'Life history of the Hawaiian Monk Seal' Pacific Science 23:215-52 (1959)

    & SCHEFFER, VICTOR B. 'The seals, sealions and sea otters of the Pacific coasts' *US Fish and Wildlife circular* No. 32 (1955)

    et al Reports of the Standing Committee, Marine Mammals. Annual meetings of the American Society of Mammalogists Seattle, Washington (1964 onwards)

KING, JUDITH E. *Seals of the world* British Museum (Nat. Hist.), London (1964)

LAWS, R. M. 'The seals of the Falkland Islands and Dependencies' *Oryx* 2(2):87-97 (1953)

LILLY JOHN C.* *Man and dolphin* Doubleday, New York 1961; Gollancz, London 1962

LOCKLEY, R. M. *The seals and the Curragh* Dent, London 1954

    Grey Seal, Common Seal André Deutsch, London 1966

LOUGHREY, ALAN G. 'The Polar Bear, and its protection' *Oryx* 3(5):233-9 (1956)

MANSFIELD, A. W. 'Seals of Arctic and eastern Canada' *Fisheries Preservation Board of Canada* Bulletin No. 137, Ottawa (1963)

MARINE FISHERIES REVIEW, April 1974 Special Number: 'The Californian gray whale' 36(4):1-65; National Marine Fisheries Service, Dept. of Commerce, USA

MATTHEWS, L. HARRISON *British mammals* (New Naturalist Series) Collins, London 1952

    Sea Elephant Macgibbon & Kee, London 1952

    The whale Allen & Unwin, London 1968

MAXWELL, GAVIN *Seals of the world* Constable, London 1967; Houghton Mifflin, Boston 1968

MELVILLE, HERMAN* *Moby Dick* 1851

MILLER, R. C.* *The sea* Random House, New York 1966; Nelson, London 1967

MOORE, J. C. 'The range of the Florida Manatee' *Quart. Journal Florida Acad. Sci.* 14(1):117-58 (1953)

MORRIS, DESMOND *The mammals* Hodder & Stoughton, London 1965

NORMAN, J. R. & FRASER, F. C. *Giant fishes, whales and dolphins* Putnam, London 1937

PAYNE, ROGER (sound recording) *Songs of the Humpback Whale*, Capitol, Hollywood

PEARSON, R. H.* *A seal flies by* Rupert Hart-Davis, London 1959

PERRY, RICHARD* *The world of the Walrus* Cassell, London; Taplinger, New York 1967

SANDERSON, I. T. *Follow the whale* Cassell, London 1958

SCAMMON, CHARLES M. *The marine mammals of the north-western coast of North America* San Francisco 1874. Reprinted by Dover, New York 1968

SCHEFFER, VICTOR B. *Seals, sealions and walruses* Stanford University Press, Stanford, USA 1958. Distributed in the United Kingdom by Oxford University Press, London 1958

SIMON, NOEL *et al. Red Data Book* Vol. 1 – 'Mammalia' 1966. See also entry under IUCN

SLIJPER, E. J. *Whales* Hutchinson, London 1963

SMALL, GEORGE *The Blue Whale* Columbia University Press, USA 1971

SVERDRUP, H. U., JOHNSON, M. W. & FLEMING, R. H. *The oceans: their physics, chemistry and general biology* Prentice-Hall, New York 1942

THOMSON, DAVID* *The people of the sea* Revised edition, Barrie & Rockcliff, London 1965

VAN DEN BRINK, F. H.* *A field guide to the mammals of Britain and Europe* Collins, London 1967

WALKER, ERNEST P. *Mammals of the world* Vols. 1-3. Johns Hopkins Press, Baltimore 1964

ZISWILER, V. *Extinct and vanishing animals* Longmans, London 1967; Springer-Verlag, New York 1967

ZOOLOGICAL SOCIETY OF LONDON 1960-74. International Zoo Yearbooks, various articles

Index

Acknowledgements

Cover – Francisco Erize/Bruce Coleman; title page – J. R. Seager/British Antarctic Survey; p. 15 – I. Collinge/BAS; p.16 – Fred Bruemmer; p.17 – Popperfoto; p.19 – Edward Ashpole (top); Norman Tomalin/Bruce Coleman (bottom); p.21 – Fred Bruemmer; p.25 – Francisco Erize/Bruce Coleman; p.31 – Fred Bruemmer; p.37 – Popperfoto; p.39 – I. Collinge/BAS; p.42 – Fred Bruemmer; p.43 – Dick Clarke/Seaphot; p. 50 – Popperfoto; p.55 – J. & S. Brownlie/Bruce Coleman; p.57 – Sea Library (left); Fred Bruemmer (right); p.61 – Jen & Des Bartlett/John Topham Picture Library; p.63 – Marineland of Florida/Frank Lane; p.65 – James Simon/Bruce Coleman (top); Frank Lane (bottom); p.66 – Dick Anderson/Sea Library (top); D. Bone/BAS (bottom); p.67 – Francisco Erize/Bruce Coleman (top); James Simon/Bruce Coleman (bottom); p.68 – Flip. Schulke/Seaphot (left); I. Collinge/BAS (top); Steve Leatherwood/Sea Library (centre); R. Chinn/BAS (bottom); p.70 – Rod Salm/Seaphot; p.71 – Marineland of Florida/Frank Lane; p.73 – Steve Leatherwood/Sea Library; p.76 – Jen & Des Bartlett/John Topham Picture Library; p.81 – Francisco Erize/Bruce Coleman; p.85 – Robert Burton/Bruce Coleman; p.86 – R.I.L. Smith/BAS; p.87 – Jeff Foott/Bruce Coleman (top); B. Kellett/BAS (centre); I. Collinge/BAS (bottom); p.88 – Heather Angel; p.93 – Fred Bruemmer; p.94 – J. R. Seager/BAS; p.98 – J. Brook/BAS; p.103 – Fred Bruemmer; p. 107 – Popperfoto; p.109 – S. McCutcheon/Frank Lane; p.110 – K. W. Kenyon/Frank Lane; p.117 – Fred Bruemmer; p.126 – Fred Bruemmer; p.128 – A. Christiansen/Frank Lane; p.129 – I. Collinge/BAS; p.131 – I. Collinge/BAS; p.133 – I. Collinge/BAS; p.135 – Popperfoto; p.137 – I. Collinge/BAS; p.138 – Francisco Erize/Bruce Coleman (top); G. Laycock/Bruce Coleman (bottom); p.139 – M. F. Soper/Bruce Coleman; p.140 – Leonard Lee Rue/Bruce Coleman; p.142-3 – Fred Bruemmer; p.144 – I. Collinge/BAS (top); Fred Bruemmer (bottom); p.145 – J. R. Seager/BAS; p.150 – Dr. Roland Eichler; p.151 – Dr. G. C. L. Bertram/World Wildlife Fund; p.157 – Sven Gillsater/Bruce Coleman; p.158-9 – Seaphot; p.160 – Jeff Foott/Bruce Coleman; p.163 – Ben East/Frank Lane; p.169 – L. M. Chace/Frank Lane; p.170 – Marineland of Florida/Frank Lane (top); Fred Bruemmer (bottom); p.173 – Popperfoto; p.174 – Popperfoto; p.175 – US Naval Photographic Center; p.176 – Fred Bruemmer; p.179 – I. Collinge/BAS; p.181 – Jack C. Stewart/Sea Library; p.182 – Popperfoto; p.184 – Marineland of Florida/Frank Lane; p.185 – US Naval Photographic Center; p.186 – Popperfoto; p.189 – S. McCutcheon/Frank Lane; p.190 – I. Collinge/BAS; p.193 – Fred Bruemmer; back cover – Popperfoto.

The maps in this book have been prepared by Ron Hayward.